THE LIBERATION OF THE LAITY

D1430527

The Liberation of the Laity

In Search of an Accountable Church

PAUL LAKELAND

continuum
NEW YORK · LONDON

2004
The Continuum International Publishing Group Inc
15 East 26th Street, New York, NY 10010

The Continuum International Publishing Group Ltd
The Tower Building, 11 York Road, London SE1 7NX

Printed in the United States of America

Library of Congress Cataloging-in-Publication Data

Lakeland, Paul, 1946–
    The liberation of the laity : in search of an accountable church /
Paul Lakeland.
      p. cm.
    ISBN 0-8264-1483-4
    1. Laity—Catholic Church. 2. Catholic Church—Membership. I. Title.

BS1920 .L37 2003
262'.152—dc21

                                2002151509

This book is dedicated to my good friends
Sally and Joe Cunneen,
in recognition of all that they have done
for more than half a century
for the American Catholic Church.

Hope has two lovely daughters: Anger and Courage.
Anger that things are not what they ought to be;
Courage to make them what they might be.
—*Attributed to St Augustine*

True theology begins with indignation.
—*Jon Sobrino*

Contents

PREFACE AND ACKNOWLEDGMENTS   1

INTRODUCTION: THE IDEA OF THE LAITY   7

Part One
How We Got to Where We Are

CHAPTER
1. The Road to Vatican II   17
   Laity: The Decadence of an Idea   17
   Modernism versus Neoscholasticism   19
   The "New Theology"   23
   The Beginnings of a Theology of the Laity   44
   From Humani Generis *to Vatican II*   47

2. The Achievement of Yves Congar   49
   Laypeople in the Church   52
   Stress Points in Congar's Thought   62
   Congar and the Concept of "Ministries"   70
   The Radicalism of Congar's Ecclesiology   75

3. Collegiality, Coresponsibility, and the Council   78
   The Council and the Laity   79
   Suenens and the Council   82
   The Council Documents   87
   Evaluating the Work of the Council   101
   Schillebeeckx and the Need for Theological Reflection   107
   In Conclusion   109

4. Theology and the Laity since Vatican II   111
    From the Runaway Church to Restoration   113
    The Roman Synod of 1987   120
    Christifideles Laici   125
    Meanwhile, in America . . .   131
    The Theological Debate on the Laity   135

Part Two
Where We Go from Here

5. Secularity   149
    What Is "the Secular"?   149
    Resources for a Theology of Secular Reality   158
    The Secularity of the Church   171
    A Lay Spirituality of Secularity   177
    A Note on Ordained Ministry   184

6. The Liberation of the Laity,
    the Liberation of the Church   186
    The Crisis of Leadership in the Church Today   188
    The Liberation of the Laity   192
    A Note on Lay Theologians   205
    How Democratic Should the Church Become?   207
    Rescuing the Church   215

7. Mission in the (Post) Modern World   220
    Communion Ecclesiology and Vatican II   220
    Reading the Signs of the Times   227
    The Church in Face of Modernity   235
    The Mission of the Church Today:
        Combating the Anti-Human   242
    Laypeople and the Mission of the Church   255

8. An Accountable Church   257
    Does the Church Have a Future?   259
    Beyond Vatican II   262
    The Structures of the Church   266
    The End of the Laity?   282

NOTES   286

INDEX   303

Preface

and Acknowledgments

W HEN I BEGAN TO THINK ABOUT WRITING THIS BOOK some four years ago, it was not a fashionable topic. I knew that relatively little had been written on the topic of "a theology of the laity," as I first described the task, since Yves Congar's magisterial work *Lay People in the Church*, in the mid-1950s. But I was convinced that theology needed to take another look at the role of laypeople. I was certainly not thinking of any particular crisis, merely of the general malaise that seemed to hang over the church, stemming I thought then (and now) from an outmoded understanding of ministry and a failure to harness the apostolic potential of the laity. Many of the most active and educated of the laity seemed to me to be mildly depressed, for the most part faithful to their local community of worship but frequently frustrated with the larger church and occasionally plain angry at the powerlessness they experienced in the church. I was also dimly aware that this was not the vision that the Second Vatican Council had presented of lay apostolic life. And I could not fail to see, like any of us, that despite these restrictions the American Catholic Church exhibited a rich array of lay ministries.

Putting the finishing touches on this book in the summer of 2002, it is hard to believe that so much has happened in so short a time to clarify the issues and to motivate large numbers of laypeople to action as never before. It is, of course, inexpressibly sad that it took the terrible tragedy of clergy sexual abuse of minors to "conscientize" Catholic laypeople. But if any good has come out of this particular crisis, it

must surely be that through the spectacle of episcopal shortsighted-
ness, incompetence, and the arrogance of power the Spirit has revealed
to us in no uncertain terms that the time has come to take another
look at patterns of ministry and the lifestyles that have grown up
around them. The efforts the bishops eventually began to make to
address the problem of sexual abuse and their own complicity in its
scale have been at best inadequate. However, they have also been
important for the admission—under pressure—that laypeople not
only legitimately have a voice in the church, but that solutions to such
problems cannot be left in the hands of the ordained ministers.

As the work of writing this text unfolded, it became apparent to me
that it could not fairly be described simply as a "theology of the laity."
First, it is quite impossible to write a theology that reflects on the
ecclesial role of over 95 percent of the church's members without it
simultaneously being an ecclesiology—a theological reflection on the
whole church. This is true not only because of the overwhelming
numbers of laypeople in the church. More importantly, once you pass
the point of thinking of laypeople as simply the recipients of the grace
of God and the services of the ordained, their common priesthood
and heavy responsibility for the church's mission rapidly leads you into
deep theological waters. Second, every word of theological reflection
on the role of the laity is replete with implications for priests and bishops. To think through the role of laypeople is to think anew about the
church as a whole. Accordingly, while the point of entry of this work
is a theological reflection on what it is to be a layperson, the exit point
turns out to be a vision of a future church in which patterns of ministry must be radically rethought. In this respect, the book is about the
end of the laity as we have known it.

The book is divided into two parts. In the first, I try to lay out the
recent history of the church as it reveals the slow growth of interest in
theological reflection on the role of laypeople. The introduction takes
a very brief look at the understanding of "lay" and "cleric" in the early
church. Chapter 1 begins in the nineteenth century at the time of the
First Vatican Council (1869–70), where the idea of the laity seems to
me to reach its theological nadir. Here, laity are simply defined by
what they are not, "not clergy," and that is the end of the matter.
Then I examine some of the real changes in theological reflection that
come about in the church in response to the modernist crisis at the

beginning of the twentieth century. I am particularly taken up with the standoff between the neoscholastic Roman establishment and the more progressive approaches to theology that neoscholastic orthodoxy tended to label "neomodernist." Here I focus on the French church, not only because many of the leading modernists were French but also, and more especially, because it was in France that a new way of thinking theologically came to be fashioned in the mid-century. Sarcastically dubbed the "new theology" by its opponents, this theological outlook was intensely pastoral, even missionary, and devoted also to *ressourcement*, that is, to a return to the classical sources of the tradition. In the second, I look in detail at the work of one of the "new theologians," Yves Congar, on the question of "laypeople in the church." Through a critical review of his important work, and a consideration of his own second thoughts on how to talk about laypeople, the text prepares the ground for examining the fortunes of the laity at the Second Vatican Council, where Congar's thinking was very influential. Chapter 3 looks at the council's work on the laity and at the early disappointment at its failure to fulfill its promise, particularly as expressed by Cardinal Leon Joseph Suenens. In the final chapter of this first half of the book we turn to examine the fortunes of the laity in the last quarter of the twentieth century, the pontificate of John Paul II. Here we find the curious paradox that while on the one hand there is a wonderful flowering of lay ministry in the church, perhaps particularly in North America, there is a concurrent effort to set limits to reflection on the ecclesial implications of these ministries.

In the second half of the book, I shift to a more constructive effort to reflect theologically about the laity, in the face of a postconciliar Roman orthodoxy that has remained, at least in terms of ecclesial vision, distinctly neoscholastic. The fundamental problem of neoscholastic polity, like neoscholastic thought in general, may be its lack of a sound pneumatology. There is little or no room for the work of the Holy Spirit, unless it be to confirm the structures themselves.[1] The relationship of church to Spirit in the neoscholastic polity is something I can illustrate no better than by telling a brief story. Many years ago I was acquainted with a Latvian Jesuit priest of great zeal, who had a considerable reputation as a preacher, but who was no great friend of Vatican II. One day he arrived home in high dudgeon. "I was saying mass for a big crowd," he said, "and I got to my sermon, and it was going well. Then, right in the middle of the sermon a woman stood up in the middle of the Church and shouted 'Praise the Lord!'" I responded enthusiastically at this evidence of the Spirit at work, only to be met with blank incomprehension. "But no," said the good father, "I pointed straight at the woman and I shouted 'Sit down! I will tell you when to say Praise the Lord!'" Thus does the neoscholastic church see the relationship between the institution, the Spirit, and the individual believer.

The four chapters that constitute part 2 address the situation of the church today and examine the nature of the lay role within it. As Congar did in his later years, these chapters try to rethink lay/clergy in terms of different ministries, rather than positions in some essentially hierarchical relationship. Each chapter examines one aspect of the church in the world today. In chapter 5, the starting point is the common depiction of the laity as "secular" or as oriented to the world, while the clergy are supposedly oriented to the church. Chapter 5 puts this distinction into question by suggesting that both clergy and laity, and indeed the church itself, are immersed in the secular. Chapter 6 turns to the present-day church and suggests a need to apply the rubric of "liberation" to the current condition of lay Catholics, arguing that their liberation from structural oppression will be the liberation of the whole church. Chapter 7 reflects on the mission of the church. While the church's mission is always complex and many-sided, its mission in the world as a mission of humanization means today, I argue, a consistent struggle against the antihuman pressures of global capitalism. Finally, in chapter 8, we indulge in a thought experiment on the future of the church. I offer one vision of how the polity of the Catholic Church might be quite radically changed without compromising anything essential to the tradition.

Because this text is addressed to all sectors of the Catholic Church and not simply to the laity or to trained theologians, different readers may want to customize its apparently straightforward structure. The more theological education the reader possesses, the more I would hope she or he would begin at the beginning and work through to the very end. Those with less acquaintance with theology might want to hold the first and second chapters aside and read those—if at all—after completing the rest of the book. Obviously, if a reader just wants to see what all this will lead to, then a brief glance at the final chapter might be a place to start, after which it is hoped that the reader would be moved to go back and find out why the conclusions we come to there are not half so radical as they may seem. If a reader is a lay minister, then chapters 3 and 4 could come first, with chapters 7 and 8 to follow. A theologian may find most to chew on, and perhaps disagree with, in chapters 2 and 5. A historian might find chapter 1 the most immediately accessible. But whoever you are and however you read what follows, be prepared for some chapters being more of an intellectual stretch, others calling more for leaps of imagination. In my own mind, I have moved from the historical to the theological, from the more didactic to the more speculative, from the theoretical to the practical. The overriding purpose of this book is the service of the church and, through the church, the world. I hope it inspires some readers to take up the same issues, whether to press them forward or to correct them. If so, I will be satisfied.

I have many people and institutions to thank. First, I must express my gratitude to Fairfield University for two research awards, the Senior Summer Research stipend given in 2000, and the grant of a semester's sabbatical leave in 2001–2002. Second and in equal measure, I am indebted to the Louisville Institute for a Faith and Life Grant, which enabled me to broker the sabbatical semester into a whole year in which to write the bulk of the book. I am also deeply grateful to the Cardinal Suenens Institute at John Carroll University in Cleveland for a summer stipend in 2001, which allowed me to do much of the research on Suenens that has found its way into these pages. After Yves Congar, no single individual has had more influence on this book than Leon-Joseph Suenens. I am thankful too to Pastoral Press, for permission to use material previously published in *Changing Churches*, edited by Michael Warren. The chapter I wrote in that book, much revised, appears as part of chapter 6 of the present work. And, of course, it goes without saying that you would not be reading this book without the enormously helpful advice of my editor at Continuum International, Frank Oveis. This is a better book because of him.

A number of individuals, all of them laypeople, have read portions of this text in preparation, and to them I am mightily thankful: Liz Keenan, Janice Mattioli, Joe O'Callaghan, and Beth Palmer. I am especially grateful to Michael Warren for an invitation years ago to participate in a conference on "The Material Practices of the Local Church," which began my thinking along these paths. Rick Gaillardetz gave me of his time and expertise to help me deal with some problems in the first two chapters of the book. Joe Komonchak generously supplied me with a bibliography of works on the "new theology," which simplified the task of writing chapter 1 and enormously enriched my own theological understanding. Finally, as always, my good friend and colleague John Thiel read and reread these chapters, even though sometimes they were in shamefully early versions, and even though their slant and style did not always appeal to him. I also applaud the effort of my twelve-year-old son, Jonathan, who salvaged an early manuscript copy of the entire book from the wastebasket and placed it on his desk, writing on the cover, "Found in garbage. Must read." I am also grateful to Beth Palmer, who had to put up with my being around the house much more than usual. I have written many of these pages to the sound of her piano as she played the same concert pieces over and over and over again. Her perfectionism as a musician has inspired me to make this work a little better than it otherwise might have been. Last and by no means least, I have dedicated this book to Joe and Sally Cunneen, Catholic intellectuals of a kind rare in this country. In their work founding and editing *Cross Currents* for half a century, they and their colleagues brought the intellectual riches of the European Catholic tradition to generations of American Catholics. To all these people and to so many others who have enriched my life to a point where simple gratitude is not even remotely enough, I say thank you for your efforts to make this book better, while of course I take final responsibility for its inevitable warts.

Introduction

The Idea of the Laity

W HEN A THEOLOGIAN SITS DOWN TO WRITE, the history of an idea is always an important consideration. Theology is never just created. Instead, it grows out of what tradition has bequeathed to the church. Good theology adds to the collective understanding of the community, modifying the tradition it has inherited and of which it is a part. Bad theology is more like an unsuccessful graft, destined sooner or later to have the body expel it. So theology that is not to be rejected must be respectful of its host, the faith community. But it must also be conscious of its responsibility to reinvigorate the community that, like any other body in history, can become tired, even lifeless. The new life that theology breathes into the tradition comes, most often, from the interchange between the tradition we possess and the gift given us by the times in which we live. The role of the theologian is to fuse these two together in an act of theological imagination. But the theologian does not do this alone. Her or his work is conducted within, and hopefully in dialogue with, the faith community that the theologian serves and participates in.

Choosing to write about "the laity" involves the same kind of respectful attention to the tradition that would be the case if this were a work in trinitarian theology or christology. But there are significant differences. Unlike the Trinity or Christ, the tradition's account of the "laity" is thin, even perhaps impoverished. Why is this the case? It would be possible to construct a sort of Marxist analysis, blaming the poverty of theological reflection on the laity on the oppressive ideo-

logical practices of an elite clerical class. At moments in history, there
may even be some truth to this idea. There is also an obvious plausibility to the claim that the clergy have done most of the theologizing
throughout the centuries, and that the theological status of the laity
was invisible or unimportant to them. But the probability is that the
church did not feel the need for this kind of theological attention and
drifted into a history of silence. In the beginning there were no laity,
only Christians. When distinctions came to be made between what we
would now call clergy and laity, it was the special responsibilities of the
former that seemed to need more definition, not the general responsibilities of the latter, which grew out of their baptism alone. Eventually, this would lead to defining the laity as "not clergy."

In the heady days after the Second Vatican Council (1962–65),
Avery Dulles wrote his best book, *Models of the Church*. Centrist and
cautious, the American Jesuit theologian (now a cardinal) yet drew
attention to the fact that the church has always needed to modify its
understanding of structures and offices "so as to operate more effectively in the social environment in which it finds itself."[1] The five
models for understanding the church that he scrutinizes in the book
are all important. But in the moment, the logic of the book was to
dethrone the model of "institution" from its preeminent position and
to balance it with images of communion, servanthood, sacrament and
prophecy. For too long, said Dulles, the model of institution has been
thought of as defining the reality of the church. The council had put
it in its place, as one important image among others.

Dulles, unfortunately, did not go on to point out that the preference for institution shows a particular form of historical amnesia to
which the church is prone. The church has a tendency to represent
any present moment in church life, even more so the recent past, with
the way things have always been and—by implication—the way things
shall always remain. The institution may have its own particular reasons for encouraging this habit, busy as it inevitably is with preserving
stability and security, and the community as a whole is not possessed
of sufficient historical knowledge to dispute it. So while the Catholic
tradition is two thousand years old, the memory of present-day
Catholics is only a couple of generations long. Our grandparents define
the good old days, and change is often thought to be messing with
age-old truths when it is just as likely to be abandoning nineteenth-
century or, now, twentieth-century presuppositions.

The greatest achievement of twentieth-century Catholic theology and philosophy may well have been the recognition of the role of the historical process in the formulation of ideas, the evolution of structures, and the articulation of doctrine. Recognizing historicity has at least two consequences. On the one hand—and liberals must never forget this—it means that we cannot canonize the prevailing wisdom of the present moment. The gospel will always in part be a refreshing blast of what Johann Baptist Metz has called "productive noncontemporaneity" (it may sound better in German!). We never stand under the hegemony of the *Zeitgeist*. But at the same time—and conservatives must never forget this—we are also precluded from a slavish attachment to the structures and formulations we have inherited. Instead, we have to participate in a complex process of historical discernment as we try to figure out how to follow one of the few changeless precepts of the Christian church, "preach the gospel!"

One clearly changeable element in the church is how we understand the respective roles of ordained ministers and the nonordained who make up the overwhelming majority of its members.[2] Throughout history there have always been leaders and led, and this is unlikely to change. But who shall lead and how leadership shall be practiced are not set in stone. The church is founded on the apostolic tradition, on apostolicity. But what it means to be apostolic today involves a more subtle discernment than a simple imitation of the recent past. All, of course, are called to witness to the gospel. But beyond that the church is not bound to any particular description of what a witnessing community shall look like. As a matter of fact, having spoken in terms of ordained and non-ordained is already misleading, since the early church did not use this kind of language. Terminology is complex and ever changing. Words like laity, clergy, priest, presbyter, deacon, bishop, ordination, hierarchy, ministry, believers, the faithful, people of God, and so on all come and go in the church's history, often shifting in meaning as they do. Moreover, as words go in and out of favor and structures adjust to circumstances, they also reflect changes in the church's whole self-understanding. The self-understanding of the church (its "ecclesiology") is different in the first two centuries from that which develops in the third. The ecclesiology of the early Middle Ages is not that of the Counter-Reformation. That of the nineteenth century and much of the twentieth is not ours in these first few years of the new century.

It is helpful to think of distinct stages in the development of a "lay/clergy" structure in the church. The first stage corresponds to the first two centuries of the church, when there was no clergy and there was no laity. The terms were not much used and, when they were, did not correspond to the way they are used today. The ideas of clergy and laity in any terminology were foreign to the early Christians. A second stage in which ideas of laity and clergy slowly formed can be discerned in the third century and reaches its full realization only in the twelfth. From that time onwards, the laity are considered in a primarily negative fashion, as those who live in the world in a lower state of holiness than the clergy. Of course the claim is never made that all clergy are holy and all laity are not, but the states of lay and clerical life are contrasted in such a fashion. Increasingly, as we move through subsequent history, we see the decadence of these ideas, which reach their nadir in the vision of the church at Vatican I (1870). However, like all periods of decadence, the inner ferment that will lead to a renewal in a subsequent stage is already at work at the end of the period, in the nineteenth and early twentieth centuries. Finally, today we stand in a new stage, which has been upon us for less than half a century. It is still forming, as our present-day church struggles to digest the theology of Vatican II.

We begin with words, and with the New Testament. The words "lay" and "laity" (from the Greek *laos*) and the words "cleric" and "clergy" (from the Greek *klēros*) were very little used in the early church and did not at all mean what we take them to mean today. The word *klēros* means "portion" or "lot." In the First Letter of Peter we find the author addressing the elders or presbyters:

> Tend the flock of God that is your charge, not by constraint but willingly, not for shameful gain but eagerly, not as domineering over those in your charge but being examples to the flock. (1 Pet. 5:3)

This passage is interesting above all for its understanding of ministerial leadership, which is as freshly relevant today as ever. However, the *klēroi* referred to here are not the presbyters but the "charge" which has been given to them to tend. In other words, the *klēroi* are actually what we would call the laity. Moreover, these *klēroi*, all Christians in fact, are those of whom Paul speaks, telling the Galatians that "if you are Christ's, then you are Abraham's offspring, heirs [*klēronomoi*] according to the promise" (Gal. 3:29). As Alexandre Faivre concludes, "the term *klēros* is applied not simply to the ministers, but to the whole of the believing people."[3]

Turning to the word *laos* or *laikos*, we can be even more succinct. *Laikos* (whence our word "lay") is not found anywhere in the Bible. *Laos*, on the other hand, is frequently found in the Bible, where it means "the people," but not just any people. It refers to the people of God, "the sacred people in opposition to those who were not consecrated."[4] *Laos* as used in the Bible, like *klēros*, is a word for the whole community, not for a segment of it. While the word *laikos* comes to be used in the early church to refer to those who are not especially qualified or assigned some office in the church, it always retains the sense that these "laypeople" are the ordinary members of the people of God, *all of whom* constitute a consecrated, holy people. The term is not used to distinguish the ordinary people from the holy minority to whom office has been assigned, at least not at this formative stage of the church's life. It is rather the case, as Congar points out, that "there is no distinction between 'laypeople' and 'clerics' in the vocabulary of the New Testament."[5]

The words "lay" or "laity" are not used in the texts of the Christian church between the New Testament and the writings of Irenaeus in the latter part of the second century, with the exception of two passages in the late-first-century letter of Clement of Rome to the church in Corinth.[6] This very important early testimony to the need for church order seems to have been occasioned by the Corinthian church's having deposed some of its leaders. The references to "laity" actually occur in a discussion of the levitical priesthood, and it is not clear that the analogy would carry over to the community in Corinth. At the same time, there is no doubt that the point Clement is making is that, full members of the community as they are, the "laity" of the Old Testament are distinguished from the priests in virtue of their not possessing certain powers. On the other hand, Clement's principal criticism of the Corinthian church is that it has removed people from ministerial leadership when they were not unworthy. This would clearly seem to imply that, had they been genuinely unworthy, the local community would have been within its rights to force them out (*1 Clem.* 44).

It is not entirely obvious what we are to conclude from the almost complete silence of the early church about the laity. Yves Congar avoids the question, suggesting that we should simply stick to examining the places where the word does appear, namely, in third-century texts.[7] Faivre is less cautious, insisting perhaps rightly on the theocentric or christocentric character of the early communities of faith, in which God's gifts have been so freely bestowed on the whole people that it would seem churlish to spend time arguing about how they were to be shared or distributed.[8] Either way, it is safe to say that the language of laity and clergy was apparently not current in the early church. But at the same time we cannot make an assumption that the emergence of such language in the third century simply came out of nowhere. The reality for which the language was apparently found useful must already have been forming, and Clement of Rome's letter is a good example of that.

In the work of Irenaeus of Lyons we can see an important transitional moment. On the one hand, he does not use the language of lay and cleric, and he considers the whole people to be a priestly people. "We" are all "disciples." But within this context Irenaeus was led by his polemical purposes against the Gnostic heretics to single out the presbyter as a particularly outstanding example of a disciple. The judgment, however, is existential rather than juridical. The one who is the "presbyter, the disciple of the apostles," is in virtue of his calling graced with the likelihood of being an outstanding disciple. But this does not mean that all presbyters are so in virtue of their office, still less that those who are not presbyters may not also be such outstanding disciples. For Irenaeus, we are all called to be "spiritual disciples," but the presbyters show us the way. They become "masters" for the community. Thus is the path laid for the emergence of a "clergy" that Irenaeus never mentions.[9]

From some indeterminable point in the second century, there slowly developed distinctions between clergy and laity, but the situation was complicated in the third century by the emergence of a third group, the monks. This point is at the heart of Congar's discussion of the problem of lay status, and it deserves close attention. Clerics and monks were "sharply differentiated," the former term indicating a function, the latter a state of life. So when laity were compared to clergy, the distinctions were those of function or office within the church. But monks and the laity were contrasted in terms of different states of life. Hence, "lay" could sometimes refer to a function in the church, at other times to a state of life—and frequently the two could be confused. Moreover, the differences between clergy and monks could become occluded. Congar gives three good reasons. First, it was thought fitting that those dedicated to the altar should possess the virtues and spirit of the monks. Second, in the Western church in particular, monks came to have clear liturgical roles, though this is not of the essence of the monastic life (and by no means so common in the Eastern church). Third, as late as the twelfth century, we find monks insisting on the title of cleric. The consequences are well stated by Congar. The church moves from a "triple division" of laypeople, clerics, and monks to "a double division into men of religion and men of the world."[10]

From the twelfth century onwards two notions—one monastic and one more juridical—conspire to cement the unfortunate understanding of the laity as passive and defined negatively, which the church largely held until the Second Vatican Council. The first stresses the differences in state of life and can be seen in the writings of the twelfth-century theologian Gratian. He divides Christians into two kinds, placing clerics and monks in one category, and the laity in the other. But as Congar points out, Gratian sees the very existence of the laity as a concession to human weakness and assigns them "no active part in the sphere of sacred things."[11] The second, canonical notion of the laity reflects a general movement in the twelfth-century church. The laity are defined by function: they are those who live in the world, unlike the monks, and they are those who receive spiritual goods from the clergy. Left thus, says Congar, "laypeople . . . are negative creatures."[12] It will be a major part of Congar's life work to develop a more positive characterization of the laity. But until he does so, in the middle of the twentieth century, the laity's status is admirably exemplified in the doubtless apocryphal story of the German theological encyclopedia of the nineteenth century. Search its index for "laity" and you will find the following entry—Laity: see "clergy."

Part One

How We Got to Where We Are

1

The Road to Vatican II

It follows that the Church is essentially an unequal society, that is, a society comprising two categories of persons, the Pastors and the flock, those who occupy a rank in the different degrees of the hierarchy and multitude of the faithful. So distinct are these categories that with the pastoral body only rests the necessary right and authority for promoting the end of the society and directing all its members towards that end; the one duty of the multitude is to allow themselves to be led and, like a docile flock, to follow the Pastors.

—*Pope Pius X, Vehementer Nos* §8

LAITY: THE DECADENCE OF AN IDEA

IN THE NINETEENTH CENTURY the subject of the laity is almost invisible in theological reflection and institutional practice. One of the things we shall have occasion to note most often in these pages is that the fortunes of "the laity" or the "theology of the laity" cannot be understood in isolation from the current working ecclesiology at any particular moment in the church's life. In the nineteenth century the church, most especially the Vatican, was engaged in a tenacious and mostly fruitless struggle with modernity, though the church of the time would have called the enemy "liberalism."[1] From the French Revolution in 1789 through the First Vatican Council some eighty years later, to the modernist crisis that marked the early years of the

17

twentieth century, the Roman Catholic Church at the highest levels conducted a systematic campaign against the "evils" of freedom of speech, freedom of religion, the separation of church and state, and many other so-called social ills that at Vatican II the same church would so heartily embrace. For the previous two and a half centuries, since the reforms of the Council of Trent, the church had slowly drifted deeper into isolationism, had become more triumphalistic, more fearful of contamination by that which was the world. But when, in the nineteenth century, its power and authority came to be directly challenged by European political developments, it reacted like the ancient King Canute, standing on the shore and ordering the tide to go back. King Canute was only trying to teach his subjects a lesson, while the church was deadly serious, but both got their feet equally wet. The struggle with French liberal Catholics, the "Syllabus of Errors," Vatican I itself, the definition of papal infallibility, and the attempt to institutionalize Thomist philosophy all in their different ways relate to the peculiar blend of fear and aggression that characterizes the church of the nineteenth century.

The quotation at the head of this chapter, though taken from a letter of Pius X written in 1906, reflects exactly the view of the church that won the day at Vatican I in 1870. It also serves well as an epitaph for a view of the church that was already, in 1870, anachronistic. Much of the church outside Rome, and very many of the world's bishops gathered at the council, were already beyond such a reactionary vision.[2] Many left Rome rather than vote for the declaration of papal infallibility. Many more spoke strongly against the definition, though they remained and—in the end—did not resist it.

It has often been said that the First Vatican Council, since it broke up with much of its anticipated program incomplete, cannot be seen in isolation from the Second Vatican Council, which almost a hundred years later consciously completed its work and reaffirmed its teachings. This is both true and misleading. The dominant tone of the two completed documents of Vatican I is juridicist and triumphalistic. The preparatory schemas for Vatican II were couched in similar language, but were thrown out by the assembled bishops and replaced with documents of a far more pastoral character. In that sense Vatican II consciously corrects Vatican I. True, it reaffirms the definition of papal infallibility. But it places it where it belongs, in a discussion of the role of the Holy Spirit in the faith of the church, and counterbalances the doctrine with a statement of the way in which infallibility resides both in the collective teaching of the episcopacy and in the faith affirmations of the whole church. Had Vatican I continued beyond 1870, it would undoubtedly have produced more documents. But there is no evidence that it would have been able to break out of the hierarchical and inward-looking mind-set of the dominant papal party. Of course, there were plenty of prescient and independent-thinking bishops and theologians at the time. But they were unable to shift the balance toward their point of view. At Vatican II, the same two groups were still discernible, but there were differences. The balance had shifted, and the "papal party" of curial bishops and their conservative supporters from around the world were in the minority. More importantly, of course, the pope of the time, John XXIII, was not one of them. The papal party was without the pope, and thus destined to fail.

I have called the idea of the laity implied in the schema for Vatican I "decadent" because it is the end point of the twelfth-century juridicizing of ecclesiology, and because it is already long out of date by the time it is written. Obviously, the vision expressed therein is that of a church defined by hierarchical assumptions. However, it is not the mere mention of hierarchy that is problematic—Vatican II will reaffirm the hierarchical character of the church—but the juxtaposition of clergy and laity, power and rights in the context of language denying equality. The laity are those who are sanctified, governed, and taught through the work of the clergy. The clergy possess these powers and the laity do not. The only right that the laity have, by implication, is to receive the ministrations of the clergy. This vision is at best paternalistic, at worst a theological justification for an ecclesial caste system. And while it is dressed up as theology, it is at least as much about denying the vision of the human person as possessor of rights and dignity independent of the church that was espoused by the liberalism that was, at this time, the church's enemy.

MODERNISM VERSUS NEOSCHOLASTICISM

The closing of the First Vatican Council seemed only to polarize the church still further into those liberal and ultramontane camps that had warred against one another through most of the century. True, with the definition of papal infallibility and the conservative tenor of the council, the ultramontanes were firmly in the ascendant, while the more liberal bishops and theologians had retired to lick their wounds. A neoscholastic orthodoxy reigned in Rome even more firmly than it had before. But the triumphalistic church of Vatican I was weak at the core, straining still to rail against the modern world with which it would, willy-nilly, have to come to terms. In the ninety years that must pass between Vatican I and Vatican II, the losing battle with modernity would continue, but it would involve more than the intransigence of Rome in face of the modern world. Now, much more than before, the battles would be conducted within the church itself, as voices of reform, both moderate and extreme, battled for intellectual freedom in a church determined to maintain an unhistorical orthodoxy.

The modernist crisis that broke upon the church in the years after Vatican I showed very clearly what would be at stake throughout the twentieth century and is best seen in the French context for a number of reasons.[3] First, the primary locus of modernism, at least as it was defined in Pius X's condemnatory encyclical *Pascendi*,[4] was France. Though no names were mentioned in the encyclical, Alfred Loisy was envisaged as the type of the modernist theologian. Second, it is in France that we can most easily see the transition from modernism proper to what later came to be called by its witch-hunting enemies first "neo-modernism" and then the "new theology." Third, the theologians who were derisively labeled "new," and who were largely French (with some Belgian and German additions), had an enormous impact on the work of the Second Vatican Council. Fourth, the new theology, while it was deeply involved in the renewal of liturgical and biblical studies, was primarily directed toward ecclesiological questions. Fifth, prominent among the ecclesiological issues examined was that of the nature of lay participation in the life of the church. Sixth, because these theological discussions and intraecclesial political machinations took place against the background of the struggle for the evangelization of the French proletariat, the pastoral intent of the new theology is clear. The new theology was no mere academic exercise, and it is as pastoral theology that it comes to have such an influence on Vatican II.

In many ways, however, the most important reason for examining modernism and neo-modernism in some detail is because we still live in the church today with the remnants of the battle between a neo-scholastic orthodoxy at the structural center of the church and a far more liberal and devolutionary kind of theological thinking at what we can only call, structurally speaking, the periphery. It is far too facile to think of Vatican II as having brought final resolution to these controversies. In one way or another, they continue. As we think, in these first years of a new century, of the future of church governance in general, and of the meaning of "laity" in particular, it is an unhistorical neoscholastic orthodoxy that will insist that these matters are settled.

Scholars have long recognized the problem of accurately describing and assessing modernism.[5] The movement and its name were an invention of the Roman document in which it was denounced.[6] There was no modernist school. The same documents compound the problem by naming no one as perpetrator of the heresies they set out to condemn. In fact there is no doubt that one of the principals targeted by Rome was the French priest Alfred Loisy (1857–1940), and in this short discussion Loisy will serve as representative modernist. Loisy was an outspoken advocate of attention to the new biblical criticism and in general to the consistent application of the historical method to Christian theology. He insisted that theological reflection must bow before history. He taught for a time at the Institut Catholique in Paris, but was forced to resign in 1893 as a result of controversy over his views on historicity and exegetical method. In 1902 Loisy published *The Gospel and the Church*,[7] a Catholic reply to the immensely influential work of Adolf von Harnack (1851–1930), *Das Wesen des Christentums* (The essence of Christianity).[8]

Loisy attacked Harnack's views in part by challenging his exegesis, but in principle set out to defend an evolutionary hypothesis that saw contemporary Catholicism as the authentic development of the "essence" contained in the original Gospels. Unfortunately for Loisy, this meant challenging the reigning neoscholastic intellectual orthodoxy in the church, which vigorously fought any notion of historical development. According to this unhistorical mind-set of neoscholasticism, Jesus established the church very much as it is today, with its same understanding of sacramental life, of authority, and of doctrine. Loisy's challenge to the establishment was intensified in the second edition of his work a year later, where an additional chapter on Gospel sources set out to show that the Gospels themselves were to be understood as expressions of the faith of the community at the time of their composition. Further, he argued, Jesus himself must have shared the eschatological vision of his times and was therefore in the end mistaken about the imminent coming of the kingdom of God. But the whole of the Catholic Church is a necessary development out of the Gospels. Even dogma, though it is not contained in the Gospels, may proceed from the Gospels.

Loisy's works were placed on the Index, and though he tried hard to accommodate his Roman judges, by degrees he moved away from the church and steadily lost influence. Pius X acted in 1907 to condemn "modernism" in the strongest possible terms, calling it in his letter *Pascendi* the "synthesis of all heresies." In many ways a saintly man, Pius seems also to have been possessed by a virulent and obsessive determination to eradicate this "modernism," to the point at which a classic witch-hunt marked his entire papacy. In 1910 the "anti-modernist oath" was established, to be required of all candidates for ordination and leadership in the church (and revoked only in 1967). The struggle against what Etienne Fouilloux calls "the specter of Modernism" was orchestrated from Rome, led everywhere by representatives of neoscholasticism, many of whom came to be known as "Integralists," taking up as a name the general label that had been applied previously to antiliberal and usually promonarchical Catholicism favoring strong papal authority. Pius even favored the deplorable crusade of Umberto Benigni, who established a kind of secret society, the *Sodalitium Pianum,* to ferret out and denounce the activities of modernists.[9]

For what follows in the development of Catholic thought, it is important to keep two separate yet related issues in mind. On the one hand, the return to Thomism offered a valuable intellectual resource to the church, whose twentieth-century history is one of a rich pluralism. The work of scholars as different as Jacques Maritain and Reginald Garrigou-Lagrange in one camp, Pierre Rousselot and Joseph Maréchal in a second, and Marie-Dominique Chenu (1895–1990) and Yves Congar (1904–1995) in a third testifies clearly to the vitality of the Thomist tradition.[10] On the other hand, there is also a kind of "political neoscholasticism" which harnesses itself, largely for temperamental reasons, to a rigidly unhistorical approach to Thomism, and which had by far the most power and influence in Rome (Maritain toyed with this approach for a time but later turned away from it, while Garrigou-Lagrange became its theological spokesperson, to his intellectual discredit). In consequence, the vitality of Thomism stands in stark contrast to the sterility of neoscholasticism. Thomism simply shows the diversity of a rich intellectual tradition. Neoscholasticism illustrates the natural affinity that exists between a univocal and unhistorical approach to truth, on the one hand, be it scholasticism or any other system, and a rigidly authoritarian attitude to difference in church life, on the other.

THE "NEW THEOLOGY"

No group of individuals had a greater impact upon the work of Vatican II than the French Dominican and Jesuit theologians who flourished from the 1930s onwards; Chenu, Congar, Henri de Lubac (1896–1991), and Jean Daniélou (1905–1974), to name just the best known of them, illustrated in the shape of their professional lives the course of mid-twentieth-century Catholic ecclesial life. Chenu was removed from his position of leadership at the seminary of Le Saulchoir and sent to work in a convent in Paris. His pupil and friend Congar was silenced for several years and sent into exile in England. De Lubac was deeply suspect and the primary target of Pius XII's 1951 encyclical letter *Humani Generis*.[11] Daniélou's 1946 article in the French Jesuit journal *Etudes*, "Les orientations présentes de la pensée religieuse," which argued that the modernists had been asking the right questions, even if they had come up with the wrong answers, was removed from circulation.[12] Yet all lived to exercise enormous influence, and Congar, Daniélou, and de Lubac ended their days as cardinals of the church. None of them liked the term "new theology" to describe what they did, and, like the modernists before them, they were not self-consciously a school or a movement. But they had all known the fury of antimodernism in one way or another; they had all been formed in the controversies of neo-Thomism; and they had all grown up in a France troubled by Action Française. They knew firsthand the struggles for a place for Catholicism in French public life and in particular in the life of the ordinary working people. It is no surprise that they had so much in common.

The new theologians (for such we shall have to call them, despite their dislike of the name) were, like the modernists before them, primarily motivated by an apologetic, even pastoral, purpose. Deeply scholarly to a man, they were all aware that the French proletariat had come into existence in the nineteenth century in times of profound anticlericalism and that this class of people had truly never been evangelized. They had not so much been lost to Catholicism as never even touched by it. The urban underclass was largely pagan, and if the church was to evangelize these people it had to break out of its bourgeois and aristocratic forms of life and reach out to a new audience. So, as we look at the intellectual accomplishments of Chenu, Congar, de Lubac, and Daniélou, we have to see them against the background of the new French evangelism, if we are not mistakenly to classify them simply as reforming academics.

Is France Mission Territory?

In the early days of liberation theology, in the years immediately following the Latin American Bishops' Conference in Medellin, Colombia, in 1968, numbers of priests and religious all over Latin America left their comfortable houses to live with the poor in the slums of the cities. If their purpose was to evangelize the masses, they soon discovered that sharing the lives of the poor gave them an appreciation for the dignity of the people they had come to serve and often led them to see that the poor had as much to teach them as they had to teach the poor. Human solidarity in the face of great deprivation and the continuing struggle for lives of dignity led the religious professionals to see the gospel with new eyes. It also opened the eyes of the Latin American church to the strength of popular religion and the limitations of the elite form of Catholicism.[13]

What is less well known is that in France in the 1940s, this aspect of liberation theology—as well as a number of others—was clearly anticipated. Catholicism in France in 1940 was largely the preserve of sectors of the aristocracy, the bourgeoisie (though the latter were often fiercely republican and anticlerical), and the rural peasantry. The masses of the French proletariat were unchurched, not in the sense that they had lapsed from a historical Catholicism, but rather that the proletarian class had emerged in a time of great socialist and anticlerical fervor in nineteenth-century France and had found no discernible need for religion in general or for Catholicism in particular. The old alliances of French Catholicism with monarchical and conservative political movements were so entrenched that even had a need for religion been perceived, the chances of large-scale conversion to Catholicism would have been very small.

While discussions of the need to evangelize the workers had gone on for some considerable time, little progress had been made. Then in 1943 a short book written by two French priests, Henri Godin and Yvan Daniel (always associated more with Godin), burst upon the scene—*France, pays de mission?* This book changed all previous thinking about the evangelization of the workers by offering a cogent explanation of the previous lack of success and a vision of how future work needed to be conducted.[14] Born in 1906 of a poor rural family, Henri Godin was sent to the *"petite seminaire"* at the age of twelve and was ordained in 1933. From his journal notes kept during his years of study it is easy to tell that even in the earliest years he saw himself called to serve the workers, "because I desire the apostolate of the poor whom Jesus preferred, whose outlook I share more than that of the rich and who are too often left on one side."[15] He was acutely aware, too, that priestly training tended to make the seminarian into a kind of class traitor, perhaps against his better wishes. In an early thesis, which later became material for *France, pays de mission?*, Godin reports on a worker complaining about his former friends who entered the seminary, "They're bourgeois now. They don't care about the working classes. They're deserters. There ought to be a seminary for workmen where they'd stay workmen when they become priests. All priests are bourgeois."[16] Mission, the authors wrote in their startling book, is about creating not individual believers but communities. The missionary's responsibility is to create a church. The reason why so many previous efforts have failed is that the conversion of individuals inevitably means incorporating them into existing communities. The parish hardly touches the pagan world, and the newly converted must leave their culture behind to be incorporated into the already existing parishes. This is a "false conquest" and does not evangelize the "real milieux." "What is needed is a small Christian community living in the milieu and radiating Christianity from its very midst. This the existing parishes do not provide."[17] There must be clergy specially trained for this very different world, and the gospel must be as inculturated here as it would have to be in a traditional mission land of Africa or Asia. But also "we must change our outlook and seek out in the community Christians with a missionary vocation. . . . We must send them, well prepared, into a world that is not their own world."[18]

Godin's many books, of which this was the most influential, were a product of thinking fashioned in his daily contacts with the *Jeunesses Ouvrières Chrétiennes* (Young Christian Workers), the JOC as they were known, or the *"jocistes."* They had been founded in Belgium by the great Cardinal Cardijn (1882–1967), as a kind of youth wing of Catholic Action. Cardijn encouraged a form of reflection and analysis based on the "see, judge, act" trilogy to which the methodology of liberation theology's "base Christian communities" is deeply indebted. Godin was also connected to the *Mission de France,* led by Cardinal Suhard (1874–1949), who had formed a seminary to train both seminarians and priests for the special conditions of this missionary work (where Godin himself studied for a time in 1942). It was Suhard's call to Godin and Daniel for a report on the relations of the proletariat and the church that led to the book *France, pays de mission?* Godin seems in the end to have been closer to the methodology of the *Mission de Paris* than to that of Catholic Action, which he appears to have suspected of too deductive an approach to problems. Maisie Ward quotes one writer on Godin remarking on his deeply inductive sensibilities. He always "started from a lived experience. . . . He never started from what is commonly called a 'critical study.'"[19]

In 1943 Godin began work establishing a Mission de Paris, to match the work of Suhard's Mission de France, but to be independent of it. Both Godin and Suhard were in agreement that while the Mission de France was primarily parish-based, the Mission de Paris would not be. It was also the case that the former was entirely clerical, but the Mission de Paris employed laypeople from its beginnings. Cardinal Suhard went to Lisieux, where Godin and his collaborators had spent December 1943 in study and prayer, and gave his blessing to the Mission. On Saturday, January 15, Godin and the others returned to Paris to begin work. The Mission was to start on Monday morning, but Godin died of asphyxiation from coal-fire fumes during the previous night. For four days following this tragedy, a line of people visited the apartment where he died, to view the body and to pray, and thousands attended his requiem mass. Godin was buried in the cemetery of Pantin, in an area of graves for poor workers. The Mission de Paris energetically began its work.

Long before Godin, the church had seen the need for "internal mission." Popes since Leo XIII had been aware of the growing divorce between working people and the church, but it was Pius XI who directly addressed the problem. Alarmed by the secularization of Europe, Pius XI had promoted "Catholic Action" as the solution throughout the 1930s. The movement flourished in French-speaking countries above all others. His famous definition of Catholic Action as "the participation of the laity in the hierarchical apostolate"[20] not only indicates the character of this lay movement but also hints at some of the problems that came to be associated with it. On the one hand, as the pope himself frequently pointed out, he was starting nothing new but only adapting to new circumstances the age-old "help the laity brings to the apostolic work of the hierarchy." Of course, this may be a little disingenuous on the part of the pontiff, since the differences were enormous. The need for Catholic Action was directly connected to the shortage of priests, and it was envisaged as a mass movement of loyal lay Catholics, something that "lay participation" had never before been. But its apparent move in the direction of a genuine lay apostolate seemed to some to be anything but that salutary development. If the lay apostolate were to be understood as lay "participation" in the work that belongs directly to the hierarchical apostolate, could this truly be said to be lay ministry? In his 1922 encyclical *Ubi arcano,* Pius XI explained to his fellow bishops that as the laity participate in the work of bishops and clergy "by carrying abroad the knowledge of Christ and teaching men to love Him . . . then indeed they are worthy of being hailed as 'a chosen generation, a kingly priesthood, a holy nation.'"[21] Does this papal statement imply that the laity only share in this royal priesthood when they share in the ministry of the hierarchy? As we shall see when we turn in the next chapter to the work of Yves Congar, a very vigorous discussion arose on precisely this point. Is there not in fact a specifically lay apostolate that is theirs in virtue of their baptism, which is not collaboration in a hierarchical apostolate, and which they conduct without direct ecclesiastical oversight?

The positive stimulus for Catholic Action, beyond strategic considerations about the need for assistance to a dwindling clergy, was the sense that a revolution was needed in Catholic lay life. The laity needed to get beyond a passive understanding of their role in the church, to "turn their lives upside down . . . to co-operate with the Spirit because they have been baptized into an apostolic church, a church which is sent, a church with a mission."[22] In part, this call for change was a product of anxiety about the waning strength of the church, particularly in the industrialized world. But it also had theological roots, especially in the revived interest in St. Paul's ecclesiology of the church as the "mystical body of Christ."[23] Perhaps the difference between the call to lay ministry then and now might be a reflection of which image of the church is given priority, the "Mystical Body" of the first half of the twentieth century, or the "People of God" of the second.

The Jocists were one important offshoot of Catholic Action, particularly in France and Belgium. The Jeunesses Ouvrières Chrétiennes, or Young Christian Workers, were exactly what their name suggests, namely, young Catholic laypeople who conducted a ministry within the urban working world that was their métier. It was with these individuals that Abbé Henri Godin was particularly involved, and a glance at his relations with the Jocists is instructive about the relationship of lay ministry to the hierarchical apostolate. Maisie Ward points out that Godin attended many meetings of the JOC, but "spoke little, listening, bringing things to a point, awakening enthusiasm, and leading his boys to ardent and practical resolutions."[24] In other words, he was what today we would call a "facilitator." More telling still:

> [H]e would not make the decisions for his Jocists: that was to go outside what, in his judgment as well as by the theory of the movement, was the chaplain's province. It was also a profound instinct of leadership. . . . "He loved," says a Jocist leader, "to pose problems . . . and not offer solutions, for according to him that was the leaders' own job."[25]

Clearly, Godin was aware of the very delicate balance that had to be preserved between offering inspiration to the JOC and depriving it of its own lay leadership. The same struggle to achieve this balance always afflicted the work of Catholic Action in general. Given that Catholic Action refers not to the individual's apostolic endeavors in her or his own walk of life but to coordinated organizations operating independently of but under the auspices of the hierarchy, the question of the limits of their independence is always going to be tricky. Catholic Action was at one and the same time a marvelous means of harnessing lay enthusiasm and expertise in the service of the gospel, particularly in what was called the "social apostolate," and also at times a convenient mechanism by which lay movements could be controlled, if not suppressed.[26] A renewed outburst of anticlericalism in the early twenties had led to the formation of the *Fédération Nationale Catholique* (FNC) in 1924, which five years later Pius XI confirmed as the model of Catholic Action, despite its possessing a similar raison d'être and modus operandi to Action Française. Of course, unlike Action Française, it was subject to ecclesiastical control. But the approval for the FNC backfired in the end, as it and similar movements, some connected to Catholic Action, stonewalled papal internationalism and concern for the poor as it shone through the social encyclicals from Leo XIII onwards.[27]

Chenu and Congar: "Theologians in Action"

At the same time as the new evangelical fervor was coursing through the veins of the JOC, the Mission de France, and even the more traditional work of Catholic Action in general, developments in French Catholic intellectual life kept pace. In the fields of historical studies, philosophy, and theology, we can for simplicity's sake see two constellations of reforming activity clustered around two houses of study, the Dominican house at Le Saulchoir and the Jesuit foundation in Fourvière. While many other notable figures were involved, the former will always be associated with the work of Marie-Dominique Chenu and his student and colleague Yves Congar, while the movement associated with Fourvière inevitably brings to mind, above all others, both Henri de Lubac and Jean Daniélou. We turn first to the Dominicans.

Marie-Dominique Chenu and Yves Congar exercised incalculable influence on twentieth-century theology, the former primarily through his work as a historian, the latter essentially in the two areas of ecclesiology and ecumenism, though it is perhaps in pneumatology, the theology of the spirit, that his fundamental insights are to be found.[28] The roots of their approach to theology lie, however, in the work of a previous scholar, Ambrose Gardeil, whose attention to the nature of faith (along with Rousselot) inspired so much of the new theology.[29] Gardeil's question was of the nature of the relationship between theology and faith. Much neoscholasticism had tended to see faith primarily as an intellectual assent provoked by contact with the truths of revelation. This approach, as we saw earlier, also colored the understanding of the task of apologetics, making it in essence a species of intellectual combat, where the individual is constrained to believe by the weight of the evidence in scripture and dogma. But Gardeil, obviously influenced by Maurice Blondel (and to a lesser extent Rousselot), argued that faith is primarily a gift of the Spirit, who enlightens the individual and creates those interior dispositions through which the truths of revelation are perceived as religious values. Faith, in other words, is prior to and seeks the understanding offered it through theology.[30] Theology, which is then "the science of faith," is in constant dialogue with revelation; its method is historical, its formulations analogical. Chenu and Congar (and later another Dominican, Edward Schillebeeckx) were to broaden and elaborate this direction.

Marie-Dominique Chenu's life and work mirror the changes in the church in the twentieth century. Born in 1894, he entered the Dominicans at the age of eighteen and was sent to Rome to study at the Angelicum from 1914 to 1920, where he completed a dissertation on contemplation under the direction of the very conservative neoscholastic Reginald Garrigou-Lagrange, who dearly wanted to keep him in Rome as his assistant. But he was sent instead to Le Saulchoir. There he studied and wrote a number of influential texts on the history of scholasticism, as well as essays that tried to address the issues that modernism had raised in such an unhappy way. As prefect of studies at Le Saulchoir, in 1937 he published a short book outlining his views on priestly formation and on the relationship between theology and history, declaring in conversations with Jacques Duquesne that he opposed a "timeless" understanding of theology and offered instead "theology enmeshed in relativism, that is in the complex to and fro of interactions which continually modify not, of course, the root content of faith, but its expressions."[31] The book immediately drew the attention of Rome, and in 1942 it was placed on the Index, drawing the following comment from the great Cardinal Suhard: "Dear Father, don't worry. In twenty years everyone will talk like you."[32] Twenty years later exactly, Chenu was instrumental in drafting the Vatican Council's "message to the world," through which the bishops of the opening session voiced their dissatisfaction with what Chenu called the "inflexible line of abstract and theoretical statements" in the preparatory schema, through which "the intellectual thought police" (Chenu's phrase) were seeking to control the world's bishops.[33] Clearly, the battle in 1962 was essentially similar to that of twenty years earlier, but the power was in the process of shifting.

There are three main steps to Chenu's discussion of theology in the second chapter of *Le Saulchoir*.[34] First, he outlines his understanding of the nature of theology and its relationship to faith, which built on the work of Ambrose Gardeil. For historical reasons particularly connected to the rise of scholasticism and to the polemical purposes of Counter-Reformation Catholicism, the primacy of revelation in theology had lost out to a proof-texting approach "from Scripture, from tradition, from reason."[35] To counter this, Chenu suggested that everything in the life of the church can be a site of theology, including behavior, devotion, spirituality, philosophy, institutions, and sacraments. Thus, to turn to his second step, the historical-critical method needs to be employed in the work of theology. Theological utterances are always of their nature more or less inadequate, since they are expressed through imperfect human words and share in the weakness of human nature. A theology that believes it possible to present the word of God in unhistorical and authoritarian formulae is a theology that has forgotten the transcendence of God's word. Chenu's "theological sites" clearly refer to historical events and are close to the notion of "signs of the times" promoted by Vatican II. It is a matter, says Chenu, of "being present to revelation in the life of the church today and in the current experience of Christianity." The theologian's eyes must be "wide open to Christianity as it struggles today," and so he looks with a "holy curiosity" on the following phenomena: missionary expansion, cultural pluralism, the East, ecumenism, social unrest and the role of popular cultures, and the new movements of lay involvement in apostolic life. They are bad theologians, he comments, who fail to take all this seriously, not only in "the pious fervor of their hearts" but "formally in their science." Third and finally, Chenu insists that a theology is an expression of a spirituality, of a way of life. Because a way of life is dynamic, any theology, even Thomism, fails when it becomes an orthodoxy. Rather, theology should be "a courageous and creative expression of a 'style' of faith."[36]

Among those involved in the initial Roman response to Le Saulchoir were Fr. Reginald Garrigou-Lagrange, O.P., and the new assessor at the Holy Office, Monsignor Ottaviani, later to lead the conservative curial forces into their crushing defeat at Vatican II at the hands of Chenu and others. Chenu was summoned to Rome for "discussions," and there he was eventually presented with a handwritten text of ten short propositions, which had neither heading nor signatories, and was asked to agree to them.[37] While they were products of the "baroque" theology he opposed, he was able to assent to them, though one can only imagine that it cost him considerable intellectual gymnastics. The propositions begin with the terse statement that "dogmatic formulations state absolute and unchanging truth" and proceed to a series of similarly poorly nuanced pronouncements about the superiority of Thomism, its indispensable role in interpreting scripture and tradition, and the need to see that if theologians or theological schools differ with one another, they cannot all simultaneously be correct. Collectively, the ten principles represent an attack on the more historically sophisticated form of Thomism associated with Rousselot, Etienne Gilson (1884–1978, an outstanding historian of medieval philosophy), Maréchal, and others. Chenu's book strikes us today as an important and creative approach to theological studies, but it also had the effect of putting Rome on its guard, of warning it of the advent of the "new theologians," as Rome sarcastically called them.

Chenu's former student, friend, and collaborator Yves Congar probably had more influence on the Second Vatican Council than any other single theologian. In the twenty-five years before the council he wrote on ecumenism, tradition, reform in the church, pneumatology, and the theology of the laity; was silenced by Rome for a time; and was rehabilitated when John XXIII called him to work on preparations for the council. In the next chapter we shall study Congar's theology of the laity in considerable detail. For now, let us look briefly at some of the strains of the "new theology" emerging in his early ecumenical writings.

Congar's first major work was *Chrétiens désunis,* published in France in 1935.[38] As any text on ecumenism must, it presents a vision of the church. Congar's conception of the church is of a spirit-filled community, and his talk is always of reunion and not "return" of the "separated brethren" to the fold. The work is subtitled "A Catholic Study of the Problem of Reunion." He anticipates several emphases of Vatican II, notably contrasting the visible, earthly institution with the Mystical Body of Christ. Christendom is more extensive than the visible reality of the church, he argues, and while critical of the ecclesiologies of both Anglicanism and Orthodoxy, he insists that membership in the church is realized in different ways and to different degrees, by different people and different churches. The language and, more importantly, the tone of Congar's book is more or less exactly mirrored in the documents of Vatican II wherever other "ecclesial communities" are discussed. The book was a revelation to non-Catholics, who had come to expect something much more patronizing in Catholic outreach. It was the first genuinely ecumenical text from the Catholic tradition. Not surprisingly, perhaps, it was much less well received in certain quarters within the church.

Congar himself has written about the reception of his book in a lengthy autobiographical introduction to a later collection of essays on ecumenical themes.[39] His vocation to work for ecumenism, he says, dates from the time of his ordination in 1930, though "the seeds of it had been sown in me for many years, no doubt even from my childhood."[40] He writes with affection about many of these early influences, from his parish priest and his mother to significant figures in French liturgical renewal. He is aware that his contribution was to be primarily doctrinal and that ecumenism would for him be closely tied to ecclesiology. As the time for writing *Chrétiens désunis* approached, he became aware that

> ecumenism is not a specialty, and that it presupposes a movement of conversion and reform co-extensive with the whole life of all communions: It seemed to me, also, that each individual's ecumenical task lay in the first place at home among his own people. Our business was to rotate the Catholic Church through a few degrees on its own axis in the

direction of convergence towards others and a possible unanimity with them, in accordance with a deeper and closer fidelity to our unique source or our common sources.[41]

Hence, the program of the new book, which would give rise to his works on reform in the church, tradition, and the theology of the laity. It came as no. 2 in a series that Congar founded with Éditions du Cerf to be called *Unam Sanctam,* intended to revive traditional ecclesiological themes. The series was to begin with Johan Adam Möhler's *Die Einheit,* which eventually appeared as no. 1, but in practice Congar's book was the first to appear, in July of 1935. The first hint of problems came the same month, when Congar was invited to be present at the Oxford Ecumenical Conference as a Roman Catholic observer. Having requested permission from the master general to accept the invitation, he received a negative response, but from Cardinal Pacelli (the future Pius XII), then secretary of state to Pius XI. In April 1939 he was called to Paris by the master general of the Dominicans to be told of "very serious difficulties" which had arisen with his book. In 1940 *L'Osservatore Romano* published an article by Père Cordovani that was critical of Congar's work (without, of course, naming him). The problems went on hold for the duration of the war, most of which Congar spent as a prisoner of war in Germany, though of course it was during this time that Le Saulchoir and Chenu in particular were struck down. Congar always believed, probably correctly, that he was saved from the fate of Chenu only because he was in captivity. "The ground I trod, however," he wrote, "had trembled and the tremors were to continue for many long years.[42]

While 1946 and 1947 were in Congar's estimation "one of the finest moments in the life of the Church" in France, his own troubles continued. Writing of his relations with Rome, Congar comments that from 1947 until the end of 1956 he "knew nothing from that quarter but an uninterrupted series of denunciations, warnings, restrictive or discriminatory measures and mistrustful interventions.[43] He was forced to cancel a Catholic ecumenical conference planned for Easter 1947. After Congar had thoroughly revised *Chrétiens désunis* for a new edition, the Dominican master general took the manuscript away for censorship (a common practice) and then sat on it for two years, returning it only in August of 1950. Obviously knowing of the imminent appearance of *Humani Generis,*[44] he warned Congar of the dangers of "false irenism" and told him that one of the two readers had demanded some alterations to the text. But Congar was not told what the needed alterations in fact were. He eventually abandoned plans for a new edition.

During all of his difficulties with Roman censorship in the early 1950s, Congar was allowed to publish one major work, *Jalons pour une théologie du laicat,* which "came back from Rome without any veto and ultimately received the *nihil obstat* of the French censors."[45] It is not unreasonable to wonder why this particular work should have so thoroughly escaped the censor's concerns, and it may be the subject matter rather than the treatment. At the Vatican Council, too, one of the less controversial preliminary texts was that on the laity. There were perhaps two reasons for the limited concerns about a theology of the laity. On the one hand, there was a common feeling across the political spectrum in the church that the subject of the laity was something that needed to be treated with expedition. Catholic Action had become a major force in the church, particularly close to the heart of both Pope Pius XI and Pius XII, while no serious theological consideration of the lay role had accompanied it. On the other hand, so little previous work was available that what did get published was starting from scratch and was not challenging any particularly entrenched traditional theological position. Furthermore, and this certainly applies to Congar's work, what was said in the text was relatively moderate, while the more radical theological implications were only hinted at (and at the time Congar himself was probably unaware of some of them). In the council, the theological questions of the lay role were for the most part shelved in favor of the much easier question of their pastoral responsibilities.

Daniélou and Ressourcement

> It is impossible in our world to separate thought and life; a thought which is not at the same time a witness seems to be something of no account.
>
> —*Jean Daniélou*

In an article in the Jesuit journal *Études* in 1946, Jean Daniélou commented on the new theological directions in France.[46] Like Chenu's book, it was influential, courageous, and immediately suspect. Daniélou wanted to reclaim a voice for theological reflection in the intellectual life of his times. He maintained that modernism was an unhappy effort at solving real problems. The movement had correctly identified two deficiencies in religious thought, namely, the weakening of a sense of God's transcendence and the "mummification" of scholastic thought, which meant that it lost contact with contemporary developments in both philosophy and science. Because modernism's responses were inaccurate but its identification of the issues was correct, it was a factor in causing a renewal in religious thought, if not actually helpful in formulating the thought. Of course, modernism had to be opposed, and both Thomism and the Biblical Commission had been suitable barriers, but, said Daniélou, "it is quite clear that barriers are not answers."[47] Insisting that "theoretical speculations, divorced from action and disengaged from life, have had their day," Daniélou identified three needs for contemporary theology: to treat God as God, not as an object; to speak to the experiences of the people of the day and to take account of developments in science and philosophy; and to offer a response to contemporary life that would attract human beings, with all their hopes for life. Theology is not alive, he thought, if it does not do these things. He then proceeded to outline the ways in which theology was responding to these needs.

First among the signs of hope Daniélou placed the return to the sources of the Christian tradition, that is, scripture, the fathers of the church, and the liturgy. This contact with the sources had been lost since the emergence in the thirteenth century of theology as an autonomous science and its eventual "desiccation." While acknowledging the invaluable work of Catholic scripture scholars in the previous fifty years, Daniélou argued that it was time for a renewal of biblical theology. Wrestling with the way in which the Old Testament might be a source of theology, he proposed a return to the figurative exegesis of the fathers, as opposed simply to the "scientific" exegesis promoted in Pius XII's 1943 encyclical letter *Divino afflante spiritu*. In the return to patristic thought, comments Daniélou, we can uncover a number of "categories which are those of contemporary thought but which scholastic theology had lost." The idea of history, for example, while foreign to Thomism, is important to Irenaeus, Origen, and Gregory of Nyssa. Even more importantly, the Greek fathers correct the Latin fathers on the matter of salvation. Conversion today, says Daniélou, does not come from being confronted by the question, "How can I save my soul?" but by the imperative, "I must save the soul of my brothers." This emphasis on salvation as the salvation of humanity, not of the individual, is the contribution of the Greek fathers. It is what Catholic Action exists to promote, he says, and it is an attitude strengthened by a return to the theology of the Mystical Body, which suffuses the patristic literature.

If Daniélou's first point was likely to arouse the ire of many more conservative scripture scholars and even a few of those more "scientific" exegetes who had been heartened by Pius's encyclical, his second and third points were a direct challenge to the neoscholastic establishment. He argued, for example, for a sustained encounter between theology and modern philosophical currents of Marxism and existentialism, because they give priority to questions of historicity and subjectivity, which are so important to modern human beings, while "scholastic theology is a stranger to these categories." "Locating reality in essences rather than in subjects," Daniélou continued, "[scholastic theology] ignores the human world, the concrete universals that transcend all essences and are distinguished only by existence, that is, no more through intelligibility and intellect, but through value, love and hatred."[48] He wrote approvingly in this context of the work of the Jesuit paleontologist and theologian Pierre Teilhard de Chardin, whose works had all just been placed on the Index.[49] And if we recognize that Marxism and existentialism confront us with the themes of history and the goodness of the world, freedom and the absurdity of the world, we should also note that it is in the Christian mystery that this conflict finds its highest expression. Further, he argued, rubbing neoscholastic noses still deeper into the dirt, existentialism offers a method that resists the reduction of concepts to Aristotelian logic or Hegelian dialectic and so is allied with those like Rudolf Otto, Gabriel Marcel, and Max Scheler, who insist on the irreducibility of notions of the sacred, of Christian love, of faith, and of hope. This admittedly incomplete method "must now become the basis for all theology which founds itself on descriptions of concrete religious realities."[50]

Daniélou's third and final broadside attacks the separation of theology from real life. Theology, he says, must be apostolic and "totally occupied in building up the Body of Christ," though, in typical fashion, he supports this unexceptional claim by quoting Marx's distinction between understanding the world and changing it. Effectively,

Daniélou makes the case here for the inseparability of theology and spirituality, once again calling on the example of the fathers. Applauding the publications of Catholic Action and particularly of the JOC, he makes numerous references to current French works that particularly aided laypeople in understanding sanctity as love of neighbor, in better appreciating the theological dimensions of marriage, and in coming to terms with the place of political activity in their faith. Theologians, he concludes, have a double role. First, they must appreciate the value of human reality. Daniélou challenges an unhealthy dualism that has crept into French Catholicism, born of a confusion between spirituality and theology. There is legitimacy, he says, to the depreciation of creatureliness from a spiritual point of view, but "this becomes illegitimate when it is transformed into a theological judgment."[51] Second, they must at the same time place human values in the context of the Christian mystery of Christ's death and resurrection. It is this, he says, that is in danger of being forgotten. Further, Christian thought must move beyond its European dress and open itself to other cultures. This is not the development of Revelation, which was closed with Christ, but the development of dogma, as each cultural milieu expresses the riches of Christ in its own way.

Daniélou was not a man to mince words. Nor was Reginald Garrigou-Lagrange, who in a letter of July 17, 1946, had referred to Daniélou's article as "the manifesto of this new theology." Garrigou-Lagrange followed up with an article entitled "La nouvelle théologie: Où va-telle?" published in the Dominican journal *Angelicum* in 1946, after it had been rejected by the *Revue Thomiste*.[52] In twenty pages of misquotations and quotations taken out of context, Garrigou-Lagrange offered a vicious *ad hominem* attack on the "young Jesuits" and a series of clear criticisms of unnamed others, including his former student, Chenu.[53] Many were shocked by the intemperateness of the elderly Dominican. Philip Donnelly wrote in *Theological Studies* in 1947:

> One could have wished that a theologian of P. Garrigou-Lagrange's international standing had been more objective, not to say conclusive, in his charges of unorthodox tendencies directed against individual theologians of outstanding merit, before linking their views with those of anonymous proponents of open heresy.[54]

In all probability speaking for Rome, Garrigou-Lagrange called the new theology a "return to modernism." While subsequently there was some published correspondence with Maurice Blondel, the Jesuits attacked in the article were forbidden by the Jesuit general to publish replies to Garrigou-Lagrange. Perhaps this emboldened him, since in the next few years a series of articles by the same author appeared in *Angelicum*. The titles alone tell the story: "The Truth and Immutability of Dogma" (1947), "The Need to Revisit the Traditional Definition of Truth" (1948), "The Immutability of Dogma According to Vatican I, and Relativism" (1949), and "Relativism and the Immutability of Dogma" (1950). Perhaps the most telling of all comments is Garrigou-Lagrange's remark in an unpublished and undated report, probably written for internal use in the Dominican order, where he refers to "the campaign of the young Jesuits against St. Thomas."[55] But during these final years of the decade of the 1940s there was a relative and perhaps uneasy calm, to be broken in 1950 by the publication of Pius XII's encyclical *Humani Generis*. While this letter was an attack on the new theology in general, its clearest target was the work of Henri de Lubac, to whom we must now turn.

De Lubac and Le Surnaturel

While the debates about the need for a historically sensitive reading of St. Thomas were real enough, and while much of the opposition to this was the work of individuals whose security and intellectual complacency would be punctured by a denial of the normativity of the neoscholastic synthesis, the fundamental issue was theological. At the same time, this theological question was an instance of the need to return to Thomas himself, and of the folly of assuming that later commentators were necessarily faithful representers of the thought of the master. It is Henri de Lubac, above all, who tackles the vital question, whether or not the human person is invested with a natural desire for God.[56] Is the human person by nature open to the supernatural, or is the desire for God itself only real as a result of a free act of God? It will be necessary to outline briefly the technicalities of this debate, since so much of Vatican II's theology, and in particular the theology of the laity, depends on it. We shall then be able to view the "new theology" in all its glory, to see what it was that seemed so threatening to Rome.

Shortly before de Lubac's book, a work by Henri Bouillard had shown very convincingly that the understandings of grace possessed by Augustine, Thomas, and the later scholastic commentators were not identical to one another but reflected differences in the questions they were asking and the resources they had to answer them.[57] Furthermore, they showed an understanding of the dynamics of theology quite different from the notion of a serene development from a less adequate to a fuller expression of the same fundamental truths. Of course, the fundamentals of faith are immutable, while theology demonstrates different expressions of these fundamentals. This was not controversial. What was so challenging to the neoscholastics was the claim that the "development" of theological reflection could also include moments of loss as well as gain, that later developments could "forget" the truths of earlier times.[58] Coupled with the devastating clarity with which Bouillard showed that Thomas's account of grace is quite different from that of his later commentators, this book could not but leave neoscholastics in disarray.

De Lubac's *Surnaturel* was the second salvo in the battle, addressing more directly the question of "double finality," namely, whether there was in the human person "a state of pure nature" to which God added a second in which was given the orientation toward deification. This view, which nineteenth-century neoscholasticism attributed to Thomas, was in fact an invention of his sixteenth-century commentators Cajetan, John of St. Thomas, and Suárez. Thomas's view, argued de Lubac, was that no such thing as a state of pure nature had ever existed. Of course the possibility of an orientation to the beatific vision, of deification, had to be a gift of God, since human beings could not of themselves become deified, but it was a gift given in the creation of human beings. There is no double finality; there is only one, and thus the human being has a natural desire for the beatific vision. Both patristic and medieval theology, said de Lubac, concurred in this judgment. For human beings, there is no such thing as a natural order and a supernatural order. There is only one, that of "graced nature."

The theological implications of the defeat of the "double finality" interpretation of St. Thomas are considerable. Formally, in the first instance, de Lubac and Bouillard have clearly shown that the nature of theology is, like other academic disciplines, subject to history and hermeneutics, distinctly evolutionary, with all the uncertainties and false paths that evolution itself takes in its progress. Only looking backwards can the theological tradition track the faithfulness of its conceptions to the truths of faith. Only looking backwards can it see the difference between false paths and steps forward. And it cannot be sure, since it is cannot look back at the present moment, whether contemporary theological reflection is also straying from the truths of faith.[59] Such thinking, dubbed "relativism" by Garrigou-Lagrange, totally undermined the security of the neoscholastic system beloved of the Roman "baroque theology." Frankly, it also reminded the neoscholastics of the modernists, correctly so if Daniélou's judgment is upheld, that the modernists had the issues right though their solutions were erroneous. The new theology could not be allowed to pass without comment.

De Lubac's reading of tradition was also profoundly unnerving to the neoscholastics. In the realm of Christian anthropology, it affirmed a much more positive evaluation of human cooperation with divine grace, moving the church further away from the assessment of the Reformers. By rejecting the idea that human history is made of two layers, secular and sacred, or natural and supernatural, de Lubac clearly prepared the ground for all the work that Vatican II would do on the church–world relationship. But above all de Lubac's theology dealt a crushing blow to the rationalist apologetics that had ruled Rome for centuries. Where the rationalist apologetics imagined the chasm between belief and unbelief as crossed through the exercise of reason, responding to the claim to authority through scripture and tradition, the "new" apologetics showed that a sounder and earlier tradition supported a different understanding. Because God has from the moment of creation infused the human person with a capacity, even a thirst, for the infinite, so faith springs from the heart, not the intellect, and there really is no chasm to cross.

All that we have seen in these few pages about the growth of the new theology out of the modernist crisis and the evolution of Thomism has a political as well as a theological face. There is much to be said for the hypothesis that the antimodernist fury of Rome in the early part of the twentieth century was largely a product of papal insecurity in the face of cultural modernity, which had destroyed the papal states and encouraged the growth of secularism and atheism. We should not forget the strange position that the Vatican was in during the worst years of antimodernism, no longer a church-state, not yet the Vatican City State of the 1929 Concordat. The modernists, on this account, just chose the worst possible moment to suggest that it was time for the church to accommodate itself to modernity. Their point, however, was in its turn more pastoral and apologetic, but political considerations made it even harder for Rome to hear them than did the theological clamor of their neoscholastic opponents. By the time of the new theology, also strongly pastoral in motivation, the same could not be said.

Servant Theologians

One of the most striking characteristics of the French church after the Second World War was the way in which intellectual life and apostolic activity went hand in hand. There were, in the first instance, large numbers of Dominicans, Jesuits, and secular clergy involved in the youth movements, both in the Boy Scouts, where the Dominicans were strong, and in the JOC, where the Jesuits seemed most active. But even the most distinguished theologians of the time were involved in one way or another. All of them wrote frequently in the great French journals which carried French theology to a wider public than simply theologians, *Études, Esprit,* and *La Vie Intellectuelle* in particular.

This meant of course that they had to write in a different style, no less erudite but considerably less technical than they might have done for their *confrères* in the academy. This style of writing, which the French call *haute vulgarisation,* is an honorable pursuit. The English translation "popularization" does not quite capture the nuances, suggesting something seedier. But Daniélou was easily adaptable to this way of writing, and Congar learned to do it with facility. (Even Karl Rahner, that densest of theologians, practiced it in his published sermons.) Beyond their writing, what is noticeable about Daniélou, Chenu, and Congar in particular is the degree to which they spread themselves widely in the cause of direct apostolic activity. Congar for very many years, for example, always devoted January to a preaching tour in the cause of the Octave for Christian Unity. Year after year for an entire month in the dead of winter he crisscrossed France, giving

sermons in churches in towns big and small, to congregations of ordinary Catholic layfolk. Daniélou managed to combine his professor-
ship at L'Institut Catholique with work with a number of lay groups
and chaplaincy to a girls' high school. Chenu in his turn was devoted
to all kinds of everyday apostolic contact with ordinary people, particularly during the twelve years he spent at the Convent Saint Jacques,
after his expulsion from Le Saulchoir. And the sympathy of all of them
with the vibrant "worker priest" movement, which was itself crushed
by Rome in 1954, was well known.[60]

Fouilloux has suggested that what came into being in these individuals was a new understanding of the role of the theologian, one of
the most distinctive characteristics of the French church in the twentieth century. Dubbing him a "servant theologian," Fouilloux writes
that such a person was "neither an agent of the magisterium nor a simple seminary professor, not an Anglo-Saxon scholar nor a German
academic."

Rather he was "an apostle whose desire to preach the gospel leads
him to put his professional skills at the service of the Christian community, the most humble and the most distinguished (*huppées*)."[61]
While this conception certainly looks back to the days of the early
church, and while Chenu at least saw parallels between the French
church at this time and the theological ferment of his beloved thirteenth
century, it also anticipates the way in which liberation theologians
would understand their relationship to the believing community. It is
particularly close to the notion of the theologian as "professional
insider" developed by Ada María Isasi-Díaz in her *mujerista* theology.[62]

Deep down, it may well be that it was this close association between
professional theology and the daily life of the church that most
unnerved Rome. Traditionally, theologians have been given considerable latitude to develop their thinking in directions that might seem
at times to border on plain heresy, so long as they restrict the dissemination of these ideas to their academic colleagues and the technical
theological journals in which they exchange opinions. Only by
stretching, by trying out ideas, by arguing with one another, can the
theological community move forward. Sometimes some of these ideas
will be abandoned, while others will meet with approval and move by
degrees toward the point at which they will enter the mainstream of
church life. But when theologians gain the ear of the ordinary faithful

for their risky notions, Rome is not happy. Why did Karl Rahner and Edward Schillebeeckx fare better than Congar and de Lubac, than Hans Küng and Leonardo Boff and Charles Curran at a later date? Those who came under censure were all of them theologians whose writings were read well beyond the professional theological community, and so, from Rome's perspective, whose speculative notions were being put into the minds of those untrained to evaluate them.

Moreover, the success of French Catholicism in bringing lay movements, lively intellectual journals, and major theological figures together, while it produced a new spring in the minds of people like Congar and Chenu, presaged disaster in Roman eyes. Something had to be done, and something was done.

THE BEGINNINGS OF A THEOLOGY OF THE LAITY

Given the prominence of lay activity in the work of the French church at this time, it was unthinkable that there would not be sustained theological attention to the place of laypeople in the apostolic activity of the church. The definitive statement on the theology of the laity during this period is undoubtedly Congar's *Jalons pour un théologie du laicat*.[63] But this must be seen as the climax of considerable earlier work, both in France and in Belgium, much of it inspired by the need to make theological sense of the phenomenon of Catholic Action. François Varillon (1905–1978) and Yves de Montcheuil (1899–1944) are good examples.[64] The former saw, on the one hand, that discussion of the laity implies consideration of the role of the priesthood and, on the other, that the power held by the ordained ministry must be relaxed to allow the flowering of the work of the laity called for, for example, in Pius XII's encyclical *Mystici Corporis*. The latter, de Montcheuil, is emblematic of the rise of lay theology in the French church at this time. A learned man capable of enormous academic contributions to theology, he in fact spent most of his short life working with lay groups across France, especially the young, for whom he wrote a number of short and more popular works addressed to their needs. He was executed by the Gestapo, perhaps for his involvement in a series of underground publications, *Cahiers du Témoignages chrétiennes*. He is the subject of a very moving tribute by Henri de Lubac in his little book *Three Jesuits Speak*.[65] De Montcheuil wrote of the idea of the church as the Mystical Body, but in order to point out that, unlike members of a physical body, the members of Christ's body are "thinking members." They have not only the right but also the responsibility to reflect on their place in the work of the church. Christians must not talk of what affects "me" or "them," he says, but of what affects "us." If there is a "care for all the churches" proper to church leaders, "there is also a universal care common to all Christians."[66]

The one major figure other than Congar who puts the laity at the center of his work is a Belgian theologian, Gerard Philips. Mostly forgotten today, he was very significant in his time and, like Congar and Rahner, highly influential on the work of Vatican II. In 1955 he wrote a short but powerful book, *The Role of the Laity in the Church*.[67] Though appearing a couple of years after Congar's great work, and paying close attention to Congar, Philips's book is far less concerned with developing a theology of the laity, much more taken up with an examination of the nature and limits of lay apostolic activity. Congar and Philips are very much of one mind, though Philips is not without his criticisms of Congar. But Philips's area of interest is more directly reflected in Vatican II's efforts to evaluate and promote the lay apostolate. Congar's concerns, on the other hand, clearly address a theological evaluation of the laity as such, a topic not dwelled upon by the council, though considered after a fashion in *Lumen Gentium*. Overall, as we shall see later, the council's words on the laity skirted the question of their theological status and concentrated on their apostolate.

Philips, more cautious and certainly more conservative than Congar, nevertheless applauds the Dominican's distinction between the church as institution and as community of life. Philips perhaps shows a little too much deference to the hierarchical element in the church, observing that even in heaven where there will of course be no masters and servants, "many pastors and teachers will shine there forever like the stars, a reward for fidelity to their tasks."[68] But to do him justice, he is equally concerned for the holiness of the laity. If we view the laity "merely as an inferior part of a well-organized society," says Philips, then the laity are condemned to passivity, "and then we would have no Christianity." On the contrary, baptism and confirmation bring the layperson "into the *laos* or people of God." And this theology has practical implications, demanding a particular lifestyle. The layperson will not only practice obedience but also cultivate a spirit of initiative, without which submission "will not save . . . orthodoxy." But the layperson must also deepen faith through serious reflection, the opposite of passivity. It is not enough to rely, says Philips, on the pastor's directives: "[t]he faith of a coal miner can be inspired by a praiseworthy sense of mystery, not by a disguised spiritual sloth."[69] Moreover, there must be an ecumenical spirit that shows a true catholicity, rather than the all-too-common "collective egoism" that "is often presented as a virtue." Above all, says Philips, the Catholic layperson must be able to recognize the role of hierarchical authority in decision making, while also exercising freedom and initiative. Moved by the Spirit, the Catholic must also never substitute individual judgment for the collective wisdom of the whole church, as voiced by the hierarchy. Above all, the need is to awaken in the layperson a sense of her or his truly apostolic status. As one "descends" (an unfortunate, preconciliar choice of word) through the organization of the church, "the concept of apostle diminishes without ever becoming completely diluted."[70] It is not just about ruling or sacramental ministry, but in the last instance relates to spreading the gospel. Hence, anyone with that mission—and that means the layperson as well as the cleric—is in some sense an apostle, challenged to responsible activity. We are none of us "marionettes on strings," but invited by the Spirit "to a generous co-operation that changes subjection to adherence."[71]

While Philips's book is an important text, it is a reforming rather than a potentially revolutionary work, and it aroused few of the suspicions that Congar seems to have inspired. A call to the laity to recognize their spiritual adulthood, *The Role of the Laity in the Church* is also a resounding appeal to the clergy to relate to the laity as adults to adults, to expect and reward responsibility and initiative. It utilizes the language of the church as "people of God," anticipatory of Vatican II. But nowhere does Philips envisage any real change in power relations in the church, nor does he investigate the nature of the priesthood and episcopacy in which that power is totally invested. In this sense, his vision seems quite close to that of Pius XII, whom he quotes approvingly at length in his opening chapter. Addressing the new cardinals in February 1946, Pius spoke of the need for the laity to see that they "are stationed in the front ranks of the life of the Church, and through them the Church is the living principle of human society." They must come to understand, said the pope, that they do not just belong to the church; "they are the Church." But all of this is said in the context of a highly centralized, militant army of Catholic Action and "auxiliary pious associations." Philips goes beyond this, but perhaps not so very far beyond.

FROM HUMANI GENERIS TO VATICAN II

On the publication of Pius XII's encyclical *Humani Generis* in 1950, his secretary of state Giovanni Battista Montini (the future Paul VI) explained that this was not another *Pascendi:* "Indeed one could say that the Holy Father's intention is to avoid the need for another *Pascendi*."[72] Outsiders could be excused their skepticism. The pope attacked relativism and historicism in theology, naming no names but clearly targeting the French Jesuits and Dominicans. Many of them, including de Lubac, were promptly removed from their teaching positions, most of them forbidden to publish further. While it is true that the aftermath of *Humani Generis* was neither so long nor so painful as that which had followed Pius X's 1907 attack on modernism, it was not at the time clear that the encyclical was the last gasp of a weakening but still virulent antimodernism. To those affected directly, it seemed that the antimodernist crusade continued unabated.

Having opened by outlining the spirit of rationalism, dialectical materialism, and existentialism that has come to infect the modern world, the pope turns to those within the church who are affected by these same currents of thought, declaring that they are "desirous of novelty and fearing to be considered ignorant of recent scientific findings" (*Humani Generis* §10). "Concealed beneath the mask of virtue," there are many who advocate an "irenism," by which the pope means a relativism in theology, such that ecumenical disagreements could be brushed aside (§11). Could he have been thinking of Congar? Some want to abandon the perennial philosophy of Thomism "to bring about a return in the explanation of Catholic doctrine to the way of speaking used in Holy Scripture and by the Fathers of the Church" (§14). Did he have Daniélou in mind? The more audacious among them actually favor the idea that the mysteries of faith are only ever expressed analogically, never "by truly adequate concepts but only by approximate and ever changeable notions" (§15). Were Bouillard and de Lubac his targets? The pope sees all these unnamed theologians as really targeting the teaching authority of the church. While theologians should return to scripture and the fathers of the church, this is primarily because "it belongs to them to point out how the doctrine of the living Teaching Authority is to be found either explicitly or implicitly in the Scriptures and in Tradition." Quoting Pius IX, the pope comments that "the most noble office of theology is to show how a doctrine defined by the Church is contained in the sources of revelation 'in that sense in which it has been defined by the Church'" (§21). The letter, says Pius, is written to nip these problems in the bud rather than to be forced "to administer the medicine after the disease has grown inveterate" (§40). He concludes by demanding that bishops and the superiors of religious orders take appropriate disciplinary measures to ensure that all these harmful opinions are not taught any longer.

The generals of the Jesuits and the Dominicans were ready to do the pope's bidding. Fr. General Janssens acted almost immediately against Daniélou, de Lubac, and Bouillard. Bouillard and de Lubac were sent to Paris, admittedly not a terribly onerous exile for a Frenchman, but it removed them from their work at the seminary of Fourvière, near Lyon. Henri Rondet, the prefect of studies at Fourvière, was also dismissed. The Dominicans took a little longer to act, but in 1954 Chenu was sent to Rouen (and allowed a month every year in Paris!) and his license to teach was suspended. Congar was sent off to Cambridge, where his English Dominican brothers treated him as more or less under house arrest and kept careful tabs on his ecumenical contacts. The impact on Le Saulchoir was, if anything, greater than that on Fourvière. Nor did everything end here.

The last years of Pius's pontificate maintained the pressure on the French church, and even in the headier days of John XXIII, many of the curial officials who had run Pius's campaign were still at their respective helms. Admittedly, most of their energies were being expended on figuring out how best to undermine John's convoking an ecumenical council and to limit the damage to the church.

2

The Achievement of Yves Congar

T HE STORY OF THE GREAT DOMINICAN THEOLOGIAN Yves Congar is in many respects the tale of the twentieth-century Catholic Church. Born in France in 1904, Congar grew up in a church in the aftermath of the modernist crisis. He joined the Dominican order in 1925 and was attracted to the historical retrieval of the work of Aquinas, favored by the Dominicans. He also came to believe that much of the thought of the modernists, albeit purged of excesses, could be rehabilitated for the church, specifically the attention they had given to history and to personal experience. Two of his greatest works, *True and False Reform in the Church* and *Lay People in the Church*, published in the early 1950s, were followed shortly by his silencing by the Holy See, a ban that was not really lifted until in 1959 Pope John XXIII called him to serve on the preparatory commission for the Second Vatican Council. A number of the council documents, above all the chapter from *Lumen Gentium* on the laity, were drafted by teams in which Congar was prominent, and naturally reflect much of his thought (and that of Philips). During the pontificate of Paul VI, Congar served on the Catholic-Lutheran Commission and the International Theological Commission. In Congar's last years, Pope John Paul II named him a cardinal. In the previous chapter, we noted how a number of theologians who fell into disrepute in the times of antimodernist purges were eventually rehabilitated, Congar among them. Rehabilitation, however, does not necessarily indicate that all the theologian's views have been embraced by official Roman theology. There is a vein of radicalism in Congar's theology of the laity that has yet to be fully explored, and whose implications the author himself may not have fully realized at the time of writing.

While all of Congar's work can profitably be read by anyone interested in a theology of the laity, the focus of attention will inevitably be on *Lay People in the Church*, first published in French in 1953 and in English and American editions just two years later. Congar added some material for the revised edition published in French in 1964. The revisions, while not extensive, are sometimes quite important, reflecting not only the development of Congar's thought over a ten-year period but also the new ecclesial climate of the era of Vatican II.[1] Two further short pieces illustrate the later development of Congar's thought and show how he came to question some elements of his earlier work, namely, a 1972 article in *The Jurist* and his introduction to the French edition of the papal apostolic exhortation *Christifideles Laici*.[2] Finally, there is a series of late essays on "ministries," the category through which he came finally to want to understand the respective roles of laity and clergy.[3]

From the beginning, there is a tentativeness to Congar's work on the laity that goes beyond the prudent moderation of the scholar, or that can even be explained by the difficult situation of theology in the first half of the twentieth century. The very title of the major early work, "signposts" (*jalons*) for a theology of the laity, suggests that Congar did not think of this (450-page) book as a comprehensive study of the topic. He later referred to it as a "patchwork" and pleaded guilty to two failings, "a rather rigid framework" and having been too "schematic," focusing on the structure of functions in the church more than "their actual working in practice." If he had paid more attention to activity and mission, he says, "the results might have been more satisfactory."[4] This hesitancy about the final product recurs in later writings. In "My Pathfindings," for example, he declares that "the inappropriate element in my procedure of 1953 was perhaps to distinguish too nicely . . . to define the ministerial priesthood purely in itself."[5] Toward the end of his life, in a conversation with Bernard Lauret, he returned to this topic, referring to the "deliberately modest title" of the book and admitting that despite the positive valuation of the laity therein, he had to a degree fallen into the trap of defining "the laity in relation to the clergy." Remarkably, he added that "[t]oday it is the case, rather, that the clergy need to be defined in relation to the laity, who are quite simply members of the people of God animated by the Spirit."[6]

Congar's theology of the laity is a magnificent achievement, but there is a still better work hidden within its covers. Congar pleads pressure of time as the reason that he never wrote the complete ecclesiology that he wished to produce and never subjected the first version of his book to a thorough revision. There is no doubt that he is speaking the truth. His profound commitment to apostolic and particularly ecumenical activity did indeed limit the amount of time he had for writing. Other factors also contribute to the explanation. One, undoubtedly, was the personal crisis he went through as a result of his silencing by the Vatican, only to be lifted at a time when he immediately plunged into the preparatory work for Vatican II. In later years, his increasing physical debility was a contributory cause. But it is clear that even within *Signposts* one can trace an ambivalence about some of its albeit tentative conclusions. We know that from as far back as 1936 Congar was working under a cloud of suspicion that only grew darker and more threatening after his return from internment in Germany during the Second World War. It is reasonable to conclude that he was exercising considerable caution in the way in which he approached the topic. In itself, this goes a long way to explaining the claim that the work is only exploratory and preparatory and shows why the later regrets are entirely understandable. While it would be interesting to speculate about what the finished text of that other, hidden work might have been, we will follow a different path. After briefly reviewing the remarkable achievement of *Lay People in the Church*, we will focus on those areas of the text which seem less satisfactorily concluded, connecting them to Congar's own later thoughts on the same or similar topics. In that way, we may be on firmer ground in seeking the book he might have written, or might have wanted to write but didn't, than in attempting some wholesale and inevitably fanciful reconstruction. There are more than a few hints in this book of a far more radical theology of the laity than it actually presents.

LAY PEOPLE IN THE CHURCH

In *Lay People in the Church* Congar explores the complexity of the lay role. In the first place, the laity are secular. That is to say, while the clergy are primarily occupied with direct service of God in the church, the laity serve God in the world by loving and using the things of the world in and for themselves. Now this is most emphatically not a rigid separation of the clergy and laity, in which one is ordered to heavenly things, the other to earthly things. It is a matter of degree. Two truths must be maintained. First, that "as members of the people of God, lay persons are, like clerics and monks, by their state and directly, ordered to heavenly things" (p. 18). Second, that "the layman . . . is one for whom, through the very work which God has entrusted to him, the substance of things in themselves is real and interesting" (p. 19). But this sense of an ordering to earthly realities is immediately qualified:

> [A] lay person is one for whom things exist, for whom their truth is not as it were swallowed up and destroyed by a higher reference. For to him or her, Christianly speaking, that which is to be referred to the Absolute is the very reality of the elements of this world whose outward form passes away. (p. 24)

Nevertheless, in the 1964 additions Congar admits that his way of writing led to some misunderstandings. He recognizes the superiority of Karl Rahner's way of putting things,[7] since Rahner makes it clear that the world "only provides the conditions of Christian activity," while Congar's discussion "appears to affect the *matter* of what is done for God." Moving beyond this point, he affirms the council's preference for the language of the People of God, the community in which the "hierarchical fact" is situated. "There are particular forms of exercise of the Church's mission," he writes in *Lay People in the Church*, "but there is no particular mission differentiating the faithful and the ministerial priesthood." Referring the world to God is also part of the hierarchical ministry, and "the lay faithful in their own way carry on the Church's evangelizing mission" (p. 25).

In Congar's view, laypeople exercise multiple roles. Although he does not use this phrase, we could say that, for Congar, laypeople's secularity consists in their "loving the world for God." But at the same time, in virtue of their baptism and confirmation, laypeople exercise roles within the church both sacramentally and apostolically. They have an important, active place in the eucharistic worship of the church. They are not merely passive spectators at worship conducted by the clergy. Rather, they bring the world into the worship of the church, offering it back to God. Moreover, through Catholic Action they can participate in the work of the hierarchical ministry, work that is not to be confused with the roles that laypeople have in the world, simply as lay Christians. We can identify in Congar's thought the following four aspects of lay life:

1. The layperson is called to life in the world, showing "respect for the true inwardness of things," though referring them to God.

2. The layperson should exercise a role in the eucharistic worship of the church, actively bringing the world and its concerns before God in Christ.

3. The layperson may cooperate, through Catholic Action, in the work of the hierarchical apostolate.

4. The layperson is called through baptism and confirmation to a direct evangelization of the world that is exercised independently of the hierarchical apostolate.

All four of these characteristics of lay apostolicity are priestly roles. While the hierarchical ministry is a priesthood of a different order from that of the priesthood of the laity, lay priesthood is real in itself, and most certainly not derivative of ministerial priesthood. The laity who engage in apostolic actions are not mini-priests, but rather "lay priests."

Congar challenges the clericalization of the church, believing that throughout the second millennium the church has failed to understand the important role the laity play. He frequently speaks disparagingly of the flippant remarks of ecclesiastics about the role of the laity, to "pray and pay" and so on. This emerges most clearly in the lengthy chapter on priesthood. Even though Congar was uneasy himself about the degree to which he defined laity in relation to clergy, and even though his friends and critics, notably Jean Daniélou, took him severely to task for this weakness, his presentation of the role of the laity represents a pronounced advance over what went before, and is in some ways today still ahead of much of the thinking in the church. It is true that the Second Vatican Council and subsequent documents of the Vatican and Roman synods clearly show the extent of his influence. But it is equally the case that there are dimensions to his work that Rome did not take up. For example, while it is never in doubt that Congar saw ordained priesthood as much more than just a function within the church, it is striking how insistently he stresses the fundamental parity of clergy and laity. First, all are Christians; then, some are lay, some are ordained. There is also a clear sense that lay activity in the world is not something delegated to them by the clergy, but theirs by right and responsibility as laypeople. Neither of these insights gets much play in the various texts on the apostolate issuing from Rome since the council.

Before we turn to the "stress points" in Congar's work on the laity, credit should be given for the mighty advances he makes. In addition to the general assertion of the nature of lay activity outlined above, there are many specific points in the text that are worthy of note. In the first place, discussing how the kingship of Christ is complete in principle but is to be worked out in history, Congar distinguishes Christ's spiritual authority in the church, where he reigns, from his temporal authority in the world, where he does not yet reign (pp. 79–107). If it is in the work of the laity in the secular realm that Christ's temporal authority is forwarded, it is important to see that this temporal authority is not mediated through the spiritual authority within the church. Moreover, Congar allows some soteriological significance to this "building the Kingdom" in history. Preferring an incarnationalist to a "dualist-eschatological" perspective, in which the world strives for "the state of integrity," he writes beautifully that "final salvation will be achieved by a wonderful refloating of our earthly vessel rather than by a transfer of the survivors to another ship wholly built by God" (p. 102). It would not be wrong to see here some anticipation of the ecclesial soteriology of liberation theology, where the precarious balancing act between a proper evaluation of secular activity and a due deference to the final power of God to save is also successfully maintained. It is also unquestionable that this vision locates lay apostolic activity at the heart of the church's mission.

Further positive elements in Congar's book can be found in his lengthy chapter on the priesthood of God's people. A thorough examination of the role of the priest in Hebrew Scripture, in the New Testament, and in the fathers of the church precedes his theological interpretation, in which Congar juxtaposes the more common under-standing of the priest as mediator with that of priesthood as sacrificial. By "sacrifice," Congar means not so much the ancient blood sacrifice now re-presented as the one sacrifice of Christ, but more the self-sacrificial dimension of the priestly role. At first reading, the insistence that priesthood is both mediation and (self) sacrifice can seem like a preparation for a claim for the moral superiority of hierarchical priest-hood over lay life. But it turns out not to be so. Not only is the medi-ating role of lay activity in the secular world so important. It is the (self) sacrifice of both clergy and laity (the cross) that is united with the sacrifice of Christ in the mass.

The laity's priesthood is a true priesthood (Congar's preferred term is "spiritual-real"), which has its place both in "the order of the holi-ness of life," and in "the order of sacramental worship."[8] Congar offers a diagrammatic representation of the priesthoods of the church, both hierarchical and lay (pp. 192–93). This shows clearly that while the ordained priesthood has particular responsibilities not shared with the laity pertaining to the celebration of the sacraments other than baptism and Eucharist, all other aspects of priesthood are shared by clergy and laity. The diagram and subsequent commentary also indi-rectly illustrate, in the degree to which it limits the specific functions of the ordained ministry, why the postconciliar period has been dis-tinguished by a crisis of identity among the clergy (pp. 192–93).

In general in this chapter on the priestly role of the laity, really a small book in its own right, Congar reveals a very high ecclesiology. Although later chapters eventually restore some kind of balance, for Congar at this point the church seems to be far more about the rec-onciliation of all things to God than it is about the evangelization of the world that needs that reconciliation. It is not unreasonable to ask whether the mediating role of the priesthood, both clerical and lay, is not as much about the mediation of God to the world, as it is about the reconciliation of the world to God. But it is perhaps of overriding importance for Congar at this point in his argument to stress that even when we attend to the worship and holiness of the church in itself, lay priesthood is of immense importance. The laity, in other words, are not just taught in the church and sent into the world. They exercise a positive, active role within the church.

In the later and shorter chapters of this huge book, three particularly important steps are taken to assert a balanced relationship between the roles of clergy and laity. First, in the relatively short but masterful chapter on the laity's place in the church's "kingly function" (pp. 234–70), Congar discusses kingship both as a form of life, and as power. Congar first offers a brief spiritual treatise on kingship over self (over our own powers and deeds), and kingship over the world. Kingship over the world is a matter of spiritual freedom, a dialectic of "refusal and engagement" through which we serve, challenge and even at times withdraw from the world. But when he turns to the question of kingship as power, he has to examine the place of lay involvement in authority within the church. Here he makes a crucial distinction. If we look at the history of the church, he says, there is never a question of the laity having any ecclesiastical rule. The laity "has never been looked on as giving the Church her structure as Church." This "is the business of the episcopate alone" (p. 246). In fact, arguments about this have tended to occlude the real role of the laity, thinks Congar, which resides in "the principle . . . of consent, as a principle, not of structure but of life, as a concrete law of all the great acts of ecclesial life, beginning with that of designation to the highest offices" (p. 247). Although Congar goes into considerable historical detail to show the extent of lay involvement in consent and even decision making in this history of the church, for clarification he returns to the structure/life distinction. The important thing here is balance, preserving, on the one hand, the hierarchical constitution of the church and, on the other, the cooperation of the faithful, which gives the structure life. The texts of early Christianity are "both resolutely hierarchical and indefeasibly communitarian." The law of existence of the church, says Congar, is "the meeting and harmonizing between an hierarchical communication from above and a community's consent" (p. 263).

Reading this chapter today, the contemporary Catholic might face a challenge or two. The huge role that Congar sees for lay consent in order to make the church not just a structure but a living community is greatly heartening. But perhaps not so the vigor with which Congar defends the notion that power in the church, the power of decision making, rests entirely with the hierarchy. The church is no democracy, he insists. Looking at laity in the church today, however, the issue is not primarily one of democratic structure. It is voice that is the greatest concern, and that the voice be heard. Congar's thinking on the importance of consent does a lot to help clarify the issues. In our days of extraordinary capacity for communications, when no corner of the world is beyond scrutiny from any other, we might reasonably ask, If consent is so vital to the life of the church, what mechanisms are in place to garner that consent? And as for the democracy issue, which certainly surfaces at times in the rhetoric of worthy organizations like Call to Action, this can be misunderstood. In the end, it seems, the concern is not so much the location of decision-making power with the clergy, or the hierarchical principle, but the vesting of that principle in a hierarchical priesthood to which are attached nonessential characteristics, such as celibacy and gender. Congar is correct that democratic decision making, at least on the Western model of one person, one vote, is not the way of the church. But what we might call a "democracy of access" to the ranks of ecclesial leadership cannot be so easily brushed aside. We shall discuss these matters at greater length later in this chapter.

In the chapter entitled "The Laity and the Church's Communal Life," Congar makes a second important constructive contribution. We have already referred to his "high ecclesiology," but here he balances it with an "ecclesiology from below." There is one source of the church, says Congar, and that is Jesus Christ, but the one source flows in two ways. "The stream can come directly from above, transmitted through the apostolic ministry, and the sacraments, and through them alone," but "it can also come through the personal life of the men [*sic*] who have received God's gifts." This mystery of divine grace builds the church "from below." In this respect, the fullness of Christ's mission is lived out more by the layperson than by the monk, in "the whole process of the world and its history," and we are returned to "the idea of the laity as the *plēroma* [fullness] of the hierarchical priesthood" (pp. 327–28). Here the church makes its members and is made by them as community. And here the contribution of the layperson is distinct from both that of the monk and that of the hierarchical minister.

The issue is that of the unity of the church, which Congar describes as woven from the warp of the hierarchical ministry, which gives structure, and the weft of the human contribution, which brings life. We have to be concerned in the church, he says, both for the relationship between the parts (life) and the relationship of the parts to the principle of order (structure). Unfortunately, for complex historical reasons the church has tended to overstress "communion with," to the detriment of "communion between." All Catholics can attest to the truth of this observation. Asked to define Catholicism, the overwhelming majority will do so in terms of relationship to the center of the structure. Most will see "fellowship" as a Protestant emphasis, though many will add that it is a much-needed corrective to the imbalance within Catholicism. This is exactly Congar's point, and he buttresses it with the usual impressive display of historical erudition. Cajetan, the great commentator on Thomas Aquinas, outlines three aspects of the unity of the church. First, there is agreement in faith and worship. Then there is common recognition of the same head of the church, the pope. Both of these together, says Cajetan, are not enough to constitute the church as a single community. Real fellowship rests in the will of the parts to behave as one, as members of one body, a single community "whose regulating principle is none other than the Holy Spirit." Unfortunately, says Congar, modern voices invoke the first two elements of Cajetan's triad and omit the third. Official theology will tend to play down pneumatology, since the Spirit is notoriously fickle with respect to ecclesial structures and not easily confined within canon law. There is no better-known illustration of this than Robert Bellarmine's famous definition of the church:

> The community brought together by the profession of the same Christian faith and conjoined in the communion of the same sacraments, under the government of the legitimate pastors and especially the one vicar of Christ on earth, the Roman Pontiff.[9]

The product of this one-sidedness is that the faithful of the church lack a consciousness of their role in ecclesial life. Congar is frequently quite critical of lay passivity, but the roots of it, beyond the sin of sloth, lie here in a one-sided presentation of the church. For this reason above all, the laity are unaware of the church as something that needs to be made, and made by them, in what Pius XII called "a give-

and-take of life and of vigor between all the members of Christ's mystical Body on earth" (*Lay People*, 323).

Within this general discussion of the need to reweave the active involvement of laypeople into the building-up of the church, Congar highlights two or three particular opportunities. First, he points to "the living reality of basic communities," a term primarily associated today with liberation theology. While Congar was obviously not thinking of liberation theology in 1953, the basic communities he applauds are essentially similar to those that sprang up in Latin America some fifteen to twenty years later. He finds these more informal cell-groups to be not only elements of great vitality within the local parish communities but also both a protest against overrigid ecclesiastical structures and a means of return to the church for those to whom "the Church's machinery, sometimes the very institution, is a barrier obscuring her deep and living mystery" (p. 339). Second, he suggests the importance of recognizing that the rebuilding of the church as community is a work that can only be done "from the bottom." A community begins with persons and elementary communities, whereas "the more authority is exercised at a higher level, the more it tends to become external and to substitute the impersonal bond of law for the ties of community" (p. 340). Third, he tackles the sensitive issue of the relationship between the community and its priest, particularly the common wish of "spontaneous partial communities" to choose their own priest. Congar, of course, is fully committed to the Catholic understanding of the structure of training and ordination to the hierarchical priesthood, but this *ex officio* dimension, he points out, can only be a confirmation of what is there *ex spiritu*. There is no opposition here, he says, and "in the New Testament there is no hierarchical ministry without charisms." Veiled and qualified as it is, Congar is obviously appealing for a new attitude to priestly formation and a recognition that you can't make a silk purse out of a sow's ear. Training and ordination confer the gifts of hierarchical spiritual power, which are "decisive" and which suffice "in the order of validity" (p. 342). But the ancient tradition of the church was not to accept an *ex officio* "unless it were not merely complemented by, but grounded in, an *ex spiritu*" (p. 343).

The final chapter of the book is on spirituality, and here we find the third element of particular note. Congar begins by declaring the uni-

versal call to holiness, a note taken up in Vatican II's document on the
church, *Lumen Gentium*. But what colors his entire chapter is the
consistent effort to recognize the universality of the call, the oneness
indeed of the call, while simultaneously articulating the specific conditions that mark the call of the layperson. The primary mark of "laicity," to use the unfamiliar term that Congar uses (less unfamiliar but
still not transparent in French), is secularity. Indeed, as Congar stresses
over and over again, there really is no lay apostolate or lay role in the
church, perhaps even no real laity at all, until the secularity of the
world is recognized. Although changes are afoot, through the Middle
Ages the daily life of people in the world is not truly secular, because
daily life in the world is not understood as possessing its own autonomy. There is a kind of ecclesiastical hegemony which consistently
relativizes earthly life to the spiritual realities of the life to come. The
emergence of the secular is not primarily, for Congar, the triumph of
the Enlightenment, but rather the combination of the rise of humanism with a theology that takes seriously the incarnation. He quotes
Charles Péguy to good effect here. Writing of the way in which a certain kind of Christian spirituality is world-hating, Péguy observes that
"if one would raise oneself to the eternal, it is not enough to depreci-
ate the temporal." Those who fall prey to this path are full of miscon-
ceptions. They imagine, he says, that they are godly, when they are
just too timid to engage the world. "Because they love nobody," he
adds, "they believe they love God. . . . And yet Jesus Christ was a
man."[10] Congar actually locates the emergence of a humanist spirituality in the writings of St. Thomas. Thomas adapted the pagan virtue
of *magnanimitas* to the service of an understanding of the Christian
life that seeks God as firmly as does the approach of the monk, but
through human beings and the human world, not in the monk's
immediate address to God.[11] Of course, today a really lay world has
emerged in a way that was not true in the time of Thomas or for long
afterwards, since it took the Enlightenment and atheistic humanism's
experimentation in a world without God, before "the inevitable character of the process" of uncovering a true laicity was complete (*Lay
People*, 413).

    Congar's lengthy discussion of the process of sanctification in the
world, or a spirituality of lay life, identifies several stages. It begins with

the recognition of the will of God and proceeds to a sense of vocation. But having called us from the "tyranny of the world," says Congar, God now gives it back to us "with the vocation to co-operate with Love's design for his creation" (p. 432). This leads on to engagement in the world and responsibility for the world, as the specific charge to the lay apostle, and both engagement and responsibility call for the exercise of personal judgment and decision making. The layperson is faced often with moral choices and must utilize "an ethic of God's immediate will," that is, a prudential discernment of the demands of God's will in this or that particular circumstance. Congar does not shirk calling this a "situation ethic," linking it to Thomas's theology of action, in which are combined prudence and the gifts of the Holy Spirit. If this is true, says Congar, then the layperson is called to the necessary discernment in the particular circumstances and is not simply executing some list of ethical principles drawn up in the abstract:

> Accordingly, the job of priests with respect to lay people is not to make them the *longa manus* of the clergy, telling them what they've got to do; but to make them believing men and women, adult Christians, leaving them to meet and fulfil the concrete demands of their Christianity on their own responsibility and in accordance with their own consciences. (p. 441)

The prudent person will look for advice when it is needed, but the adviser must never become a dictator, says Congar. The church must clearly leave room for the exercise of the virtue of prudence.

At the very end of this final chapter, Congar makes a theological point of enormous importance for understanding the lay apostolate as central to the mission of the church. In Jesus Christ, he says, we see God's self turned to service through love. In Christ, God "has shown a pattern not of exaltedness, but of lowly service." Congar gives a different twist here to the common understanding of *kenōsis,* or self-emptying. The idea is usually employed to stress the truth of God's self-identification with lowly humanity, the incarnation as a precondition for the redemptive acts of God in Christ. But here Congar uses *kenōsis* to highlight the structural similarity between God's descent and the apostolate of the laity. "We begin to scale the heights," he says, "when we go down to the lowest place, moved by love to serve in love. That is the mission of the Incarnate Word" (p. 451). And, in a very real sense, that is the mission of the lay Christian at work in the world, loving the world for God.

Apostolicity and the Origins of the Church

Turning now to the stress points in Congar's argument, we begin where he is at pains to establish that the church is not merely fellowship, which he would see as a Protestant position, but also "the totality of means provided by the Lord to bring men to his fellowship." There is the communal or fellowship dimension of the church, and there is the structural or institutional element. There is the *res* and the *sacramentum*. For historical—actually largely for polemical—reasons the church has overemphasized the institutional element with a resultant sterility. Later in this same book, as we already saw, Congar appeals with great force to the understanding of the church as communion. But here in the distinction between the two elements there is a curious ambivalence, which in some ways marks his whole endeavor. Arguing largely from Christ's commissioning of the Twelve in the Gospel, Congar concludes that the *sacramentum* precedes the *res*. Of course, the community of faith is the more fundamental reality, and the structural element is destined one day, in an eschatological perspective, to disappear, but there is a certain inescapable priority, he argues, to the structure (pp. 110–11).

While we could certainly mount a philosophical challenge to the notion that a sacrament can precede the reality of that which it signifies, in this particular case the stronger argument is historical. On the one hand, historical-critical study of the Gospels would caution against pinning an entire ecclesiology on the story of Jesus commissioning the Twelve. How much this particular story reflects the actual chain of events in Jesus' life, and how much the priorities of the evangelist, is extraordinarily difficult to discern. But still more, the notion that the Twelve were appointed out of thin air, as it were, and not drawn from a larger band of followers, is not sustained by the text itself. Congar himself seems to have recognized this problem with his argument. In "Pathfindings" he contrasts the two theologies of the laity that will emerge from two different points of entry to the issue. Start from "the door of the hierarchical priesthood," he says, and the laity will be seen as participating in or cooperating with the hierarchical apostolate. But enter "by the door and concept of community" and you avoid making the hierarchy a mediating agency that puts the laity in a position of passivity, as you also avoid that "democratism" that is sometimes wrongly ascribed to Protestant polity. Congar certainly maintains what we would have to call a "high" ecclesiology, that is, a belief that "Christ willed a structured community." But, he insists, "it was *within* the community of his disciples that he chose the Twelve."[12]

Congar cannot quite leave the issue here, however, and adds that "[t]he Twelve are the seeds of a new people of God. . . . What is founded in the Twelve is not only the hierarchy but the Church."[13] This is definitely a step back from the immediately previous claim that "it was *within* the community of his disciples that he chose the Twelve." Is it the case that he feels constrained to the more restricted statement by the text of the missionary letter *Ad gentes divinitus*, which he is all but quoting here? In any case, there seems to be confusion between the first calling of the disciples and the later commissioning of the Twelve. As Congar has rightly said, the Twelve are selected from a larger group of disciples. If we want, with Congar, to argue for Jesus' intention having been to create a structured community, we do not thereby have to accept that the community exists only when the structure exists. The coming into being of the church is a dynamic process, perhaps gestating slowly in Jesus' mind, certainly not really fully developed until sometime after his death, and even today not a fixed and settled entity but something growing and changing in response to circumstance and the movement of the Spirit. There is no reason to see the commissioning of the Twelve as the definitive moment in the church's coming to being, unless, of course, one wants to insist on apostolic authority as the principal reality in the church. If the Spirit were held to be the primary reality at work in the church, then Pentecost would be a better choice. But it is surely the case, whatever moment we wish to choose as definitive (and I would argue for no single defining moment), that the coming into being of the church, historically speaking, has at least begun to happen before the commissioning of the Twelve and perhaps even before the calling of the disciples at the outset of Jesus' public ministry. So, while the Twelve are certainly originating members of the new people of God, if we argue that they become so at the moment that Jesus commissions them, if we say with Congar that "what is founded in the Twelve is not only the hierarchy but the Church," we seem to lock ourselves into an irremediably subordinationist role for laypeople. A perhaps simpler way to make the point would be to suggest that in Congar's use of the image of stalk and ear of corn to describe the relationship between the structure and the community (the *sacramentum* and the *res* one more time), he overlooks the fact that stalk and ear are obviously a chicken-and-egg kind of problem.

The Lay Role in Teaching Theology

A second set of stresses and strains can be located in the chapter on the prophetic element in the church. This chapter is baffling, not because what it has to say is not valuable, as we shall see, but because Congar construes prophecy almost exclusively as the teaching office of the church. After an initial recognition of the wider meaning of prophecy, including the more common understanding today that prophecy is "speaking the truth to power," Congar proposes leaving this meaning aside and concentrating instead on the lay role in the teaching ministry of the church, since "[t]hat is the heart of matter where these questions are concerned" (*Lay People*, 321). This is doubly puzzling, since "speaking the truth to power" corresponds more closely to the Hebrew prophetic tradition that Jesus inherited and would also fit more smoothly with the general mission of the laity in the world than does the attention to teaching. "Teaching" immediately gets us into questions of authority and magisterium, and the role of the laity here is always secondary. But they can and often do take the lead in speaking the truth to power.

If we leave aside the puzzling absence of attention in this chapter to the common meaning of prophetic speech and action, what Congar actually says is rich and helpful. He has two principal aims, both laudable. First, he examines how laypeople teach and develops an understanding of the *sensus fidelium*, which once again anticipates what Vatican II will say. The "faithful maintain tradition by fully living their Christian state," he says, laity and clergy in their different ways; and the whole faithful "also develop [the tradition], instinctively reacting against whatever is harmful to it." So, says Congar, "they teach mankind, the Church, the hierarchy itself" (pp. 293–94). His second objective is to outline specific teaching activities in which the laity may be involved, both in the area of witness in the world through word and action, and in what Congar calls "scientific teaching," by which he means teaching in the narrower sense, holding professorships, writing books, and so on. He is clear that there is a kind of personal witness which belongs to the laity in their private capacity and is not derived from the hierarchy. And he frankly recognizes the existence and value of laypeople engaged in scientific teaching in the church, past and present, including even the teaching of theology.

Although there are problems with the distinction Congar makes between witness as personal fervor and the communal witness which may take place under the auspices of hierarchical authority, it is his remarks on "scientific" teaching that cause most concern. Let it frankly be said that Congar wrote strongly to support a role for the laity in teaching theology. But let it also be noted that in one or two curious passages he implies that this is not their real role, and that indeed priesthood has a certain privilege here. While he argues that as far as competence is concerned, "the lay man is on exactly the same footing as the cleric," yet "it cannot be said that priesthood, with its accompanying celebration of the mysteries, brings nothing in the spiritual order to a theologian's work" (p. 307). So, it seems, other things being equal and the competence of the layperson not being impugned, yet there is a special "spiritual something" that makes the way a priest does theology at least different from the way a layperson would do it. Congar returns to this idea a couple of pages later, stating more bluntly that laypeople "can never handle theology like priests." It is not simply, he adds, that the priest because of his work is likely to be more in touch with the "pastoral effects and consequences of his words and works," but that "having the priestly charisms, celebrating the mysteries, he has to a greater degree living contact with the realities of the tradition." So, he concludes, "[t]heology properly so called is preeminently a clerical, priestly learning," and the more appropriate work for lay activity is not so much "in the domain of theological science" as "in the immense field that lies between the Church's dogmatic tradition and man's most actual problems" (p. 310). He sees the laity, in other words, having their proper role in apologetics, and in the "auxiliary sciences" of history, philosophy, and so on. But "no attempt should be made to put them in the clergy's place and turn them into doctors of divinity" (p. 311).

If Congar were simply saying that, as a matter of fact and on the whole, the clergy are likely to be better situated to engage in theological science, he would be making a historically conditioned judgment that has a certain logic and plausibility, and that has largely been true for the life of the church thus far. But he is saying more than this, suggesting a necessary and essential connection between priesthood and theology that admits of the lay theologian only grudgingly and by way of exception. That this claim is open to challenge was recognized by Congar himself in "Pathfindings." He notes the two reasons from the earlier text mentioned above—that the priest will tend to more balance because his ministry makes him more "conscious of the pastoral effects and consequences of his words and works," and that the possession of the priestly charisms means that "he has to a greater degree living contact with the realities of tradition." Rightly defending his position as a proponent of lay involvement in theology, he allows that his reasons for arguing that priests bring "particular conditions and resources to theological activity" do not possess "the status of metaphysical necessity." Nevertheless, he says, "I still think they possess concrete truthfulness." His own personal experience and the history of the church, he adds, "seem to me to bear this out."[14]

For Congar to argue, as he does, that it is experience and history that lead to the judgment that priests, on the whole, are more appropriately involved in theology than laypersons, is obviously a historically conditioned judgment. Fifty years on, it is no longer possible to be so confident. Allowing, with Congar, no metaphysical necessity to the association of priesthood and theological learning, and bowing to more recent history and to the actual experience of the church, particularly in North America, one would have to pronounce Congar's judgment "dated." But more, one would also have to say either that he was mistaken in arguing that the priest more appropriately does theology because of a better "feel" for pastoral issues and a greater closeness to tradition, or that he was correct in his judgment. But if he was correct, then one would also have to opine that the growth in lay expertise in theology, which in the United States has certainly shifted the balance between lay and clerical theologians, is regrettable. One would not have to say, and Congar would certainly not want to say, that an individual layperson's theological skill is regrettable, but that overall the fact that the clergy are no longer "properly" preeminent in theological science is a loss for the church. Congar might perhaps see this shift in the context of the problem of declining numbers of clergy, thus allowing that lay theological expertise would be a relative good, one of those examples he likes of laypersons stepping in when necessary to take up the work that is properly the work of clergy. But of course such an argument would then need to introduce a third factor beyond history and experience to substantiate the claim that this change is only a relative good, and what third factor could there be, other than some essentialist claim for a connectedness between priesthood and theology?

Lay Ministry and Catholic Action

A third stress point in Congar's great work on the laity can be found in the chapter on the apostolate. As we noted earlier, this chapter is a largely positive evaluation of the apostolic activity of the laity. Congar understands very well that apostolic activity may not be directly evangelical, that sanctification of the world can be forwarded through the struggle for humanization. The bulk of the chapter, however, is a discussion of the value of Catholic Action, and it is here that questions arise. The term "Catholic Action" refers to a whole range of apostolic endeavors, especially prominent in continental Europe and in Latin America in the thirties and forties of the last century. What distinguishes Catholic Action is that it is lay-led work conducted under the auspices of the hierarchical church, with ecclesiastical sanction and "mandate." In the formulation of Pius XI, Catholic Action is "the participation of the laity in the hierarchical apostolate" (p. 362). It does not refer to devotional organizations, or to such things as professional associations or trade unions, which are "temporal and secular," but, it would seem, to lay associations with a more narrowly religious apostolic purpose" (p. 363). The theological problem here, which Congar immediately recognizes, is the danger that the apostolic activity of laypeople will come to be understood only as collaboration with the hierarchy, in which case, he says, that will imply that without this particular kind of activity, they are merely passive. But, Congar insists, "a lay apostleship exists, and had always existed, anterior to Catholic Action . . . based on the sacramental and extra-sacramental gifts which make the Christian" (p. 366). Thus Congar saves the specifically lay apostolate in the secular world. However, the question remains, What then is the relationship between this anterior apostolic activity and the participation in the hierarchical apostolate that goes by the name of Catholic Action? Congar struggles to express this clearly (pp. 362–75). He comes in the end to the conclusion that the ecclesiastical approval that makes a preexisting lay association into an authentic example of Catholic Action moves the association from the status of being work in the church, to being the work of the church. It is this sanction that places the work in the context of the hierarchical plan, as it were. "In Catholic Action," he says, "this apostleship is raised to the level of a fully ecclesial activity" (p. 366). The mission of the laity that is *ex spiritu* becomes *quasi ex officio* (p. 369).

The amount of space Congar devotes to the question of Catholic Action is testimony not only to the importance of this notion in the church of mid-century France, but also to the unease the author seems to have felt in establishing it as truly lay apostolic endeavor. It was on exactly this point that he and Karl Rahner disagreed. For Rahner, if it was an apostolate that required ecclesiastical sanction and mandate then it was not, in the strict sense, a lay apostolate.[15] Congar's argument in this chapter is long-winded, oversubtle, and, in a remarkably rare occurrence in his work, somewhat confusing. Following Pius XI, he argues that organizations with purely temporal purposes (for example, trade unions) cannot be Catholic Action, because it would not be "properly religious activity" (*Lay People,* 363). Catholic Action is an appropriate lay activity, but it is a collaboration with the hierarchical mission, which is not directed toward temporal affairs. Properly lay activity in the temporal world does not fall within these religious activities, lies outside the competence of the church, and so, presumably, requires no explicit mandate from the hierarchical church. Lay Catholics can "join together in order to form themselves integrally to Christian life" and thus prepare themselves to exercise Christian influence over secular institutions. This step of organization is Catholic Action. But the activities they engage in as professionals in the world are "intrinsically temporal" and so not Catholic Action, though "in living continuity with the Church's work." He concludes:

> When properly and intrinsically religious things, things, that is, within the Church's spiritual competence, are done in order to influence the temporal in a Christian direction, then *what is done* is Catholic Action. The temporal matter influenced and its conduct do not pertain to the Church's sphere, or, then, to Catholic Action, but to the sphere of this world; they are properly a matter of the temporal activity of Christians. (p. 387)

The discussion of Catholic Action raises a number of questions of method. Congar himself came to believe that he ought to have started by examining Catholic practice rather than structure and function, and it might well have produced a healthier result in the case of discussing apostolic activity. While laypeople would certainly see a difference between teaching catechetics or RCIA (the Rite of Christian Initiation of Adults), on the one hand, and earning a living by teaching physics, running a plumbing business, or being employed as a secretary, on the other, the fundamental objective of both types of activity is the same, the sanctification of the world. As a layperson, I spend some of my time working within church systems and structures, and some of my time outside them. It is not the case that the former is religious and the latter is irreligious; better to say that the former is intraecclesial, and the latter is missionary. The intraecclesial will share in the systemic components of the particular structure, and in the church as we have it today, that will mean some kind of ecclesiastical approval. The missionary will be guided by the Spirit. The distinction between properly religious and secular not only founders on the impossibility in some cases of making a clear distinction (organizing to prepare for temporal activity is Catholic Action, while the temporal activity itself is not). It also seems to suffer from far too rigid a separation between religious and temporal. Precisely where Congar positively evaluates the specific ministry of laypeople as "engagement in temporal tasks," he subordinates the secular to the religious. "The priest apostle lives among men and their affairs," says Congar, "but in order to refer all things spiritually to God." The layperson, on the other hand, "has to live for God without being dispensed from doing the work of the world." The priest (*a fortiori* the monk) makes his way directly to God; the layperson does so indirectly. Both aspects of mission are necessary, and "the laity's mission complements that of the priesthood, which would not be fully effective without it" (p. 390).

CONGAR AND THE CONCEPT OF "MINISTRIES"

Congar's later remark that "today it is necessary for the priest to be defined in relation to the layperson" testifies to his growing awareness that all was not well in the treatment of lay ministry in the earlier work. While we have seen three stress points in the argument, in each of which he has tended to subordinate lay ministry to the hierarchical ministry, that is certainly not his conscious intention. As he said himself, he is "spontaneously" clerical, no doubt a product of upbringing and a result of a life lived very much within the institutional church. But Congar is not a clericalist. Over and over, he shows sensitivity to the scandal to the church that has followed the progressive reduction of the laity to mere sheep. It is in part this genuine common sense and lack of ecclesial cant that make reading Congar such an enjoyable experience. Here is a professional theologian, unafraid of complex argument and minutely detailed historical investigation, who yet has his feet on the ground.

His most extended later attempt to correct his being "spontaneously clerical" can be found in his writings on "ministries."[16] Congar first moved to address the problem of defining laity in relation to clergy in the revision he made to *Signposts*, published in French in 1964. Criticizing his own earlier definition of laypeople for its lack of clarity, if not for any inaccuracy, he turns to the image of the People of God newly made prominent by Vatican II. "The starting-point now," he writes, "is the idea of the People of God, the whole of it active, the whole of it consecrated." He recognizes that the mission of the church is exercised in different ways, but "there is no particular mission differentiating the faithful and the ministerial priesthood" (*Lay People*, 25). For Congar, of course, as we saw earlier, the different ways of exercising the ministry derive from Christ, not from a decision of the church, and so the church "is given a structure from the moment of its constitution, not *after* its constitution." But he welcomes the new recognition, at Vatican II, of "the primacy . . . of the ontology of grace over associated structures" (p. 26).

Congar offers a more developed account of the theology of ministries in the three essays written in the 1960s. In writings that are clearly digesting the significance of Vatican II, itself influenced by his earlier work and, indeed, canonizing some of that work, he rethinks the laity–clergy relationship. There are many ministries common to all, but within these common ministries of witness, of the word, of cult, of "offering a holy, spiritual, pleasing sacrifice to God through Jesus Christ," there is an "instituted" (*institué*) ministry of the clergy, established by Christ.[17] While this is a distinct ministry, it is one that has its meaning within the common ministry of all the faithful. It is instituted by Christ; thus, it is not a function of the church but is instituted by Christ to serve one function among many within the common ministry of the saints. Priesthood is not simply a personal, individual calling, but a ministry that has its full significance in the context of the whole community of the faithful. At the same time, laypersons exercise ministry in many ways, as catechists, at liturgy, in the family, and so on. There is indeed a general ministry of the faithful, seen, for example, at the time of a parish mission or retreat, where the faithful bring about in one another a renewed commitment to a deeper faith life. In such a diffused, general ministry, the faithful "exercise simultaneously both their royal priesthood and . . . the witness of Christian prophecy" in activities which, while they are not ministries in more precise senses, are "something extremely real."[18]

Resuming his work on this topic in the "Pathfindings" essay, he writes eloquently:

> Jesus has instituted a structured community which is as an entirety holy, priestly, prophetic, missionary, apostolic; it has ministries at the heart of its life, some freely raised up by the Spirit, others linked by the imposition of hands to the institution and mission of the Twelve.[19]

All ministries then come to be understood as "modes of service of what the community is called to be and to do." To illustrate the point, Congar discusses two examples. One asserts that the theology of vocation to the ministry is incomplete if it is seen simply as a personal attraction validated by superiors. He suggests that it must also be a recognition by the community of gifts that mark someone out for a mission, and, moreover, that this is as true for bishops as for priests. While wishing to maintain both sides of the understanding of vocation, Congar offers historical lessons that suggest that a return to a lay role in the selection of priests and appointment of bishops would be timely. The second example he offers is the meaning of apostolicity in this newly communitarian context. Basing himself on Vatican II (itself strongly influenced by his own work on the topic), Congar states that "the whole Church" is "apostolic" and that apostolicity is located as much in the continuing faith of the whole people as it is in the apostolic succession of the laying on of hands. And he concludes that the strengthened understanding of the lay role, coupled with the strong treatment of the episcopacy at Vatican II, has played its part in "the present crisis of the priesthood." Since the council, he adds, "it is no longer the layman who stands in need of definition but the priest."[20]

Let us for a moment take up Congar's suggestion that it is the priest who needs redefinition, not the layperson. In Congar's ecclesiology, what is left for the priest? In essence, the priest assists the bishop in presiding at the liturgical celebration of the Eucharist, in preaching the word, and additionally in the provision of the sacraments of confirmation and reconciliation. Somewhat more amorphously, the priest is also the leader of the local Christian community, with an authority delegated by the bishop—and if the later Congar is accepted—which should be in some way confirmed by the community. None of these responsibilities is removed by the understanding of ministry that Congar proposes. On the contrary, the clarification of the true role of the laity can only make clearer the appropriate responsibilities of the priest and what has unnecessarily accrued to the role, serendipitously or by design, in the course of time.

Clarifying the role of the priest produces an identity crisis not because it is clearer what he must do in the course of his ministry but because it is clearer what is not essential to priesthood. When we look at the list of responsibilities of the priest, only someone tied to the past can see in them any connection at all to the culture of priesthood as it has developed in the Western church over the last thousand years. Because there is simply no essential connection between priesthood and celibacy, the meaning of celibacy for priests who are not vowed religious becomes an enormous issue, if we are not wedded to a particular lifestyle for the clergy. While celibacy suits the current priestly lifestyle, the question of celibacy cannot be foreclosed because the institution is wedded to a particular lifestyle. While Congar does not himself make this point, at times he refers approvingly to the model of local pastor common to many Orthodox Christian communities. There, the part-time pastor serves a community that has had a big hand in his selection. Moreover, in "My Pathfindings," Congar does not even fully close the door to the idea of women participating in ordained ministry.

Given Congar's clear understanding of the nature and limits of priestly and lay ministry, it is possible to construct a clearer answer to the question he raises about the crisis of the priesthood. While priesthood is a ministry of leadership and presidency of the worshiping community—and a ministry moreover derived from God's call, not only or even mostly from the call of the community—the way of life of priesthood, even today, bears a character that has no intrinsic connection to ministry. In fact, the spirituality of ministerial priesthood, and much of the way of life expected of priests, is derived from that of religious life. But the vowed life of religious is intended to express in part an eschatological expectation, in part a level of asceticism and sacrifice that do not pertain to the character of priesthood as such. Moreover, the religious life is oriented to life in a community, providing affective and moral support. Asceticism, sacrifice, and an eye for the reign of God are expected of all Christians, and thus of priests no less than laypeople, but not in the same single-minded way that they are expected to structure the religious life. Priests in the church today have extremely conflicted lives. Celibate, they live mostly solitary existences. Surrounded by the families they serve, they have none of their own. Seen in effect by others as a species of monk, they live in the world and carry out their ministries within a clear career structure of promotion and demotion, of lines of authority and responsibility. They are neither monk nor layperson, but not a clear third species. They carry elements of both in an uncertain and confusing combination. And while the majority of them live out this particular following of the cross with grace and apostolic effectiveness, this does not mean that there is any necessary virtue to the linking of priestly ministry with the rubrics of religious life.

Once we strip away the spirituality and culture of religious life from the priestly life, much of the controversy about the respective roles of

laypeople and clergy simply disappears. Rome is not infrequently
alarmed about the confusion of roles and the "clericalization of the
laity."[21] To the degree that it shows confusion about the respective
charisms of laity and clergy, it is a problem. But at least as much it illustrates a different and altogether healthier shift, namely, an unwillingness to associate the vocation of ordained ministry with the culture of
a cultic priesthood. In the present dispensation in the church, a young
(and these days not so young), single male who was visible in the faith
community, who showed a love for the liturgy and a desire to serve,
who perhaps taught catechism, was a lector at mass, served on parish
committees and lived a morally impeccable lifestyle would be thought
by most to be demonstrating at least a potential vocation to the priesthood, albeit one that needed testing and confirmation. That same
young man, if he were married, would be considered by many to be
the ideal layman, and by some to be in danger of confusing the
boundaries between priest and layperson. Female "pastoral associates," upon whom the church increasingly depends, are always figures
of suspicion; male associates, if they exist, must be in danger of receiving a white feather for their reluctance to test a priestly vocation, at
least if they are single. All this is just to say, of course, that the confusion of roles that so alarms Rome may simply be an illustration that
there are innumerable priestly vocations "out there" among people
who are not drawn to a culture and spirituality of priestly ministry that
does not, in fact, have any intrinsic connection to what priests are
called to do and to be. If celibacy is not of the essence of priesthood,
which it is not, then it is at least possible to distinguish between a
vocation to the priesthood and a calling to celibacy. If celibacy is accidental to priesthood, which it is, then why a sense of calling to priesthood should be suspect if there is not equally a sense of calling to the
accident of celibacy is not at all clear. Congar was trapped in the earlier understanding of priesthood, but the logic of much of what he
says about laity and clergy suggests quite a different conception.

Let me be clear. The so-called clericalization of the laity derives
from two sources. There is, on the one hand, a growing shortage of
priests, which inevitably leads to a greater role for laypeople in ministries that, in former times, priests would have exclusively carried out.
(A good example of this is the current practice of laypersons bringing
the Eucharist to the sick and housebound.) This can certainly lead to

a blurring of the distinctions between clergy and laity, though the cause is as likely to be a deficient understanding of exactly what is proper to each, as it is to be the result of assigning roles inappropriately. The second source of the so-called clericalization is more controversial and more significant, namely, that the growing exercise of lay ministry is a movement of the Spirit to apply pressure to the inappropriate identification of priestly ministry with a celibate life and with the male gender. Most lay ministers may not want to exercise priestly ministry, and certainly most lay ministry is not an encroachment on priestly ministry. But remove the cultic accretions from priesthood, and then those laypersons who do feel the call can test that vocation. More importantly, with the pressure off it will be that much easier to maintain the position that there are certain roles that simply belong to priestly ministry, whether of presidency at the eucharistic assembly, community leadership, or preaching. All that Congar's ecclesiology insists upon is that ministerial priesthood originates in Jesus' commissioning of the disciples. I have suggested earlier that on historical-critical grounds such a hard and fast position may be suspect. But even if we accept it without question, it implies nothing essentially about lifestyle or gender. Ironically, the preservation of priestly ministry as distinct from lay ministry may depend upon abandoning the cultic accretions of celibacy and the exclusion of women.

THE RADICALISM OF CONGAR'S ECCLESIOLOGY

Having subjected Congar to a careful, appreciative, and hopefully searching reading, it is apparent that there are enormous riches here for theology. Clearly, the bishops of Vatican II recognized the worth of Congar's thought and consequently drew him into a central role in drafting texts for the council. The journals that he kept at the time of the council testify to his important role and to the care with which he followed and attempted to influence developments. To Congar, it must truly have seemed as if his life's work, after so many setbacks at the hands of the institutional church, was being vindicated, and so it was. But the same journals also illustrate his impatience with the curial mentality and with many little details and dramas of conciliar interactions. At much the same time, as we have seen above, he was rethinking some of his own ideas, refocusing his work on the laity in the category of ministry, a category that required him to reexamine the lay/clerical divide that he recognized had marked his earlier work. One might say that Congar came to see that a theology of the laity is indeed an entire ecclesiology, at least in implication. The ecclesiology that began to come into focus at this time was distinctly ahead of the vision of the council, for all its advances.

One way to examine the extent of Congar's radicalism would be to compare his later views with what would by general agreement be admitted to be the most radical postconciliar ecclesiology in the Catholic Church, that of liberation theology. Liberation theology as a movement in Catholic ecclesiology came to prominence in Latin America in the early 1970s. In the last thirty years it has had enormous impact upon the church in several ways, both as a pastoral movement stressing participation and as a theological movement stressing the importance of "critical reflection on praxis" as the motor of change. Its distinctiveness, though complex, can be reduced to three major principles. First, liberation theology prioritizes the experience of the poor. Second, liberation theology draws the eschatological promise of salvation and the historical project of liberation into close relationship. Third, liberation theology is an inductive, grass-roots, "bottom-up" movement that starts from the experience of the poor as analyzed, celebrated, and transformed in "base Christian communities."

Is it in fact the case that Congar's ecclesiology in general, and his theology of the laity in particular, reveals a sensibility well prepared to appreciate the development of liberation theology? There are certainly a number of places in Congar's work in which the evidence would suggest a positive response to this question, both in *Signposts* and in his later work on ministries. His understanding of the role of history in salvation, his vision of "kingship" as a spiritual freedom marked by a dialectic of refusal and engagement, and especially his call for a "communal" principle to balance the hierarchical principle are all avenues to be explored. And lest the reader imagine that this possible relationship is simply a gratuitous gambit of the author, let it be noted that the similarity is recognized by a commentator like Ramon Pellitero, an expert on Congar who is also a conservative theologian and quite hostile to liberation theology. Pellitero classifies as one of the "risks" of the theology of ministries that it might lead to "the undervaluing of the Church–world distinction and the reduction of her mission to a liberation of a socio-political type." Pellitero thinks that Congar avoids this risk, unlike liberation theology, "which implied an historical/ecclesiological monism and fell into a mix of secularism and a new clericalism." He is right that Congar avoids the risk, wrong in thinking that liberation theology falls headlong into the trap. But that he would feel the need to make the observation at all, Pellitero is obviously aware of the parallels between the two ecclesiological pictures.[22]

Congar's majestic work on the laity, *Lay People in the Church*, despite the qualifications that he later expressed, is the most influential single work ever written on the topic. Obviously, Congar himself thought that reflection on the laity was sufficiently important to spend years of his life on the project. Pope John XXIII and the majority of the council fathers seem to have thought so too. But as we turn now to the story of the council and the laity, we shall see that while much of Congar's vision was incorporated into the council documents, much of it was not. The focus on the lay apostolate was not matched by an equal attention to the theological meaning of lay life, and we still live today with the consequences of that imbalance. In North America at the turn of the century, laypeople are involved as never before in the work of the church, but we are no nearer to knowing what it is to be a lay Christian.

3

Collegiality, Coresponsibility, and the Council

Had JOHN XXIII NOT CONVENED the Second Vatican Council, the advances of the new theology would probably have had little impact on the church's consciousness. But once the council took shape, and particularly with the realization that "the church" would be its central theme, it was another story altogether. Pope John himself seems to have known from the outset what kind of council he wanted, although it is not clear that he accurately foresaw the intensity of the struggle that would ensue between the conservative curial party and the more flexible pastoral approach of most of the bishops gathered in Rome from around the world. But as events unfolded during the first of the four sessions of the council, the only session over which Pope John himself would live to preside, the writings of a handful of mostly northern European theologians, many of them the same individuals we have already encountered, came to have an impact upon the work of the council fathers that in their wildest dreams the theologians themselves could not have anticipated.

In this chapter of our story, we need to consider the fortunes of the theology of the laity at the Vatican Council. Above all this requires grasping the image of laypeople that the council sought to present, and here we will see the enormous influence of Yves Congar. We shall see that the picture of the laity presented at Vatican II is of a far more active and responsible constituency than history had typically revealed. Cardinal Suenens called this "coresponsibility," obviously echoing the language of collegiality reserved in the council documents for the relationship between the bishops. We shall need to ask just how these terms relate to each other. Is there some reason why the Vatican documents are peppered with the word *collegiality*, though mostly not in the context of the laity, but the word *coresponsibility* never appears? Are the words interchangeable? Or does collegiality have juridical connotations not shared by coresponsibility? And would coresponsibility of the laity with the clergy in the mission of the church sound just a little too much for some of the council fathers? As a kind of coda to the chapter, we shall take a look at Suenens's 1968 book *Coresponsibility in the Church*, a trenchant and at times rueful meditation on the postconciliar fortunes of the idea of collegiality in general and of the lay role in the church in particular.[1]

THE COUNCIL AND THE LAITY

In chapter 7 of *Lay People in the Church*, Yves Congar writes eloquently of the need to return to the idea of the church as a community.[2] For far too long, he writes, Catholic theologians "have thought of the church as being built up hierarchically from above" (p. 329) and have paid no attention to the equally important building from below. They have concentrated on structure, to the exclusion of life. For complex historical reasons, the early church emphasis on fellowship faded in the consciousness of the Western church. All the emphasis was placed on the relation of the parts to the center or principle, in most cases the hierarchy and the authority of the Holy See. No attention was paid to the relation of the parts to one another. In the sixteenth century, Cajetan wrote of the tripartite character of ecclesial unity as based in common beliefs, common subjection to the supreme pontiff, and fellowship, but subsequent influential commentators (Congar mentions Bossuet) leave off the third element. Thus, they effectively and sometimes explicitly adopt Robert Bellarmine's definition of the church: "The society of men on the way to the Fatherland above, united by the profession of the same Christian faith and participation in the same sacraments, under the authority of lawful pastors and principally of the Roman Pontiff." Fellowship has disappeared from the picture.

The return to fellowship, thinks Congar, requires a renewed recognition on the part of the church that the laity, like the clergy, have a major role in building up the church from below. This picture of the church, he writes, "built together by the intercourse of its members in a whole pattern of services . . . cannot be called by any other name than 'community'" (p. 339). Congar draws attention to the many forms of small groups, or what he calls "cells," growing up in church life, seeing them as an implied protest against too singular a focus on "an objective institution or hierarchical mediation." "A need is felt," he says, "to seek beneath the ready-made administrative machinery . . . the living reality of basic communities." They suggest a renewed attention to the church as "a community to whose life all its members contribute and which is patterned by give-and-take and a pooling of resources." Making the church, he adds, "is a thing which is done, and can only be done, from the bottom" (p. 340).

Congar's vision of a laity come of age (a phrase he personally disliked) is an important one, and one that suffuses the Vatican Decree on the Apostolate of the Laity (*Apostolicam Actuositatem*).[3] But just as what is said about the lay apostolate is dependent on a prior consideration in *Lumen Gentium* of what it is to be a layperson, so Congar's vision itself rests on a prior assertion of the essential equality of all the members of the church. In virtue of a common baptism, all share in a common priesthood, and the ramifications of this idea are worked out at great length in chapter 4 of *Lay People in the Church*. Drawing to his conclusions, Congar inserts a warning:

> a priest, a bishop, a pope is first of all a layman. He has to be baptized, to become a Christian, to offer his life as a spiritual sacrifice, to receive communion, to do penance, to be blessed, to work out his salvation. It is impossible to separate his personal religious life, that of layman, and the religious life of his office, that of priest or of bishop. (p. 181)

There have been criticisms of the use of the word "layman" here, and it may be better to substitute a word like "faithful," but the point is clear and a good one. Ordination to hierarchical priesthood comes later and is always related to the common priesthood of all Christians. It is the common priesthood that mandates a priestly ministry for all, lay as well as clergy, in virtue of baptism. If there were no ministerial priesthood, there would still be the common priesthood of all. But if there were no common priesthood in virtue of baptism, there would simply be no church.

The Vatican Council's treatment of the role of laypeople in the church is contained, directly or indirectly, principally in three documents. The nearest thing in the documents to a theological treatment of the lay state is to be found in chapter 4 of *Lumen Gentium*. Dependent on this is the Decree on the Apostolate of the Laity, *Apostolicam Actuositatem*. Finally, there is the vision of the church's interaction with the world in *Gaudium et Spes*. While it does not specifically treat of lay as opposed to clerical ministry, in practice it is focused on those kinds of ministries that would inevitably demand extensive apostolic involvement on the part of the laity. (There are also important ideas contained in *Ad Gentes Divinitus*, the somewhat neglected Decree on the Church's Missionary Activity.) Initially, the schema on the laity produced by the preparatory commission had been intended to gather together in one place all that the bishops would say about laypeople, but as the council sessions came and went, pieces of it were removed to places that seemed more appropriate. While this was unsatisfactory to many council fathers for a variety of reasons, it made particularly good sense to place the theological treatment of the lay state within the central document on the church. The second draft of the document on the church included a third chapter entitled "The People of God and in particular the Laity," but this was soon divided into two, and the section on the People of God became the opening chapter of the document, ahead even of the chapter on the hierarchy, to the chagrin of the curial party.

Because the discussion of the laity cannot be separated from that of the ruling and guiding image of the church as the People of God, and because the image of the People of God is so absolutely central to the council's ecclesiological vision, it is true also to say that the developing theology of the laity presented in the council documents is a central and crucial element of the legacy of the council. Any ecclesiology is an implicit theology of the laity; any theology of the laity contains within it a vision of the church. In Robert Bellarmine's definition quoted above, the layperson is deprived of any active role in the life of the church and is defined by his or her beliefs and obedience to hierarchical authority. But in the new ecclesiology of Vatican II, the layperson has the additional responsibility of exercising ministry, to borrow Suenens's cherished though problematic distinction, in the church *ad intra* and *ad extra*. That is, lay ministry involves an ecclesial responsibility within the community, and an apostolic and missionary responsibility without, in the secular sphere, which is properly the domain of the laity.

SUENENS AND THE COUNCIL

There are many excellent examinations of the ecclesiology of Vatican II. There is much less on the council's theology of the laity. My purpose here is to duplicate neither, but simply to outline the close correspondence that can be discerned from the council texts between the idea of the church and the role of the layperson within it. But before doing so, it is important to see something of the political ferment that surrounded the council fathers' discussions.[4] It is here, as we turn to this consideration, that we can begin to appreciate the extraordinarily significant role of Leon-Joseph Suenens. It was the writings of theologians that laid much of the groundwork for the council and made many of its advances possible; but at the council itself, the theologians could only have the role that the council fathers allowed them. Suenens was instrumental in gathering the expertise of so many fine theologians to the task of crafting alternative texts to those of the preparatory schemas. While not himself a true academic theologian, Suenens helped to make space at the council for the voice of the new theology. Whether through serendipity or the Holy Spirit, Suenens was positioned by both council popes in a highly influential role in the council, and he above all was the conduit by which the ideas of *la nouvelle théologie* reached the floor of St. Peter's.

Leon-Joseph Suenens was by character and talents an obvious choice for Pope John's trust. Indeed, while their physical appearances were polar opposites, with the tall and slim Suenens towering over the short and distinctly portly pope, they were in many other respects extremely similar. Neither was by nature a radical. Both were possessed of distinctly traditional piety, but both men had the kind of fearless openness to the future that only a deep faith in the power of the Holy Spirit could justify. Above all, they were both supremely pastoral individuals, possessed of precisely the same conviction that the council should be a pastoral renewal of the church and not merely a conservative theological reiteration of ancient and timeless truths. The biggest difference between the two is also quite telling: while Suenens was a youthful 58 (he lived to be 91) at the time the council first convened, the pope was ailing. If John XXIII ever thought about his mortality and the council, he might well have envisaged Suenens as a kind of executor of his will for the council, someone who would be a continuing presence after he was gone. As anticipated, when John died in May 1963, the centrist cardinal Archbishop Montini of Milan replaced him and committed himself to completing the work Pope John had begun. But Paul VI was by temperament a much more cautious individual. In the council's struggles with the idea of collegiality, Suenens's counsel to the new pope is, in a way, a dialogue on collegiality between John and Paul. And, in postconciliar years, Suenens's somewhat stormy relationship with Pope Paul can be read as a struggle between the open optimism of John XXIII and the careful, moderate reforms of Paul VI.

Bishop Suenens, as he then was, auxiliary bishop of the major Belgian diocese of Malines (which included Brussels), was active in preparation of the council almost from the day in 1961 on which Pope John declared that it was to be held in Rome in the following year. Preparatory working commissions were established, and Suenens was assigned to the Commission for Bishops and the Government of Dioceses. Suenens himself explained that this particular commission was composed of auxiliary bishops, "presumably because they were more available than bishops in charge of dioceses."[5] Two important consequences of this assignment were frequent trips to Rome in the year before the council and association with a number of other bishops who were to be influential in the future. The commission prepared a text that raised many pastoral problems, but even at this early stage their work was frustrated by items placed on their agenda by the Curia, which were "either trivial or vague" (*Memories and Hopes,* 56). Characteristically Suenens adds that since he was in Rome for the work of the preparatory commission, he "took the opportunity to get in touch with the secretaries of other preparatory commissions" and submitted a number of memoranda raising a series of issues. Among them were reform of the Roman Curia, more clarity about the role of the bishop, the permanent diaconate, collaboration with the laity, and, most controversial of all, the sensitive question of retirement age for bishops.

Suenens's position became much more influential when Cardinal Van Roey, archbishop of Malines-Brussels, died in August 1961. Three months later Suenens became his successor, and only a few weeks after that, he was elevated to the College of Cardinals. The unusually early promotion was, said Suenens, "in order to make it possible for me to be involved in the preparatory work for the Council, as a member of the Central Preparatory Commission" (p. 60). This body was composed of some fifty cardinals and a lesser number of archbishops and major religious superiors, was unwieldy, and was top-heavy with curial officials. But it played the central role in planning for the council.

Suenens's immediate reaction to the work done by the commission was one of deep disappointment; the texts and drafts prepared for the council "lacked life and vision" (p. 60). He was not alone in this judgment. Cardinal Koenig in particular had been very concerned and had asked the Jesuit theologian Karl Rahner to review the texts. Rahner's first and deeply critical report went to Koenig in January 1962[6] and must have played a part in the decision of Koenig, Suenens, Doepfner, and Alfrink, among others, to write to the pope, warning of the unsatisfactory nature of the documents and the danger that the council would reject them.[7] This letter certainly had a role in alerting John to the dangers and a greater role in the eventual orchestration of the new direction the council would chart.

Suenens did not stop there. During an audience with the pope in April 1962, he complained about the large number of preparatory schemas (about seventy); he reports that the pope asked him "to clear the ground" and prepare an overall plan for the council (p. 78). The plan was ready by the end of April, and Suenens shared it with a few cardinals, including Montini, the future Paul VI. In mid-May the pope ordered his secretary of state, Cardinal Cicognani, to distribute copies to more cardinals and asked Suenens to hold a meeting with a number of influential cardinals. The meeting took place early in July and revealed considerable support for the plan. In September the pope gave a radio address in which he generally adopted the positions in the plan. At this point, however, the pope seems to have put it aside for a time, intending to wait and see how the early deliberations of the council developed. It is a well-known story that the council floundered in its first few weeks; having been reassured of the pope's approval, on December 4 Suenens spoke in the assembly. He proposed the outlines of the plan to the council fathers, receiving, he says with characteristically optimistic overstatement, its "unanimous endorsement" (p. 87). Nevertheless, while there was still a long way to go, with much strife and drama, it is safe to say that the general will of the majority to hold a pastoral council that placed the church at its center found expression in Suenens's plan.

Suenens's plan is given in full in *Memories and Hopes* (pp. 87–100), his fascinating if somewhat self-promotional collection of reminiscences. His proposal involved opening the council with a schema on "The Mystery of Christ's Church," which would bring together some of the preparatory work done in the schemata on "The Nature of the Church Militant" and "On the Members of the Church." This seems to have been a sop to the curial party led by the indefatigable, though soon to be vanquished, Cardinal Ottaviani. Following this, the activity of the council would be divided into two parts, examining from a pastoral perspective the work of the church *ad intra* and *ad extra*. The first of these two would consider the church under four headings: as a missionary body, as a teaching body, as a community constituted by the sacraments, and as a praying community. The second, which of course eventually became the framework for *Gaudium et Spes*, the Pastoral Constitution on the Church in the Modern World, proposed a concentration on four problems: church and family, church and economics, church and social issues, and church and international issues. In conclusion, Suenens indicated three areas of dialogue: intrachurch dialogue, ecumenical dialogue, and dialogue with the modern world.

What must have been so appealing to so many of the council fathers, and probably the only thing that could have gained the support of the conservative Cardinal Siri at the July meeting, was the sense that here was a framework into which the bewilderingly large number of preparatory texts could be fitted. Indeed Suenens said as much in his introductory remarks to the plan, arguing that only in this way could the huge amount of work that had gone into the preparatory schemata be salvaged. But Suenens's own views went way beyond what many of the council fathers would have assented to. As they stood, Suenens wrote, in words at which Siri must have shuddered, "these documents are made lifeless skeletons by the legalistic, canon-istic and at times repressive manner in which they are presented" (p. 88).

This momentous intervention in the council, followed as it was by resounding support from the *papabile* Cardinal Montini, and pre-ceded as it had been by important letters to the pope from Montini and from Cardinal Bea urging a more pastoral direction to the coun-cil, effectively settled the question of the kind of council that Vatican II was going to be and determined the direction of the future work. Suenens's vision went through many stages, and the final sixteen council documents do not conform particularly well to the plan he had presented, but the centrality of the church and the pastoral nature of the council remained, as well as the vitally important insistence on dialogue with the modern world. Suenens had given voice here not only to his own convictions but also to those of many other influen-tial leaders of the non-curial majority.

What, then, of the place of the laity in Suenens's thinking about the work of the council? In the plan it is discussed explicitly only once, but notably within the section on the missionary church in the *ad intra* schema. His comments bear quoting in full:

> We need a major declaration on the role of the laity in the Church—all we have at present are three lines in the articles of canon law! A schema *de laicis* has been drafted, but it needs to be rewritten with greater breadth and soul. Moreover, this document should be harmonized with the one prepared by the Commission for the lay apostolate.
>
> Our separated brethren accuse the Church of being far too clerical and of stifling the laity. They believe in "the priesthood of the faithful," to whom they assign an important role. Quite frequently, Catholics who leave the faith to join a sect will claim to have found a religion where they are respected, and in which they can actively participate.
>
> Taking all of this into account, an important statement should be drafted, in a loving and paternal tone, recognizing the rights and oblig-ations of lay people by virtue of the baptism which they have received and through which they have been incorporated into the Church. (p. 95)

Clearly, Suenens saw a role for the laity as laity within the evangelical work of the church, not merely a role in Catholic Action as "collaborators" in the work of the hierarchical ministry. Equally clearly, the work of the church *ad extra* requires lay participation, if not lay leadership.

When the dust cleared and the sixteen documents of Vatican II were all finally approved by the council fathers, the laity loomed very large in the texts. They were discussed directly in one chapter of *Lumen Gentium,* had an entire document devoted to their ecclesial role (*Apostolicam Actuositatem*), and were central to *Gaudium et Spes.* All this followed from the central emphasis of *Lumen Gentium* on the church as the "People of God," a notion not so much democratic as communitarian. As we noted previously, in the early redrafting of the schema on the church a chapter had been proposed on "the People of God and in particular on the laity," which was intended as a third or fourth chapter to follow upon discussions of the mystery of the church and of hierarchical authority. It was Suenens again, at a meeting of the Coordinating Commission in July 1963, who proposed dividing up the chapter and moving the discussion of the People of God to a point *before* discussion of the hierarchical constitution of the church. As Jan Grootaers comments, the restructuring "meant a fundamental reorientation of ecclesiology that would put an end to the pyramidal vision of the Church."[8] From this point on, everything that pertains to the People of God pertains alike to clergy and laity, and so it is there that we should begin to trace the conciliar vision of the laity.

THE COUNCIL DOCUMENTS

To those who were acquainted only with scholastic "manual" theology, the documents of the council as a whole came as a revelation, for some a rather unpleasant one. But even for one schooled in scripture, the writings of the church fathers, and the history of the ecumenical councils as far as Vatican I, the teaching on the laity seemed to be breaking new ground. As a matter of fact, the curious thing about the council's teaching on the laity is that it is at one and the same time new and relatively uncontroversial. There was near unanimity on the need for a document on the laity. Of course there were differences about detail and whether the chapter on the laity should be part of *Lumen Gentium,* but there was remarkably little controversy about the content. Some of this can be explained by the memory of the writings of recent popes, particularly Pius XI and Pius XII, strongly urging greater lay participation in the work of the church. "Catholic Action" was such an amorphous concept and could mean so many things to so many different people that both conservatives and liberals would take no exception to it. If the council teaching on the laity had planned to venture into deeper theological waters than it did, major differences would certainly have surfaced. But the primary focus was firmly on the lay apostolate, not on a theological evaluation of the lay state. Perhaps it is a testimony to the dearth of theological thinking on the lay role in previous official church pronouncements that the modest advances the council made would be acceptable to liberals without alarming the conservatives.

Lumen Gentium

It is in this great council document on the nature of the church that the theological principles are set down for the more extended discussion of the lay role that occurs in two other documents. Whatever is said about any subgroup in the church, be it laity, bishops, or religious, needs to be understood in relation to three overarching themes of the document—the image of the church as the People of God, the universal call to holiness, and the understanding of the church as a pilgrim. Perhaps more than any other council document, *Lumen Gentium* bears witness to the character of the battleground from which it emerged. Although the document is important, at times sublime, it shows traces of two quite different approaches to a document on the church. On the one hand, the traditional sensibility would prefer a structure that began by treating of the hierarchical nature of the church and then went on to discuss each level, starting with the "highest" and proceeding to the laity at the bottom of the pyramid. A more theologically contemporary approach would want a document that started from scriptural imagery and then treated the character of the church thematically rather than structurally, perhaps stressing the marks of holiness, community, and universality. *Lumen Gentium* (*LG*) had to satisfy these two constituencies and did so by interweaving both approaches into one document. But it is the latter approach that will mark my discussion. I find myself in agreement with George

Lindbeck, who in a fine early study of Vatican II, argued that the meaning of the council is to be discovered where it breaks new ground, not where it simply reiterates the teaching of the ages.[9]

The theological discussion of the laity in *Lumen Gentium* revolves around four principal ideas: the priority of baptism, the priesthood of the laity, the specific character of lay ministry, and the solidarity of laity and pastors. As befits a primarily pastoral council, the emphasis is placed on the role of the laity in building up the church, working in concert with the members of the hierarchical priesthood. Gone is the vision of the laity as a passive flock, ushered this way and that by caring pastors. Of course, a separation remains between the kinds of pastoral responsibilities proper to ordained ministry and those that the laity should shoulder, but there is a very healthy sense that the truly apostolic role of both is vital to the well-being of the church.

The pastoral rather than dogmatic inclinations of the council in general, which we have already had occasion to note and celebrate, backfire just a little on the question of the laity. In general terms, the triumph of pastoral concern was a victory for the forces of renewal over the conservative curial inclination toward the repetition of "timeless dogmatic truths." But when we come to theological reflection on the laity, what is noteworthy is the paucity of previous teachings. Consequently, the remarkable statements of the council on the apostolic activity of the laity are constructed upon a shaky foundation of theological reflection on the nature of the lay state. *Lumen Gentium* certainly hints of a theology of the laity, but it is worked out in detail nowhere in the council's work and nowhere in the previous tradition. Defining a lay person as a baptized Christian living in the secular world only sets the stage for a true theological exploration of all that this definition might imply not only for the nature of the laity but also and more importantly for understanding more clearly the nature of the church. But once it began to come into theological focus at the council, the nature of the church could no longer be determined by the kind of overwhelming attention to hierarchy and ordained ministry that had been the norm. The specific and irreplaceable roles that the ministerial priesthood holds in the church are instrumental to God's plan for the whole. They have their meaning, in other words, only in the context of the church. They are not the meaning of the church. Leadership must always be imagined as a function of the identity of the community to be led, never the other way around.

Having placed the church as the People of God firmly in the line of ancient Israel, the first to be called the People of God, the council identifies this new people as "a kingdom of priests" who are consecrated by their baptism. In virtue of baptism, all the members of the church have the same essential responsibilities: to pray, to praise God, to offer themselves as a sacrifice, to bear witness to Christ, and to proclaim Christ "to everyone who asks a reason for the hope of an eternal life which is theirs" (*LG* 10). In virtue of their baptism and confirmation, all are given the power of the Holy Spirit, all are obliged to spread the faith by word and deed, all take part in the eucharistic sacrifice, all "offer the divine victim to God and themselves along with it," and all play their own part in the liturgical action (*LG* 11). In virtue of baptism and faith in the Lord, all share a common dignity, a common grace, and a "common vocation to perfection." In Christ and the church "there is . . . no inequality arising from race or nationality, social condition or sex" (*LG* 32). Clearly, while the bishops also affirm that the church is hierarchical, the baseline for understanding the People of God is as a community of radical equality before God, in virtue of a common baptism. The one destined for ministerial priesthood does not assume ecclesial responsibilities at the time of ordination, but has held them from the moment of baptism. The special roles of ordained ministry are exercised within the context of a truly priestly community.

What, then, is the priesthood of the laity? There are problems created by the very phrase "priesthood of the laity," since it sounds, in a Catholic Church with a highly cultic priestly caste, very much like a remainder concept. There is the priesthood (of the ordained ministers) and then there is a sort of delegated activity left over, a kind of quasi priesthood, for at least those laity with aspirations to active involvement in the ministries of the church. Such a picture is wrong on a number of counts. In the first instance, the priesthood of the laity is not derivative of the ministerial priesthood. The council is clear on this, declaring that the two priesthoods differ "essentially and not only in degree," though they are of course related to one another, in virtue of the fact that they both share in the one priesthood of Christ. Second, the priestly activity of the laity clearly overlaps with that of the ministerial priesthood. Presidency at the eucharistic assembly is reserved to the ordained minister, as are a number of other sacramental functions. But when the council enumerates the roles of the laity "by virtue of their royal priesthood," it produces a list to which ordained ministers are surely also obliged: "the reception of the sacraments, prayer and thanksgiving, the witness of a holy life, abnegation, and active charity" (*LG* 10). Third, the priesthood of the laity is not a "vocation" to which some laity are called and others not. The priesthood of the laity has nothing essentially to do with the notion of "lay ministry," understood as the various apostolic roles that some laypeople take up, either to assist the internal ministries of the church or to engage in formal apostolic activity in the wider world. The priesthood of the laity is a common possession and a common responsibility of all the laity, precisely in virtue of their baptism and confirmation. Here in passing let us note the deplorable moribundity of the sacrament of confirmation in the Catholic tradition. For all practical purposes, at least in the North American church, it serves—when not simply an empty ritual—as a rite of passage to that time when the individual is judged sufficiently mature to decide whether or not to persist in the worshiping community. In reality, it is intended as a ritual to signify acceptance of the responsibilities of the adult lay state. But in a community in which the adult lay state is not commonly understood to be one of active apostolic ministry, it is not surprising that confirmation has largely become what it is. It is obvious that confirmation ought to occur later in life than it commonly does, and that the decision to participate (or not) in the church ought to precede the sacrament of confirmation, not be identified with it. But that will require a revolution in the understanding of the lay state and, concomitantly, a revolution in understanding the nature of the church.

The priesthood of the laity, like the hierarchical priesthood, is centered on mediation. The priest ferries back and forth between God and the world. The priest, lay or ordained, holds hands with the sacred and with the secular. The church itself is priestly, standing as it does with one foot in the world, one beyond. It is both a worldly reality and a divine mystery, but what makes it priestly, and those who belong to it priestly, is the way it brings the two realms together. The priesthood of the laity requires, on the one hand, a bringing of God to the world and, on the other, a bringing of the world to God. As the council says, the special vocation of the laity is "to make the Church present and fruitful in those places and circumstances where it is only through them that she can become the salt of the earth" (*LG* 33). But at the same time, all the doings of the laity in the world, if "accomplished in the Spirit," become sacrifices to be offered to God in the eucharistic sacrifice. Remember Congar's insistence that both lay and ordained priesthoods are sacrificial. In this action, says the council, "the laity consecrate the world itself to God" (*LG* 34).

When *Lumen Gentium* discusses the specific works of the laity— while it largely elaborates upon the two movements of bringing the world before God through the worship of the church and bringing God's love to the world through a faithful living within the secular— there are places where particular ministries within the church are recognized. For example, having written of the general lay responsibility to make the church present as "the salt of the earth," the council notes that the laity can be called to "more immediate cooperation in the apostolate of the hierarchy." Laypeople also possess "the capacity of being appointed by the hierarchy to some ecclesiastical offices with a view to a spiritual end" (*LG* 33). While *Lumen Gentium* is not itself specific about these special roles, it seems that it has two kinds of activities in mind. One would be a role in teaching, liturgy, or pastoral care (see *Apostolicam Actuositatem* 24); the other would be offices like that of chancellor of a diocese or an official with a diocesan marriage tribunal. The council clearly envisages here the kinds of roles typically assumed by clergy, but occasionally, for whatever good reason, delegated to the laity.

This reference to "more immediate cooperation in the apostolate of the hierarchy" raises a number of issues. First, it is clear that there can be no such thing as a true ministry of the hierarchical priesthood that a lay person can be delegated to undertake. Of course, there are all kinds of ministries that over history have accrued to the ordained that do not belong essentially to their priesthood. Priests typically exercise financial control over a parish and often serve as teachers in the parochial school, sometimes as de facto guidance counselors. They are often, particularly in smaller parishes, coordinators of social events, music ministers, and bingo callers. All such ministries to the community can and probably should be the responsibility of laypersons. To make this change in a given parish would not be an act of delegation, since the ministries do not properly pertain to the priesthood, but rather an administrative adjustment for more efficient running of the parish. If the priest happens to be the one with most financial acumen in the parish, then let him retain that responsibility. If not, and this is more usually the case, then he ought to relinquish it. Less trivially, there is a second layer of ministries that have most commonly been exercised by the priest but which are increasingly carried out by lay-people. I am thinking here of such things as bringing the Eucharist to the sick or housebound, visiting the sick in hospitals, conducting baptisms, and leading worship. The first two of these are commonly practiced where—as in most places today—the priests available have too much to do, but they certainly fall within the understanding of lay ministry. The latter two are only practiced where a priest is not available and may be thought to be works that are delegated in cases of necessity only. But my point is that if they can be delegated, then they are not strictly ministries of the ordained priesthood or diaconate. Such would be only those roles that cannot be delegated, which might mean presidency at the eucharistic assembly, hearing confessions, ordaining priests (reserved to bishops), and administering the sacrament of confirmation.

I have skirted the most contentious issue, that of preaching. If preaching is ever delegated, then it is not a ministry of the ordained, strictly speaking. It has been the common practice of the church to reserve preaching to the ordained, but preaching does not belong to the essence of the ordained ministry. The recognition of this fact perhaps explains the sometimes tortuous steps taken in the liturgical assembly to allow an unordained person to "offer reflections" on the Gospel but not to preach. Having the priest say a few words first fulfills the canonical requirement. But what is the theological reality?

Leaving aside the question of preaching for the moment, these observations would suggest that the list of ministries that are truly proper to priesthood or diaconate are very few, as opposed simply to those which as a matter of ecclesial practice have been performed almost exclusively by ordained ministers. Certainly this is the import of the only major diagram in Congar's *Lay People in the Church*. Congar has taken his lead from Thomas Aquinas's threefold understanding of priesthood. For Thomas, there is a spiritual priesthood of the righteous, the participation of all the baptized in the priesthood of

Christ, and the priesthood of holy orders. When Congar lays out this understanding in diagrammatic form, across two pages of his text (pp. 192–93), he divides the acts of priesthood into two groups, internal and external cultus. The former relates primarily to the theological virtues of faith, hope, and charity lived out in a holy and moral life. Primary here are acts of mortification, even martyrdom, and family responsibilities, including the "priesthood of parents." The external cultus includes all those actions related to formal public worship and the celebration of the sacraments. It is notable here that most of these actions fall under Thomas's second understanding of priesthood, with the hierarchical priesthood making an appearance only in the far bottom right corner of Congar's diagram, under the rubric of "to celebrate and give baptism, marriage and other sacraments." And even here, as we have seen, there are exceptions, with baptism in particular being a sacrament not reserved to ordained ministers.

There are those who might inspect Congar's diagram, or read the previous couple of paragraphs here, and conclude that what is afoot is a scheme to reduce the importance of the priesthood to the church. There are two responses to this fundamental misunderstanding. One is the obvious point that while the ministries reserved to the ordained may be few, they are absolutely central to the identity of the believing community. If there is no Eucharist, then there is no church. But equally important, to recognize the limited number of roles truly reserved to the ordained is only the obverse of a healthy realization of how many roles and responsibilities pertain to the laity in virtue of their truly priestly status. As we have already had occasion to note in an earlier chapter, the "crisis of priestly identity" that sometimes is invoked when discussions like the present one take place has little to do with the identity of the priesthood per se. It is much more a matter of the identity of a hieratic caste of male individuals, bound to celibacy, with no other raison d'être and frequently with no other affective outlet than being a priest. Imagine a priesthood of men and women, of celibates and the married, of full- and part-time ministers. Would this issue of priestly identity still be such a problem?

The discussion of which roles are proper to the clergy and which to all Christians can obscure the more important fact that all are engaged in the one work of building up the body of Christ. The council, perhaps aware of this, devotes space in *Lumen Gentium* to the matter of solidarity between priest and people, though more is said about this in *Apostolicam Actuositatem*, the decree on the lay apostolate. Here, briefly, two kinds of points are made. First, there is the reiteration of a pastoral relationship between priest and people, such that the laity will open their hearts to their pastors, pray for them, and accept obediently what is decided by the pastors, since they represent Christ. Interwoven with these sentiments are statements that the laity sometimes possess a competence, knowledge, or "preeminence" that empowers or obliges them "to manifest their opinion on those things which pertain to the good of the Church," and that the clergy should on their part recognize the liberty and responsibility of the laity, encouraging their initiatives. The result of this "familiar relationship" will be a reciprocal strengthening in their respective missions. These passages obviously do not make a profound theological point, though they certainly express a commonsense wisdom that unfortunately has not always marked the clergy–laity relationship, even today. But the implications for parish life and structure could be considerable.

Apostolicam Actuositatem

The Decree on the Apostolate of Lay People (*AA*) opens by suggesting three reasons why the church needs widened and deepened apostolic activity on the part of the laity. First, the world itself has become far more populous and complex, while at the same time it has been shrunk by the communications explosion, and in large measure only the laity can respond to the technological complexities of such a world. Second, the legitimate autonomy of many sectors of human life (the bishops are thinking above all of political life, but also of the secularization of the world in general) has meant that moral and religious values do not play the same central role in the world as they might once have done, and this lends an urgency to the tasks of the lay apostolate. Third, priests are often scarce or are deprived of their freedom in many places, and without lay ministry the church could not make her presence felt. This third category we can lay aside. It corresponds to what a Catholic physicist colleague of mine refers to as "the apostolate of the second string." If the starting lineup (of clergy) is not available, let's go to the (lay) bench. Obviously, a serious attention to the lay apostolate cannot be based on this kind of thinking.

In general terms this document is not one of the better works of the council fathers. Like a number of others completed in a hurry at the end of the fourth session, it is underdeveloped. It bears clear signs of being a list of things that ought to be said rather than a structured whole. Thus there are sections on the nature of the lay apostolate, the objectives, the fields in which it may be exercised and the forms it may take, a discussion of relations with the hierarchy, and a plea for adequate training for lay ministers. But among the rather breathless profusion of "and thens," there are a couple of points worth special note in the introductory sections on lay charisms and in the discussion of the forms of lay apostolic activity.

The introductory chapter of the document makes two important points. First, it locates lay ministry in the notion of charisms, those special gifts of the Spirit given for building up the body of the church. While there is the customary immediate caution that "it is for the pastors to pass judgment on the authenticity and good use of these gifts," nevertheless there is a freshness about the turn to the language of charisms. The council recognizes that they are to be exercised not only to develop the church but also "for the good of men." Second, it speaks of the need for an authentic lay spirituality without which personal talents cannot intentionally be placed at the service of the church. This of course is also true and important, but the discussion of the content of this lay spirituality is a little more problematic. It must be aided by the liturgy; grounded in faith, hope, and charity; follow Jesus' way of poverty, humility, and endurance; and take Mary as its model. None of this is specific to lay spirituality. The pope could do no better than to follow the same example. The only specific references to the lay life are a comment that "the lay spirituality will take its particular character from the circumstances of one's state in life . . . and from one's professional and social activity," and the injunction to esteem professional competence and various virtues "without which there is no true Christian life" (AA 4).

The problem of identifying a distinctly lay spirituality is instructive about the character of the lay state itself. When it comes to the crunch, how many real differences are there between the lives (and hence the spiritualities) of a lay person and a cleric? Many laypeople are men, not a few are celibate, increasing numbers have advanced theological education, and some work full-time for the church. One can of course imagine that priestly spirituality might be focused eucharistically, and laypeople do not preside at the celebration of the mass. But then we are close to a lay spirituality based on exclusion, a spirituality of "not being the eucharistic presider." This would bring us far too close for comfort to the definition of laity as "not clergy." There are so many references in this particular document to humility, "hiddenness" and so on which, while often true and perhaps salutary, cannot avoid suggesting a "spirituality of the second string." Moreover, there are any number of Catholic laypeople in much more prominent positions than the average pastor, and if their professional situation is their primary apostolic métier then they may need more humility but somewhat less emphasis on hiddenness.

When the present document turns to a consideration of the different forms of the lay apostolate, a curious category emerges. It rightly distinguishes between the role of the layperson as an individual, the work of laypeople in groups and more or less formal organizations, and the thorny question of the specific difference entailed in the apostolate of Catholic Action, that is, those groups formally sanctioned by the hierarchy as collaborating "in the hierarchical apostolate." But in the discussion of the individual apostolate of laypeople, the bishops consider extraordinary circumstances that may affect what laypeople do. Here they are primarily imagining a context in which circumstances curtail the freedoms of the church. In such a situation, they suggest, the laity may "take over as far as possible the work of priests" (*AA* 17) or may do work "more closely connected with the duties of pastors" (*AA* 24). This work prominently includes teaching Christian doctrine, catechetics, and the encouragement to a living participation in the sacramental life of the church. The document on mission, *Ad Gentes Divinitus* (*GD*), interestingly adds "preaching the gospel" to this list (*GD* 21).

We have now already seen this kind of questionable distinction a couple of times. If laypeople are taking over "the work of priests" for whatever reason, then it is surely work that has been done by priests through historical accident or deliberate hierarchical decisions, not work that pertains to priesthood as such. That kind of work cannot be delegated. So, for example, even in North America the church suffers from a shortage of priests and some congregations must go without the Eucharist. They are often led in some kind of paraliturgy by a suitably trained layperson. There is never any suggestion that the layperson should celebrate the Eucharist (though there are often calls for ordaining these persons so that they could celebrate), because this liturgical action belongs to priesthood. But obviously the document imagines that the layperson can lead noneucharistic worship, or teach theology, or do catechetics, or lead the local Christian community. Hence these activities may need to be seen as legitimate branches of the lay apostolate, and not an "apostolate of the second string," called on because there aren't enough clergy to do them or because the freedom of the clergy has somehow been restricted. But if this is true, what happens to the much-vaunted distinctive "secularity" of the lay state?

Gaudium et Spes

This huge document, vast in size and enormous in postconciliar impact on the entire church, is the bible of the lay apostolate. As a pastoral rather than a dogmatic constitution, it has little or nothing to say about the nature of the lay state or the legitimacy of the lay apostolate. Another of the late documents of the council, *Gaudium et Spes* (*GS*) takes for granted everything that has been said in all the previous documents and addresses the role of ecclesial activity in and dialogue with the world outside the church. While it does not distinguish lay and clerical ministry very much, it is primarily describing the church's relationship with the secular and is thus taken up with the ambit of lay ministry properly understood. After a brief introduction, it divides neatly in two halves. The first looks at the nature of the church–world relationship. The second concerns itself with five areas in which "some more urgent problems" need to be addressed: marriage and family, economics, politics, culture, and international relations. The first lays out the vision of the church–world interaction that legitimates the depth of involvement suggested in part 2. It is with part 1 that we shall primarily be concerned.

The ambiguities we have already uncovered in the process of attempting to define the nature of the lay vocation are shadowed in *Gaudium et Spes* by ambiguities over the nature of the church–world relationship. We have seen that one of the principal challenges to the development of theological reflection on the lay state is the way in which we have to reconcile both the secularity of the laity and the role that they legitimately play in the internal ministries of the community. The development of a theology of the laity must remove any sense of conflict or lack of clarity in the relationship of these two functions. In similar fashions, at different moments in the document, the council fathers seem to see the church as addressing the world from within, while at other times they offer a vision of the church as a dialogue partner with the world, as a reality distinct from the world. Of course, this reflects two truths about the church. The church is in the world, and the church is oriented beyond the world. It is both a human reality and a divine mystery. Yet, in a pastoral document there is much to be gained from presenting one clear vision of how the church understands its relationship to the world. While the church has two faces, in a manner of speaking, it can only have one voice.

In an excellent article written in 1987, Paul J. Roy, S.J., has examined this and a number of other ambiguities in *Gaudium et Spes*.[10] First addressing the general question of the church–world relationship, he draws attention to the fact that the council fathers clearly envisage a two-way relationship between church and world, in which influence will move in both directions, which is consistent with the understanding that the church is within the world. But at other times the bishops seem to fall back into an earlier understanding, says Roy, which is "more uni-directional." So, for example, in the opening paragraphs the bishops speak eloquently of respectful dialogue with the world over contemporary problems. But they go on immediately to say that "the Council will clarify these problems in the light of the Gospel and will furnish mankind with the saving resources which the Church has received from its founder under the promptings of the Holy Spirit" (*GS* 3). Roy also considers the closely related question of the relationship between the mission of the church to convert the world and the work of the church in the world, humanizing the world. He notes that the latter is the purpose of the current document, but that both missions need to be integrated beyond the point that the council managed. Finally, in what is perhaps Roy's most telling challenge to the document, he quotes both Tissa Balasuriya and Harvey Cox to take issue with Karl Rahner's famous claim that at Vatican II we saw for the first time "the coming of a world Church."[11] The council remained a primarily eurocentric body, on this reading, and reflected the concerns and preoccupations of the so-called first world. So, for example, there is a lot in *Gaudium et Spes* about atheism and relatively little about the poor. There is ground laid for the emphasis on the theme of development in Catholic social teaching, but little sense of the role of neocolonialism or structural oppression even with the movement of development itself.

Roy's look at the tensions within what was nevertheless a groundbreaking document in the Catholic tradition possesses implications for theological reflection on the role of the laity in the church. First, the layperson is by the usual definition a Christian who lives in the secular world, and whose apostolate is closely tied to her or his secularity. If the church is primarily understood as within the world, in dialogue with the world, teaching the world, and learning from the world, then the layperson is in the vanguard of the church's mission. But if the church is primarily understood as different from the world, standing over against it if not opposed to it, offering it a saving message, then the layperson at work in the world is in a special but distinctly secondary role. Roy's second point is related to this and is particularly crucial to the understanding of the lay role in a missionary church. How does the lay person evangelize *and* humanize? How are they the same, and how are they different? If I live as a Christian in the world, in an open and responsible relationship to my fellow citizens of every faith and of none, am I evangelizing? Indeed, in a pluralistic world, how much more than that can I do before that open and responsible dialogical relationship is impeded, if not destroyed? Finally, if the church for all its opening to the world in *Gaudium et Spes,* has remained in many ways still a eurocentric community, is there not also a concomitant danger that a lay ecclesiology will also reflect the racial and gender biases of the institution and of the community from which the ecclesiological reflection emerges? There is no such thing, after all, as a generic layperson. There are lay men and women, white and black and brown, gay and lesbian, young and old. And here, of course, the much-vaunted secularity of the laity may come to the rescue of the church. Our insertion into the secular world should, though regrettably it often does not, open us much more to the demands of pluralism and to the elimination of structural oppressions that can make the very call to pluralism itself a hollow charade. There can and should be lay ecclesiologies, perhaps many of them. But perhaps there should not be *a* lay ecclesiology.

EVALUATING THE WORK OF THE COUNCIL

As the time drew near for the opening of the council, there was considerable anxiety about what it might portend, not only on the part of conservatives anxious about reform but also from reformers equally nervous that the opportunity would be lost. During the council, especially between the first and second sessions, there were many more voices raised—in alarm, excitement, or despondency. In the years immediately following the council a number of those who had figured prominently in the council's work, including especially Suenens, Congar, and Schillebeeckx, wrote not only of their warm appreciation of its achievements but also of their awareness of its limitations. They seemed to sense that the message of the council was not coming to the fruition for which they had hoped. At the same time, theologians like Congar and Schillebeeckx clearly developed their own thinking as a result of council deliberations. We saw in chapter 2 how Congar's turn to the language of "ministries" occurred in the context of Vatican II, and Schillebeeckx, as we shall see, was obviously stimulated to develop his own thinking by his disappointment at the council's failure to reflect theologically on the nature of the lay state. In this section of the chapter we need to look a little more closely at some of these responses, since they may contain important clues to how the work of a lay ecclesiology may be pursued.

Suenens and Coresponsibility

There was probably no more influential figure among the reforming majority at the council than Cardinal Suenens. He moderated many of the key sessions, and time and again he spoke in ways that moved the council fathers further toward the eventual shape the final documents took. It is also safe to say that, as a genuine liberal, he would have liked the council to have moved even further to express a fearless openness to the modern world and to the representatives of other Christian bodies and other world religions. It was perhaps because of his outspokenness in the council years that the cautious Pope Paul VI did not in the end name Suenens to the position of secretary of state, as had been widely predicted. The pope needed a less polarizing figure. And given the strong emphasis that Suenens later put in his public utterances on understanding the papacy in the context of the College of Bishops, it was perhaps wise of Paul not to have done so. Suenens was not a man to keep quiet about his opinions. He was more of a prophet, even a little bit of a demagogue, and not much of a diplomat.

As a major shaper of the council, Suenens was wonderfully appreciative of its heralding what he and many others referred to as a "new springtime" for the church. But he was also keenly aware that until the world church acted upon the council declarations, it remained a promise rather than a fulfillment. He must also have known better than most how carefully so many of the documents had been crafted to incorporate the compromises that were needed to garner the huge levels of support shown in the final vote tallies. Usually, of the almost three thousand votes cast, only a handful—rarely more than a hundred—were *non placet* votes. The result of such compromise documents, as the subsequent history of the church has clearly shown, is that they can be read in different ways to highlight either the reiteration of traditional verities or the emergence of new ecclesial attitudes. The way in which they would be influential in the church was going to depend, quite obviously, on the ways in which they were used by church leaders. Which elements in the documents would be promoted, which would be sidelined?

Suenens's best-known book, *Coresponsibility in the Church*, appeared in 1968, in both French and English editions. It was an obvious attempt to influence the way in which the council would be understood in the church, but one that was firmly grounded in the emphases of *Lumen Gentium*. For Suenens, the principal achievements of the great document on the church were a stress on communion and a call to coresponsibility. The imperative followed upon the indicative. If the church is to be understood as communion—and the undeniable preference for the model of People of God in the text of *Lumen Gentium* bears no other interpretation—then the task of preserving and perfecting this communion is one for which all sectors of the church are in their own way responsible. He writes in turn about each subgroup within the church, apologizing for the necessity of breaking the community down in this way, when the council had stressed the unity of the faithful through baptism.

When he turns to the coresponsibility of the laity, Suenens issues a sober warning:

> History will render glory to the council for having beautifully defined the nature of the church, the people of God, and for having boldly sketched the place and role of the laity in the church. History will no doubt also accuse us of not having sufficiently put into practice that which is so well defined—the coresponsibility of the laity.[12]

He writes of the role that some laypeople played in the council, but honestly admits that there was no true dialogue.[13] Recognizing that laypeople cannot be "judges in matters of faith," which is "a role reserved to the magisterium," he nevertheless quotes with approval the lesson of the Council of Jerusalem, the first in the church's history. The Acts of the Apostles, referring to the council deliberations, says that "the apostles, the presbyters, the whole church decided . . ." (15:22). "The implication," comments Suenens, "is obvious: it was the whole people of God who were engaged in making the decision."[14]

While most of the chapter on the laity is a very clear exposition of the various ways in which the laity can and should be given room to participate in the apostolic life of the church, the explosive material is to be found early on, in Suenens's discussion of the role of democracy in the church. The word "democracy" is most frequently heard in a church context, of course, in the familiar statement, "the Church is not a democracy." For Suenens, this is not true. The church is indeed a democracy, *and* a monarchy, *and* an oligarchy. The papacy, as the one principle of unity, is monarchical. The collective responsibilities of the College of Bishops are oligarchical. But "the fundamental equality of all in the communion of the people of God" is democratic. Not only are all three necessary, but they are all in relation to one another. So the papacy is "unintelligible" except in relation to the episcopate and to the whole body of the church.

Suenens's discussion of the democratic principle in the church is not merely rhetorical. There is always a relationship between the structures of the church and the historical period in which it is living. There is an "undeniable process of osmosis and imitation between the manner of ruling in the secular world and in the church, and this is to be expected." And the council "certainly was characterized by a move in the direction of 'democratization.'"[15] Suenens was well aware of public criticism of the human structures of the church, and there is surely a great deal more of it today than there was thirty years ago. But he was wise enough to see that where this stems from "lay people, devoted children of the church, whose fidelity cannot be doubted, and who suffer from the situation which they deplore," it cannot be ignored or dismissed. Questions of doctrine cannot be submitted to a vote, admittedly, and the responsibility of bishops for teaching remains intact. But on governance issues, the implications are clear: "the question of a greater or less democratization in the method of the church's government remains a valid one." "The solution to this question," he concludes, "cannot but influence the status of the layman in the church of tomorrow."[16]

Two years later, in his Pentecost pastoral letter of 1970, Suenens returned to the themes of change in the church and coresponsibility. Five years after the council, it had become quite apparent that the church was going through extraordinary upheavals, symbolized if not summarized in the dramatic number of resignations from the priesthood and religious life, themselves exacerbated by the deeply disappointed reaction to Pope Paul's encyclical in 1968 on birth control, *Humanae Vitae.* Suenens remains optimistic, calling this "a time rich in hopes for the future." He criticizes those who blame Vatican II. Instead of accusing the council of having "provoked a torrential thaw," he remarks, "it would be better to wonder where the ice came from which gave rise to this inevitable reaction." And he moves immediately to the subject of collegiality, arguing that since everything in the church is connected to everything else, collegiality needs to be exercised not only at the highest levels but also at that of "the bishop within the local church, and that of the priest at the heart of the community."[17]

Suenens clearly understands the idea of collegiality to extend throughout the church, not merely to describe the relations of bishops with the pope, and to be involved in a move toward a measure of democratization in the church, particularly though not exclusively at the more local levels. He frequently advised Pope Paul to decentralize some of his responsibilities. How could the pope be simultaneously pastor of the universal church, bishop of Rome, patriarch of the West, and so on? It would be like the president of the United States being also mayor of New York and governor of California. But Pope Paul was never persuaded. Suenens also argued that collegiality had implications for freedom of debate around controversial issues, and got into a lot of hot water in 1970 for promoting a new examination of the law of celibacy. His relations with Pope Paul were often difficult, though they seem to have respected one another's sincerity. By the time of the election of the present pope in 1978 Suenens was nearing retirement and was unlikely to be much longer a challenging presence. But some readers will surely join me in finding it ironic when Suenens reports that after the concelebrated mass to inaugurate the pontificate of John Paul II, the pope commented to Suenens, "And now, let us have some affective and effective collegiality."[18] Is it possible that the good cardinal misheard?

While an incurable optimist, Suenens was as aware as anyone of the problems that the church had in living out the message of the council. Because he was committed to the centrality of the idea of collegiality/coresponsibility in the council's teaching, he felt that the church had to address the question of democratization. The fact that it has not done so and has largely acted since the council in quite the opposite direction must raise the question whether or not Suenens's interpretation of the council is accurate. In particular, does he conflate two different ideas in so closely relating collegiality and coresponsibility, and is he wrong to believe that the co-responsibility of the laity in particular for the life of the church must involve a measure of democracy? Our consideration of his role in the ongoing concretization of the council's teachings will conclude by considering these questions.

Everything the council teaches on the nature of the church comes back to the fundamental image of the People of God. As has often been said, the chapter on the laity is chapter 4, not chapter 2. Chapter 2, on the People of God, describes the universal reality of the Christian faithful, and as Suenens never tired of saying, the term "the faithful" refers not to the laity but to all the baptized. The pope is one of the faithful before he is the pope, and one of the faithful when he is the pope. Again, one of Suenens's often-quoted remarks is that "a Pope's finest moment is not that of his election or consecration, but that of his baptism." So while someone in the Catholic tradition must hold firmly to the belief that the hierarchical ministry is not a dependent function of the ecclesial community but a divinely instituted reality, the Christian is first and always a baptized member of the faithful, sharing a radical equality with all the baptized. Understandings of the roles of hierarchical ministry in the church, and still more the personal standing of the papacy itself, have varied with the vicissitudes of history. But it has always been true, and will always remain true, that all are equal before God in virtue of a common baptism.

The question we are left with, then, is to what degree an understanding of the church as the People of God, including its hierarchical ministry, is susceptible of democratization. Suenens clearly saw that this was the question, and I believe he answered it correctly, though he did not spell out all the implications of recognizing the need for democratization. It is perfectly possible to hew to the belief that the hierarchical ministry is God-given, not a function within the universal priesthood, and to remain committed to the view that the role of proclaiming the gospel, leading the community, and teaching sound doctrine is vested in the first instance in the episcopate, while arguing that the ways in which people in the church attain these offices need to be reviewed. A pope, for example, whose election was preceded by extensive consultation with the whole People of God and marked by wider voting power than the College of Cardinals would not thereby be less a pope, less the universal pastor, even less "infallible." Perhaps he would be more so. Or, even more urgently, a bishop whose appointment was a product of genuine consultation, in which the local community he would serve was given much greater voice than at present is the case would not be a poorer bishop as a result, and perhaps would be a better one. The Holy Spirit is certainly at work in the convocation that elects a pope and perhaps even in the arcane secrecies of episcopal appointments. But these systems and structures for appointment have been quite different at different moments in history and, to my knowledge, the Holy Spirit has never expressed a preference for the present methods. If the pope were to be elected tomorrow by a simple vote of the entire body of Catholics in the church—something I am certainly not advocating—the Holy Spirit would be no less present in the process than in the secret conclaves that have elected his predecessors during the past centuries. (These and related issues will be pursued at much greater length in the final chapter of the book.)

What Suenens saw so well was that a hierarchical ministry exists for and in unity with the whole People of God of which, of course, it is a part. Another way to make Suenens's point about the place of monarchy, oligarchy, and democracy in the church is to say that papacy and episcopacy can exist within a constitutional framework. The primary problem with the structure of hierarchical ministry in the church today is not that the pope is a "monarch" or that the bishops are an oligarchy, but that the system is self-perpetuating. The whole People of God, or that enormous majority within it who stand outside the hierarchical ministry, are totally excluded from participation in the system by which people are called to the ministry, appointed to the role of bishop and, yes, elected pope. Suenens saw this process of further reflection to be something the council had left to the postconciliar church. It still needs to be accomplished.

SCHILLEBEECKX AND THE NEED FOR THEOLOGICAL REFLECTION

We have several times had occasion to note that Vatican II was in the end by deliberate choice a pastoral rather than a dogmatic council. This was the primary issue over which the curial minority and the reforming majority initially clashed, and it was this battleground to which they periodically returned as the sessions of the council came and went. But it would be a mistake to imagine that the choice of pastoral over dogmatic was a choice against theology. It was, on the contrary, a choice for one kind of theology over another, not so much pastoral over dogmatic, as inductive over deductive. Pastoral concerns are always encountered in particular contexts, and responses to them are most prudently determined in those particular contexts. So, for example, it is in the most obviously pastoral of the documents, the Decree on the Missionary Activity of the Church (*Ad Gentes Divinitus*), that the call is most clearly made for attention to local culture and custom in the conduct of liturgy and the organization of evangelization. The dogmatic impulse, on the other hand, is to mine the traditional wisdom for teaching that, because it must apply always and everywhere, cannot bear any trace of particular locations or particular sets of experiences.

The work of the Dutch Dominican theologian Edward Schillebeeckx on the council and the laity addresses the question of a pastoral theology of the laity.[19] Writing both during and after the council, Schillebeeckx elaborates one simple point. It is his belief that while what the council taught about laypeople in the church was important and indispensable, the council had missed an opportunity. For whatever reasons, the council turned away from a thorough theological examination of the nature of the lay state and instead tackled an admittedly important but easier problem, that of the character of the lay apostolate. One of the most intractable problems is to determine what a layperson is, as distinct from a member of the hierarchy. It cannot merely be determined inductively. That is, you cannot simply look at what laypeople do in the church and then fashion a description that becomes a theology of the lay state. It may be the case that certain roles have been taken up by laypeople (as also clergy) that do not really belong to them, and a merely descriptive approach would simply canonize historical error. Perhaps the council's distaste for deductive thinking meant that tackling such a normative issue as a theology of the lay state was unpalatable. But there is another possible reason, one more likely to appeal to the conservative minority, that might have cemented an unspoken and possibly unconscious agreement not to address this problem. A theology of the lay state must inevitably imply not only an entire ecclesiology but also a theology of the clerical state. Echoing words we earlier quoted from Congar, Schillebeeckx notes that the council, for all its good intentions, remained to some degree trapped in a clericalized view of the church:

> A laborious search was made for the layman's place in the church, as though this was the real subject for discussion. But, from the point of view of biblical theology, the problem is exactly the other way round— what is the place of the church's office in the people of God? From the biblical point of view, the negative definition of the layman as a non-office-bearer is bewildering. . . .

Catholics know, said Schillebeeckx, that the general priesthood of all believers is not the same as the official priesthood and that the latter is a special service performed by certain Christians. But why should those others who have a different service to perform be known simply as "nonclerical"? If we were consistent, he adds, "we should define a priest as a non-layman, an apostle as a non-evangelist, an evangelist as a non-presbyter, a teacher as a non-deacon, and so on." The weight of tradition was something the council could not defeat, and it turned away from a theological definition of the laity to a phenomenological description. It failed to define the layperson positively, though it tried.

It ended up merely with a positive definition "simply of the state of being a Christian itself," and this of course is "something that applies to all members of the church," including priests and bishops.[20] In other words, although it was a significant step for the council to locate the lay apostolate in the fact of baptism, and indeed to stress the equality of all in virtue of that baptism, that in itself is not enough to define the particularity of the lay state.

Like Congar and Rahner, Schillebeeckx tries to reconcile three dimensions of lay activity. There is the individual Christian apostolate in the world; there is the role of the lay Christian in the internal activities of the church, including but not exhausted by liturgical actions; and there are the organized group apostolates of laypeople. Some of these have received some kind of ecclesial sanction and have at times and in some places been known as Catholic Action. It is Schillebeeckx's point that the council's teaching on the role of the laity reiterated the importance of all of these roles, without developing an understanding of the lay state that would enable the church to balance the relative significance of these roles, and thus to be able to stress one or other of them more than the rest.

IN CONCLUSION

Nothing could ever be the same again for the fortunes of laypeople in the church after the Second Vatican Council. It is impossible to overestimate the theological significance of explicating the mystery of the church in terms of the overriding image of the People of God. The laity are understood to share in the mission of the church and in its liturgical life. They are called to full participation, not passive presence. The clergy are time and again reminded of the need to act in solidarity with the laity, and to recognize that laypeople are adult members of the church, sharing in a royal priesthood and gifted with all kinds of ways to assist the ordained ministers. The ordained always remain the ordained, and the laity remain laity, but Vatican II insists that on some things the laity know better, and the clergy had better adjust to this fact.

The nature of the council documents, however, and the political climate in which they were crafted, meant that the theological insights that grounded the pastoral vision were not as well developed as they might have been. Subsequent interpretation of the council's vision of the laity was thus free to go in two quite different directions. A more conservative direction would stress the importance of seeing the distinctions between the roles of clergy and laity, the former acting in the church, the latter living out the Christian life in the world. While there is much truth in this approach, dubbed the "distinction of planes" model by Gustavo Gutiérrez,[21] it has one questionable consequence. It separates church and world too clearly and leaves the laity *ad intra* with much the same passive role as it had possessed before the council. On the other hand, more liberal interpreters could expand on the implications of *Lumen Gentium* and look forward to a new age in which all—clergy and laity alike—would be coresponsible for the life and the ministry of the church.

One way to adjudicate between the two interpretations is to ask ourselves about the problems of the institutional church today. There is enormous vitality in the Roman Catholic Church. But there are problems. On the level of teaching, its social ethics is often remarkable, but it does not seem to carry the people along with it, while its sexual ethics is problematic, and it certainly does not meet with the assent of many faithful Catholics. At the level of practice, the church increasingly reveals itself to be in need of an overhaul, in the way in which bishops are chosen and how they understand their roles, in the ways in which ministers are selected and asked to live, and in the ways in which Rome understands its role as the focus of unity. Much of this will be discussed in the later chapters of the book. For now, as we turn to look at the postconciliar years, one question can be raised, if not answered. Would the church be helped or hindered in dealing with its deficiencies by a greater involvement of laypeople in its decision making and a greater sense of accountability to the laity on the part of the institution? I, for one, think there is no doubt that the answer should be in the affirmative.

4

Theology and the Laity since Vatican II

IT WILL SOON BE FORTY YEARS since the Second Vatican Council came to an end. What has happened to the fortunes of the laity in the Catholic Church during these decades? This question will be the focus of the current chapter, and in order to answer it, several matters must be discussed. There is the state of the question within the official teaching documents of the church, and in particular the vision of the role of the laity in John Paul's major statement, *Christifideles Laici,* written to summarize and respond to the 1987 Synod of Bishops.[1] We shall also need to examine some less official efforts to write theologically about the place of the laity in the church,[2] and we shall certainly need to take account of the theology of the laity implicit in the vast outpouring of words on the lay apostolate. The thesis of the chapter is a simple one, one that grows naturally from the observations we have made of the work of the council. While lay apostolic activity has flourished in the postconciliar period to such an extent that it is quite safe to say that without it the church today would be in the most serious difficulty, the theological question of the character of the lay state itself has been underplayed. To this thesis let me add a rider that will lead us into the constructive project occupying the remaining chapters of the book. Silence on a theology of the laity is to be explained at least in part by the radical ecclesiological implications of this kind of religious reflection. Some of the resistance to theologizing about the laity stems from the realization of its implications for a theology of the clerical state. When the lay state is treated as the norm in ecclesiology, rather than the clerical, the church suddenly seems very different.

What we must now squarely face, here in the first years of the twenty-first century, is that the issues that were at stake in the struggles we sketched out in chapter 1 are still live issues in the church. The council documents stand, cannot be abandoned, and indeed are invoked by representatives of both more conservative and more progressive wings of today's church. But the council itself, as a papal initiative to let fresh air into the church and to reexpress the ancient faith in a new world, must be considered an unfinished project whose final outcome remains uncertain. A hundred years from now, it may be that Vatican II will be seen as a brief progressive interlude in the history of an inward-looking church. It is my guess that if this is indeed the way that the early twenty-second century sees the church, then there will be little of the church left to appreciate. But this is by no means certain. Fundamentalisms of various kinds flourish in our world today, and perhaps the future of Catholicism is as a kind of ecclesial fundamentalism. It will be a smaller church, but it could survive quite vigorously in such a manner. On the other hand, perhaps in 2100 the commentators will be able to say that Vatican II, despite the difficulties experienced in bringing its teaching to life in the community, did finally triumph. Then, I would certainly hope, the church would still be large and vibrant in the twenty-second century, the realization of a possibility that the giants of Vatican II only dreamed of. But, again, it is also possible that it might be alive as a much smaller church, a countercultural remnant in a world divided between cynical calculation and reactionary defensiveness.

While there is absolutely no doubt that the church today has changed enormously from that of preconciliar times, it has to be said that the long pontificate of John Paul II has not been friendly to the vision of Vatican II, for all the protestations Rome periodically makes to the contrary. Of course, just as the council documents can be read to show that the council was revolutionary or that the council was simply reiterating the eternal verities, so the subsequent history of the church can be spun in at least two directions. Paul VI, they say, was either a dangerous leftist or a cautious depressive. The pontificate of

John Paul II either set out to undo the hard work of the council or to overcome the excesses of postconciliar enthusiasm in the name of a solid centrism. There have been many attempts during the past few decades to tell the story of the fortunes of Vatican II in both these directions. The truth of the matter is probably somewhere between the two. But it is also a mistake to tell the story of Rome entirely in terms of papal psychology. The Vatican is an extraordinarily complex entity, and papal control over what happens there is never complete, especially at the end of lengthy pontificates. Even if one is not given to conspiracy theories, there is no question but that popes come and go, while the Roman Curia goes on. It is also entirely possible to make too much of the Roman bureaucracy, a particularly American predisposition. It is not a heresy to argue for the abolition of the Roman Curia, and quite a good case could be made. It is easy to sympathize with Carlo Maria Martini, who as archbishop of Milan in 2002 commented acidly to one reporter that he was interested in the teaching of the pope and the bishops, but not in the doings of the Vatican. But if we are to tell the postconciliar story, we cannot leave them entirely aside.

FROM THE RUNAWAY CHURCH TO RESTORATION

The title of Peter Hebblethwaite's 1975 book, *The Runaway Church?*, nicely encapsulates the state of reflection ten years after the end of the council.[3] Hebblethwaite, a veteran writer on Vatican affairs who went on to pen outstanding biographies of John XXIII and Paul VI, was writing in the last years of the pontificate of Pope Paul. The story of those ten years is easy to tell in outline. After the council it was not long before the Latin American Bishops Conference in Medellín, Colombia, in 1968 gave strong institutional support to the emerging theology of liberation. The year previous to this, Pope Paul had issued perhaps his most outspokenly progressive social encyclical, *Populorum Progressio* (On the Development of Peoples), calling for a notion of integral development that stepped away from the narrowly economic developmentalism of the previous couple of decades. The year 1968 also saw two other momentous events for the church, the Soviet invasion of Czechoslovakia and the publication of Pope Paul's controversial encyclical letter on birth control, *Humanae Vitae*. The first of these damaged, perhaps irreversibly, the Vatican's *Ostpolitik*, the movement of accommodation with the Soviet Union, and perhaps began the process that would eventually lead to Pope John Paul's championing of the Polish Solidarity movement and the demise of the eastern bloc. The second caused even more damage within the church, leading to the defection of thousands of priests and, more significantly in the long run, to the quiet refusal to "receive" the teaching of the pope on birth control.

After 1968 the papacy of Paul VI still had ten years to run, but relatively few achievements would mark this period, which represented more than half of his entire papacy (1963–78). Pope Paul was the first traveling pope. In the first few years of his reign he visited the Holy Land, India, the United Nations, Portugal, and the Far East (where he also became the first pope of modern times to survive an assassination attempt). There were no further trips after 1970. He presided over four synods of bishops in Rome (in 1967, 1969, 1971, and 1974), only the third of which, on justice in the world, was accounted much of a success. He oversaw the enormous proliferation of consultative bodies in the universal church, from the Synod of Bishops to national conferences of bishops, councils of priests, and diocesan and parochial councils. All of these, with the occasional exception of national conferences, have proved to be largely ineffective, primarily because their status as merely consultative bodies allows them to be ignored. The national bishops' conferences, particularly in Canada, Germany, and the United States, have had more impact. The U.S. conference produced two documents of considerable weight, on nuclear weapons (1984) and on the U.S. economy (1986), though they caused great anxiety in the Vatican at the time.[4] In more recent years, Cardinal Ratzinger, prefect of the Sacred Congregation for the Doctrine of the Faith, has spearheaded a Roman attempt to cast doubt on the teaching authority of these conferences.[5]

At the same time, the achievements of Pope Paul VI should not be lightly dismissed. A Vatican official for almost all his life, and the confidant of Pius XII, he knew the Curia well and expended much energy in its reform. In the first half of his pontificate he did much to internationalize the curial workforce, shifting the proportion of Italians from about 57 percent in 1961 to only 38 percent in 1970. He established the rule that on the death of a pope all the senior curial officials had to tender their resignations. And he is well known for having instituted mandatory resignation for bishops at the age of seventy-five, and for the exclusion of cardinals over eighty from the conclave that meets on the death of a pope in order to elect his successor. More ambivalently for some, Paul VI also was responsible for considerable relaxation in the rules for the laicization of priests who wished to leave the active ministry, and for allowing—at least in the United States—a remarkable growth in the number of annulments granted to Catholics whose marriages had failed.

Paul VI has to have been by far the most complex personality to occupy the papacy during the twentieth century. He was as reserved as Pius XII but far less autocratic. He had none of the charisma or the optimism of John XXIII, but was just as personable in private meetings. He certainly did not have the clarity and drive of John Paul II, but he had a far greater capacity for self-doubt, sometimes to a fault. In fact, it seems to have been his sense of his own unworthiness to be pope, perhaps coupled with the realization that the job was too big for anyone, that was to make his later years increasingly ineffective. But the greatest tragedy of his pontificate, it would seem, was the failure to make collegiality a living reality. While a supporter of the council's moves in this direction, he was also influenced by more conservative voices to vacillate at key moments in the process, particularly on the matter of the famous *nota praevia* attached to the document on the church, *Lumen Gentium*. As a consequence, the final twelve years of his papacy included four Roman synods of bishops that failed to demonstrate true collegiality as envisaged in *Lumen Gentium*. Paul thus left the church with the council's insistence on episcopal collegiality seriously underdeveloped. When he was replaced by John Paul II, no friend of the notion of collegiality at all, there were no healthy structures in place to help resist the slow slide back into a highly centralized form of authority and decision making.

The papacy of John Paul II has often been referred to as a restorationist event, and there is really no reason to go searching for some more accurate term. The word precisely describes the move to turn back the clock, at least in some respects, to the preconciliar situation of the church. John Paul has certainly not been an enemy of the council's entire legacy, but he clearly made the choice to move back toward centralization. Both the strengths and weaknesses of Karol Wojtyla contributed to the return to authoritarianism. From the beginning of his papacy, he exuded charm and strength. Obviously a born leader, he was clearly a charismatic figure. He toured the world by plane and traveled Vatican City in a white jeep. He survived a far more serious assassination attempt than Paul VI had faced and bounced back. He was instrumental in the rise of Solidarity in Poland and the decline of the Soviet Union, the eastern bloc, and the Iron Curtain. He never seemed someone who needed any human aid. Until he was afflicted with Parkinson's disease, he did it all. Such a strong leader and fear-less moral presence in the world could not have operated so effectively, perhaps, in the context of a more decentralized vision of episcopal authority. Did he not speak for the whole Catholic world, and who would contradict him?

If John Paul II's fearlessness was a product of his Polish experience, then so—unfortunately—was his attitude to the secular world. Poland in the postwar years was a very sad place. A Catholic nation repressed by a Soviet-style government held fast to a strong church, partly at least as a form of passive resistance to successive gray administrations. Church leaders understood themselves, rightly for the most part, to be standing up for the rights and dignity of a people over against a harsh civil reality and an officially and ideologically secular state. This, of course, was one reason why the Polish episcopate was so suspicious of the "opening to the East" that marked the papacies of John XXIII and Paul VI and that was so evident in the Vatican document on the church in the modern world, *Gaudium et Spes.* But when John Paul left Krakow for Rome in 1978 he unfortunately carried with him a set of views about the relations between churchly and secular reality that in many ways did not serve either him or the church well. On narrowly political assessments, his writings were often very good. He wrote a series of social encyclicals, which, while they always spoke harshly of state socialism, were equally challenging to the materialist, capitalist West. In *Laborem Exercens* (On Human Work [1981]) he was partic-ularly acute in his criticisms, excoriating the West and the East alike for "the instrumentalization of labor to capital."[6] But as his pontifi-cate progressed and he increasingly turned his attention away from political to social and ethical issues, it came to seem that he had little or nothing good to say about the West, not only about its materialistic lifestyle but also about the Catholic people who struggled to live lives of faith in such a society. "Democracy" seemed not to figure prominently in his list of political virtues. Giant that John Paul undoubtedly was in the late twentieth century, he suffered from an almost complete failure of imagination when it came to empathy for educated first-world Catholics, particularly Americans.

The events of John Paul's papacy—the letters, the foreign travel, and the frequently remarkable moral leadership; the mending of relations with Judaism, on the one hand, but the evisceration of the International Theological Commission, on the other; the reactionary contortions of the Sacred Congregation for the Doctrine of the Faith, the ideological litmus tests for the appointment of bishops, and the stony resistance to the legitimate autonomy of the local church; the total refusal to discuss the issue of women in the ministry and the systematic undermining of the Latin American movement of liberation theology—are clearly a mixed bag, and it will be some time before we have the historical distance to make an overall assessment. But if there is one consistent thread that runs through the entire list, it is that John Paul tried to reassert a powerful centralized papacy. John Paul II's Vatican has been much more reminiscent of that of Pius XII than that of Paul VI. This seems to have been a deliberate strategy, partially a product of the papal personality, partially a sincere response to the perceived "weakness" of the postconciliar church that Paul VI left to John Paul. This has not been good for the church, and not good for the legacy of the council.

John Paul's determination to recentralize authority and reestablish control had particularly negative repercussions for the vision of the lay role in the church envisaged by the Vatican Council. The council wrote at length about the need for vigorous lay apostolic activity, and certainly the postconciliar church has shown enormous advances in this regard. The local church is increasingly run by the laity, and while this is not unproblematic, it is something that seems to have a life of its own and to be impervious to any Roman efforts to affect it. But the council also imagined a future in which clergy and laity would work together, with the skills of the laity in secular affairs being accorded respect, and with the clergy deferring appropriately to lay expertise. The structures of parochial and diocesan councils were intended to facilitate this broadening of responsibility. Cardinal Suenens, as we saw in the previous chapter, wrote in *Coresponsibility in the Church* of how "within the Church there is at one and the same time a principle of unity (monarchy), a pluralism of hierarchical responsibilities (oligarchy) and a fundamental equality of all in the communion of the People of God (democracy)."[7] In 1975 Peter Hebblethwaite commented on this same passage from Suenens, saying that it was "too neat" and that in such a schema "there were bound to be border disputes and quarrels about demarcation lines."[8] But that was before John Paul II. Today we would have to say that his papacy shows the restoration of monarchy, the subjugation of oligarchy, and the eclipse of democracy.[9]

Postconciliar history is also mirrored by the changing fortunes of the notion of collegiality. There is a general consensus, even among those not too friendly to Vatican II, that at its center stands the Dogmatic Constitution on the Church, *Lumen Gentium*. The heart of that document, as we saw in the previous chapter, is the description of the church under the guiding image of the People of God. But this is by no means all there is in the document. Closely connected to this central biblical image is the idea of the collegiality of the bishops, which we have already discussed in connection with the work of Cardinal Suenens. The new emphasis on the role of the laity in the church and the notion of episcopal collegiality stand together as to the two most significant practical applications of the image of the People of God.

The idea of episcopal collegiality, of the collective authority and responsibility of the "college" of bishops, was central to Vatican II's conscious effort to complete the work of Vatican I. Because of the pressure of war, Vatican I deliberated only on the role of the papacy in the church and had no time to proceed to pronounce on the roles that others played in the institution. Vatican II consciously committed itself to a fidelity to the words of Vatican I on the matters of papal primacy and infallibility, but placed these words in a broader context, in which the bishops exercised authority too, both individually in their local churches and collectively, though always with the pope as their head. The council fathers also wrote of the power of the *sensus fidelium*, the common commitment of the whole body of the faithful to the truths of the tradition, and they saw both episcopal teaching and the *sensus fidelium* as sharing through the power of the Spirit in the infallibility of the whole church.

Although the council fathers were explicit in their fealty to Vatican I, talk about the teaching authority of bishops made conservatives very anxious, and their very nervousness gave Paul VI cause for concern. On balance, he seems to have been firm in his support for collegiality, at least at the time of the council. But he was certainly a man of the "radical center" (Suenens's phrase) and did not want to see notions of episcopal authority spinning out of control. He also had a concern to obtain the most overwhelming votes in support of the council documents and so tended to favor language of compromise and balance. The "on the one hand . . . on the other" that marks the style of Vatican II's official pronouncements illustrates this concern. But while it made for impressively overwhelming majority votes on all the documents, it is also responsible for the kind of ambiguity that has allowed more conservative church leaders to turn back the clock in the postconciliar period, *in the name of the council itself.*

The nervousness of conservatives and of Pope Paul himself goes a long way to explain the famous, not to say notorious, *nota praevia,* or "explanatory note," added to the text of *Lumen Gentium* at the very last minute. The debates on collegiality had occupied a great deal of the council's time during both the second and third sessions. More clearly than any other topic, they had shown the seriousness of the confrontation between the conservative minority and the more progressive majority of the bishops. Collegiality was such an issue because conservatives could claim that the specter of greater authority for the bishops threatened the primacy of the pope, even if their real agenda was to protect the power of the Curia itself. So, for example, no issue raised the ire of the formidable Cardinal Ottaviani more than this one. He laid his cards clearly on the table when he announced in November 1963: "In attacking the Holy Office, one attacks the Pope himself, because he is its prefect."[10] Ottaviani drew the Holy Office (now known as the Congregation for the Doctrine of the Faith) into the debate, because he was its head, and because he was also head of the Theological Commission, which was fighting against the will of the assembled bishops on the subject of collegiality. He was also fighting against efforts by the four moderators of the council, Cardinals Suenens, Agaganian, Lercaro, and Döpfner, to assert their authority over due process.

At the opening of the third session of the council in September

1964, Pope Paul made it clear that the primary work of this session would be the ratification of *Lumen Gentium* and, in particular, the affirmation of the doctrine of the collegiality of bishops. Now fighting a rearguard action, the conservatives prevailed upon the pope to attach an explanatory note to the text of chapter 3, which dealt with collegiality. It seems clear now, as it did then, that Pope Paul did this more out of a desire to be done than out of any personal discomfort with the actual text. While the note is complex in places, its central points are to reaffirm that the college of bishops has the pope as its head and can never act without the pope, and that the pope retains full freedom to act alone. Both these points are contained in the actual text, but doubtless the conservative minority were reassured by the weight of this additional note. As a result, the nay votes on chapter 3 fell from several hundred to forty-six, and the final vote on the entire document had only five opposed, some of whom were probably progressives, upset by the presence of the explanatory note itself.

While the explanatory note certainly gained the resounding vote of approval that the pope wanted, and perhaps persuaded the overwhelming majority of the bishops that they were indeed a college vested, along with its head, with supreme teaching authority, there was a price to be paid. The effect of the explanatory note was to further shift the balance away from collegiality and back toward primacy. As a direct outgrowth of the teaching on collegiality, there was much discussion at the council about the establishment of an international body of bishops that would meet regularly in Rome to advise the pope. Pope Paul himself seemed well disposed toward this, going so far as to envisage the Lateran Palace as a sort of conference center for these meetings. The curial party was particularly upset by such plans, since their role and influence would necessarily be reduced. But in the event they need not have worried. The body that eventually came into existence, the Synod of Bishops, has turned out to be a deep disappointment, and on nothing more so than on the question of the laity.

THE ROMAN SYNOD OF 1987

The synods of bishops, which were supposed to be the principal practical expression of collegiality, have been one of the most deeply disappointing consequences of the council, at least to those who wish to take its teaching seriously. They usually meet at four-year intervals, though there have been two extraordinary synods, in 1969 and 1985. The members of the regular synods are representatives of national bishops' conferences, with a number of additional members selected personally by the pope. The synods are understood to be merely consultative bodies to the pope, which means that he can ignore whatever they say. As consultative bodies, they issue no formal conclusions of their own, but the pope himself writes a document subsequent to the synod on the theme of its deliberations. Laypeople are invited in small numbers, as *auditores* (listeners), though they are occasionally allowed to address the assembly. The laypeople are appointed, not elected, and chosen by the pope himself or by someone close to him. Overall, the synod is obviously not a genuine exercise of collegiality and is, in reality if not intentionally, a frustrating exercise for many of the participants.

The synod in Rome in 1987, called to discuss the role of the laity in the church, was preceded as usual by a working document prepared to help the bishops think through the issues they would confront. But even before this, in 1985, a *Lineamenta* was published to stimulate a wide process of consultation of the lay faithful. It rehearsed the teaching of Vatican II on the roles of laity internally to the church and externally in the world and linked the radical equality of all to the fact of baptism. But it also introduced reference to "certain problems" that had arisen in the twenty years since the council which needed to be addressed. Arising out of misreadings of Vatican II, these problems are summarized in the words of the present pope as the "clericalization of the laity" and the "laicization of the clergy" (*Lineamenta* 9). They include issues such as confusion about which ecclesial ministries are open to the laity, and also the tendency to assume that only ecclesial ministry (often construed on a clerical model) qualifies as apostolic activity. The document also mentions the tendency of laypeople involved in public life to make divisions between their faith and their professional responsibilities (one thinks inevitably here of John F. Kennedy, Mario Cuomo, and Geraldine Ferraro).[11] Further, it adds the opposite problem of that negative flight from the world that would constitute a derogation of the lay duty to enliven the temporal order with the grace of Christ.

Following upon the *Lineamenta,* the general secretariat of the Synod of Bishops prepared the *Instrumentum Laboris* (working document) by means of which the bishops attending the synod would further focus their attention. This lays out most of the neuralgic areas in reflection upon the laity, though notably saying absolutely nothing about mechanisms for allowing laity some kind of more than merely consultative voice in the church. In the end the synod would be composed of 230 bishops, with 60 lay *auditores.* The Pontifical Council for the Laity appointed all the lay observers. What is very noticeable about the document is that almost nowhere is there any reference to lay *ministry.* The language is almost entirely that of lay "participation" in the mission of the church. This telling preference undoubtedly reflects the predilections of the pope himself. On his American tour immediately prior to the synod, John Paul engaged in a dialogue in San Francisco on the role of the laity in the church and the world. He was addressed by Patrick Hughes, director of pastoral ministry for the diocese, who constantly used the term "lay ministry." This is, after all, the commonly used term in the United States. In responding to him, the pope spoke warmly of lay involvement in church life, but studiously avoided using the term ministry to describe it. He also warned laypeople once again to stick close to the ecclesiology of Vatican II or "we run the risk of 'clericalizing the laity' or 'laicizing the clergy.'"[12]

Most commentators at the time saw the synod on the laity as a struggle between two opposing interpretations of the ecclesiology of Vatican II. On the one side are those who would stress the centrality of the image of People of God, from which all further ecclesiological reflection emanates. Thus, in *Lumen Gentium,* the chapter on the People of God is placed before that on the hierarchical character of the church. While this approach could not be fairly described as democratic, it is certainly participatory and respects the legitimate freedom of the layperson to engage the world and to work in the church. The second attitude grows out of a preconciliar mentality and sidesteps the central imagery of Vatican II. As Peter Hebblethwaite illuminatingly points out in *Sources of Renewal,* his 1969 book on the Vatican Council, the then Cardinal Wojtyla revealed that for him the key passage of *Lumen Gentium* was the statement that the priesthood of the faithful and hierarchical priesthood, while interrelated, "yet differ from one another in essence and not only in degree." Wojtyla commented that this essential difference "contains in a certain manner all that the council wished to say about the church, mankind and the world." Hebblethwaite dryly calls this statement "remarkable." "Breathtaking" would be a better term. But anyone who felt this way, as John Paul clearly did in 1987, would certainly be unhappy with the term "lay ministry."[13]

The synod took place in Rome throughout the month of October. It was surrounded by the characteristic and faintly ridiculous Roman attempts at control. Bishops were forbidden to give out the full text of their speeches (but many of them did). Bishops were told that their final conclusions were to be held in secret "on pain of grave sin." The lay auditors were forbidden to see them. Any publication of these propositions would interfere with the freedom of the pope by putting undue pressure on him. They were "the personal property of the Holy Father." Somehow, the propositions leaked out, only to reveal that they showed nothing of a controversial nature and for the most part were tailored to the known preferences of John Paul, though there was a little more courage on the role of women and on the importance of the local church.[14]

In the end, the central issue that occupied the Synod was a struggle, among the bishops and perhaps in the mind of the pope himself, between the fundamental significance of the local church and the importance of "movements." "Movements" refers to international organizations set up to promote aggressive apostolic activity. For most, and certainly for the pope, this meant primarily Communion and Liberation and Opus Dei. These were papal favorites. A number of their clerical members, bishops and priests, were among those appointed to the synod by the pope himself, and the head of the Pontifical Council on the Laity, himself a supporter of Communion and Liberation, held a conference with organization members before drawing up the list of sixty lay observers. They were thus guaranteed a significant presence at the synod, but no one had counted on the firmness of the elected bishops (none of whom were representatives of the movements) in their stand for the importance of the local church.

John Paul was bound to find the movements attractive. They combine apostolic zeal with fervent loyalty to the person of the pope. More significantly, they preserve a strict division between the concepts of clergy, laity, and their respective realms of activity. The church and the world are different and separate realities. The clergy work within the church, the laity in the world. Moreover, the laity work under the instruction of the clergy. These organizations, both because of their international character and because of their highly centralized attitude to the world church, represent a challenge to the importance of the local church, as expressed in *Lumen Gentium*. Opus Dei's "personal prelature," for example, means that its members owe loyalty in the first instance to their own private bishop, and not to the bishop of the local church within which they live. As the synod gathered, bishops could be forgiven for thinking that the papal predilection for the movements meant a papal preference for a renewed centralization over the conciliar vision.

In the event, the synod was a non-event, like most of the others. Bishops were called to Rome to talk (briefly) under conditions of secrecy and then went home to await the papal response, typically published in about six months, which would take into account the opinions expressed at the synod and the final propositions ("the personal property" of the pope). That response, *Christifideles Laici*, took rather longer to appear, finally emerging in February 1989 (though it was backdated to December 1988, perhaps for appearance' sake). The bishops left a disappointing meeting whose conclusions were largely determined beforehand. The American bishops returned to a situation where two hundred thousand laypeople had been involved in the consultative phase before the synod, to tell them what? The consultation was as ineffectual as the bishops' role at the synod itself. Except that the sheer number of them who spoke in support of the importance of lay ministry, of the central significance of the local church, and of the need to explore further the place of women in the church simply could not be ignored, even in Rome. As we shall see, the papal response made one or two concessions to the bishops.

American reactions to the synod predictably covered the ideological spectrum, though on the whole reaction was appropriately muted, since the synod itself had produced very few fireworks. Perhaps the strongest response came from the liberal lay Catholic journal *Commonweal*, in an editorial of December 4, 1987. The editors began by quoting wryly the dry remark of Archbishop Weakland of Minneapolis on his return from the synod. "At least," said Weakland, "we did not pedal backward." They went on to applaud the American and Canadian bishops for getting the issue of women's ministry onto the agenda, but saw that it "drowned in the molasses of ecclesiastical rhetoric." The editorial continued forcefully:

> Still, there is a truth that needs to be spoken, and spoken plainly. The synod was a sham, an insult to the intelligence of the laity who were supposed to be the subject of its deliberations. . . . [The Synod] looked for all the world like one of those cardboard congresses periodically called by one-party dictatorships to devise filigree of verbiage around decisions made behind the scenes by others.[15]

Ending with a call for more collegiality, *Commonweal* quoted the Canadian archbishop Donate Chiffon in the *Toronto Star*, commenting on the final list of fifty-four propositions: "there was nothing to hide except the nothingness." A fitting epitaph to the synod—and perhaps to the entire synodal structure during the pontificate of John Paul II.

CHRISTIFIDELES LAICI

Christifideles Laici (CL), known in English by the rather more unwieldy title, "The Vocation and the Mission of the Lay Faithful in the Church and in the World," was published early in 1989. Although John Paul refers to the document as "a faithful and coherent expression" of the bishops' deliberations and "a fruit of collegiality," in fact it represents the state of papal thinking on the question of the laity, presumably enlightened by the deliberations at the synod. Its further purpose, says the pope in the introduction, is to enlighten and enliven the laity to understand better their roles "in the communion and mission of the Church." It is divided into five chapters, the first of which responds to the synod's call for "a definition of the lay faithful's vocation and mission in *positive terms*," that is, not simply as "not clergy." There follow chapters on lay participation in the life of the church, participation in the missionary activity of the church, forms of vocation, and finally formation.

Accurately, if predictably, the pope places the specificity of the lay state in its secular character. While the way of life of the lay faithful does not separate them from the clergy or religious, says John Paul, it sets them apart and in a manner designated by the term "secular character." The church, he says, quoting Paul VI, "has an authentic secular dimension, inherent to her inner nature and mission, which is deeply rooted in the mystery of the Word Incarnate." And all the members of the church, including clergy and religious, "are sharers in this secular dimension but *in different ways*." For the laity, the secular world is where "they are called by God" (*CL* 15). And thus it is in the world that the laity will fulfill their Christian vocations. It is in the world that their call to holiness must be lived out.

There seems to be some kind of parallel in the pope's words between the nuanced way in which all are said to share in the secular world, though the laity in a particular way, and his views on the ways in which clergy and laity share in priesthood. In virtue of our birth, we are all connected to the secular world; in virtue of our baptism, we are all sharers in the priestly vocation. But just as the hierarchical priesthood is a priesthood different in kind and not just in degree from the priesthood of the laity, so the secularity of laypeople is a secularity different in kind from that of clergy and religious. Because the church also has a secular dimension, laypeople can also take up tasks within the church. Less commonly, but also admissible, it would seem, clergy can at times be asked to engage in secular activities, since they too share in secularity, though their primary calling is to priesthood. In order to expand more practically on his view of lay ministry, for the remainder of the document the pope turns to the language of communion and mission. The nature of the church is to be communion; its task is mission. Laypeople have roles in both the *ad intra* and the *ad extra*, to borrow once again the favorite terms of Cardinal Suenens.

Given the disappointing reality of the synod itself, it is gratifying to be able to say that the bishops do seem to have influenced the thinking of the pope in two important directions. He is quite clear that "the ecclesial community, while always having a universal dimension, finds its most immediate and visible expression in the parish" (*CL* 26), and he is supportive of lay involvement in diocesan synods. To a degree, he accepts the principle of subsidiarity as applying to church structures. More significantly, perhaps, in *Christifideles Laici* he seems a little more willing than previously to use the language of ministry to describe the work of the laity. The term "ministry" is a term that John Paul has preferred to reserve to the apostolic activity of the ordained.

Thus, following Vatican II, he vastly prefers to employ the language of lay sharing in the "priestly *mission*" of Christ, but not his ministry. Now in this letter he refers to the "ministries of laypeople," though not to "lay ministers." And his primary use of the term is to cover those circumstances in which laypeople are required to supply for a shortage of priests. In extraordinary situations, then, when they are doing the work normally expected of the clergy (including the distribution of communion), they are "ministering" to the faithful. There are also several uses of the phrase "the various ministries, offices and roles" that laypeople can fulfill, but without any specificity about what these might be. The pope immediately cautions, however, against "a too-indiscriminate use of the word 'ministry,'" which would lead to the confusion and equation of the two kinds of priesthood and risk creating "an ecclesial structure of parallel service to that founded on the Sacrament of Orders" (*CL* 23). When he turns, however, to the mission of the church to evangelize, a mission in which the laity are fully involved, the language of ministry disappears once again. Accepting the command of Christ to go and preach the gospel to all nations entails a mission but not—at least for laypeople—a ministry.

In the need to warn against the clericalization of the laity, and in the determination to restrict, if not totally exclude, the language of lay ministry, John Paul is obviously exhibiting a great anxiety about the potential confusion of roles of priest and laypeople. He is clearly appreciative and supportive of the apostolic activity of laypeople. He clearly believes that baptism entails participation in the church's mission. But none of this must be allowed, in his mind, to erode the qualitative distinction between the ordained priesthood and the lay sharing in the priestly ministry of Christ. There is obviously, in the pope's mind, something enormously important at stake here. Perhaps he is concerned, as Congar was, to safeguard the Catholic belief that ministry in some way or other stems directly from Christ's commission, that it is a product of apostolicity, and not merely a function of the church. But, even if we take this to be as important a distinction as the pope and Congar seem to have thought, it is hard to avoid the conclusion that there is confusion here. Let us grant that the priesthood stems from Christ and not from the church. It is also true that the patterns of ministry in the church have developed throughout the centuries, and there is no cogent argument for claiming that history has now ceased to have an effect upon the ways in which ministry is understood. Development will surely continue to occur. Moreover, to claim that Christ instituted the ordained ministry is by no means to claim that he envisaged it operating in the way it does, nor that significant change could not continue to occur in the patterns of ministry in the future. Worries about the clericalization of the laity may simply be anxiety over changing patterns of ministry.

Pursuing the question of papal anxiety about the confusion of the roles of laypeople and clergy brings us naturally to the 1997 Vatican "Instruction on Certain Questions Regarding the Collaboration of the Non-Ordained Faithful in the Sacred Ministry of Priests."[16] The context for this curial document, says the introduction, is to provide guidance to local churches where "certain practices have often been developed which have had very serious negative consequences and have caused the correct understanding of true ecclesial communion to be damaged" (foreword). What these deleterious practices may be must be determined from the list of prohibitions contained in the body of the document. The nonordained may be asked to supply for some priestly activities that are not directly connected to ordination, but must never be given titles like pastor, chaplain, coordinator, or moderator, which "can confuse their role and that of the pastor" (1.i). In very restricted circumstances the nonordained may be allowed to preach, but never at the eucharistic liturgy (2.iv). This prohibition applies even more strictly to "priests or deacons who have lost the clerical state or who have abandoned the sacred ministry" (2.v). Councils of priests may not have lay members (5.1). Diocesan and parochial pastoral councils or finance councils are only consultative and may not become deliberative (5.ii). Laypeople may not preside or appear to preside at the liturgy and may not wear any kind of sacred vestment (6.ii). Sunday celebrations in the absence of a priest may never involve the use of eucharistic prayers (7.ii). Extraordinary ministers of Holy Communion are to be reserved for cases of real necessity. Their habitual use is to be discouraged, and they may not receive Communion "apart from the other faithful as though concelebrants" (8.ii). No one but a priest may administer the anointing of the sick (9). No one but a priest or deacon, except in quite extraordinary circumstances, may be deputed to assist at a marriage (10).

Reactions to this document were predictable, on both sides.

Conservatives came to its defense, pointing out that all it did was reiterate the regulations in place and repeat the teaching of Vatican II on the respective roles of laypeople and clergy. Some muttered darkly, like Cardinal Ratzinger himself, about the problems of "north-central Europe," which seems to have meant that Germany (and perhaps Austria) was the principal violator of the rules reasserted in the Instruction. Others repeated the need to avoid clericalizing the laity and laicizing the clergy. One letter writer suggested that the increase in lay ministry was directly responsible for the decline in candidates for the priesthood in the so-called developed world. On the liberal side, there were wild claims that the Instruction undid the work of Vatican II, that it set back the cause of the church by decades, if not more. Wiser heads did and said nothing. The U.S. bishops very sensibly sent the document to a review committee, which has never issued a public report.

The Instruction has not had much impact on the American church, not least because most of the more serious concerns discussed have not been particularly prevalent in the U.S., or at least have not been widely publicized. But as an indicator of the mentality of the Vatican on lay issues, the Instruction is seriously disturbing. By most estimates, there are well in excess of thirty thousand lay Catholics in America working full or part time in paid ministerial activities. All but a tiny fraction of them work faithfully under the supervision of a bishop or local pastor, and they are simply not guilty of the misbehavior the Instruction addresses. But the document's approach to lay ministry is one of caution and censure. The language is all gloom and doom. Of course, the overriding concern for maintaining clearly the separation between clergy and laity is one that certainly makes sense. Clergy have one set of responsibilities in the church, and laypeople have another. But the document completely fails to recognize that we live in a new ecclesial situation in which the shortage of clergy is critical, and in which the day-to-day life of the church is increasingly dependent on laypeople ministering in ways that would have been reserved to priests only a generation ago.

The myopia of the eight curial departments that signed off on this letter and of the pope who gave it his blessing is well addressed in a stinging challenge to the Instruction written by the outgoing bishop of Innsbruck, Reinhold Stecher, shortly after its publication. After admitting that there are some points that need to be insisted upon, like the responsibility of the ordained to celebrate the Eucharist, Stecher takes the Instruction to task for two related reasons. First, it completely fails to face the fact that countless thousands of Catholics around the world are unable to receive the Eucharist regularly because of a shortage of priests and that lay ministry is an honest effort to ameliorate the scandal. Second, the Vatican is clearly determined to hold access to the Eucharist hostage to its insistence upon the celibacy of the clergy. In Stecher's challenging words:

> the truly dismaying aspect of all this—no matter how embarrassing to admit—involves the astonishing theological and pastoral inadequacy of current church leadership. Office in the church, interpreted in biblical terms, constitutes an office of *serving* and not an exercise in sacred narcissism which can be unconcerned whether millions upon millions of Christians even have the opportunity to receive the grace-giving sacraments and to nurture the center of their community which according to Scripture and dogma is the Eucharist in a humanly meaningful manner.[17]

The document does not discuss celibacy, but the Austrian bishop is on to something here. What probably concerns the Vatican at bottom is that too much lay visibility in sacramental life will by degrees make the people grow accustomed to being ministered to by noncelibates, and this in its turn will lead to firmer calls for an end to the mandatory celibacy of the ordained priesthood. It was the same concern that led Rome for years to hold out against women acolytes, readers, or altar servers. Even today a pastor has the final say on whether to allow female altar servers, even over the wishes of his bishop. The issue addressed in the document, then, is not simply one of distinguishing appropriately between the functions of the ordained and the non-ordained, but also of shoring up a particular historically conditioned understanding of the ordained state. Moreover, as Bishop Stecher rightly points out, the insistence on maintaining this specific conception of ordained life is contradictory to the good of the church, because it directly deprives very many Catholics of the Eucharist, the central act of the worshiping community. True, the Vatican Instruction does indeed have a remedy for the shortage of priests. It suggests that bishops need not necessarily accept the resignations of priests, when, at the age of seventy-five, they are required to tender them! Here, surely, is another failure of the pastoral imagination.

For all its faults, the Instruction nevertheless raises once again an issue that is directly relevant to lay ministry. It brings us back to the question of the degree to which the lay minister, when taking up what are normally responsibilities of the ordained, is indeed engaging in lay ministry. Obviously, those ministries of laypeople in the church such as carrying the sacrament to the sick in hospitals or officiating at a noneucharistic service in the absence of priests, are valuable, even necessary, at this moment in the church's history. Equally clearly, if there were more priests available, laypeople would not be doing these things. Here they are "co-operating in the work of the hierarchical priesthood," to use the Vatican's term. But if they are laypeople who are doing these things, then are they engaging in lay ministry, are they acting as laypeople? Does the lay in lay ministry imply a range of activities or simply in a neutral fashion indicate that the one ministering happens to be lay? It is all going to depend on what you mean by "lay."[18]

MEANWHILE, IN AMERICA . . .

During the final quarter of the twentieth century, while Rome was showing its reservations about the apostolic activity of laypeople, lay ministry in North America—for such it was called here from the beginning—was growing apace. This rapid expansion took place without much in the way of serious challenge to the ecclesiastical status quo, unlike parallel growth in "north-central Europe." It is difficult to be exactly clear why there should have been such a difference. In all probability, it has to do with the moderately liberal, certainly not radical standpoint of large numbers of active Catholic layfolk and the moderately liberal standpoint of most U.S. Catholic bishops, at least on pastoral matters. Although many are quite conservative theologically, and not a few have the inborn caution of the Roman Curia, a preconciliar ideological conservatism toward church practices is relatively rare. The principal charge to be laid against the American hierarchy since Vatican II is probably timidity. (Even the gross failures in leadership that became apparent in the handling of the clerical pedophilia crisis seem to have stemmed more from incompetence than any more Machiavellian impetus.) And when this is coupled with an active laity that is supportive of the postconciliar church but in the main is neither theologically radical nor institutionally polarized, it happens to make for good growing conditions for lay ministry. The more radical Catholic movements like Call to Action are persistent rather than aggressive, with fairly modest platforms for church reform.

In the United States, the two church organizations responsible at a national level for promoting lay involvement in the apostolate have been the Bishops' Committee on the Laity and the Laity Secretariat of the U.S. Catholic Conference. The Secretariat, established in 1977, and the Bishops' Committee worked rapidly in the early years with a series of conferences, and in 1980 the bishops produced a brief report, *Called and Gifted: The American Catholic Laity*, which has been treated by all subsequent documents as a kind of blueprint for progress.[19] The heart of this document is the series of four "calls" to the laity identified by the bishops as stemming from *Apostolicam Actuositatem*. They are the call to adulthood, the call to holiness, the call to ministry, and the call to community. What is interesting about the bishops' treatment of these four lay calls is the insistence on the special quality of the *lay* call.

The call to adulthood, say the bishops, "which flows from baptism and confirmation," is a call to laypeople to behave within the church with precisely the same "mature independence and practical self-direction" that characterize them in other areas of life. The lay call to holiness is "a unique call requiring a unique response."

> It is characteristic that lay men and women hear the call to holiness in the very web of their existence, in and through the events of the world, the pluralism of modern living, the complex decisions and conflicting values they must struggle with, the richness and fragility of sexual relationships, the delicate balance between activity and stillness, presence and privacy, love and loss.[20]

The bishops see a particular benefit flowing from the acceptance of this call, in the involvement of the laity in the liturgy. "As lay persons assume their roles in liturgical celebration according to the gifts of the Spirit bestowed on them for that purpose," the bishops confidently assert, "the ordained celebrant will be more clearly seen as the one who presides" over the community of faith at worship. The third call, the call to ministry, occupies the most space in the letter, as the bishops carefully examine both "Christian service ministry in the world," and "ministry in the Church." In the first case, the laity have both the right and the responsibility to engage in Christian service in the world, bringing their special competencies to bear on the new challenges presented by the contemporary world. In facing these challenges, "lay people are at the cutting edge." They are "an extension of the Church's redeeming presence in the world."[21] In the case of ministry within the church, the bishops express gratitude for volunteer work of all kinds, but concern themselves particularly with "ecclesial ministers," that is, "lay persons who have prepared for professional ministry in the Church." These are "a new development" and we must all face the challenges of working out how they will function in the church, including practical difficulties like availability of positions, procedures for hiring, and just wages and benefits. Breezily unconcerned about the language of "ministry," the bishops also call for special attention to an "increased role for women in ministries of the Church to the extent possible." Finally, the call to community is invoked. Placing the stress firmly on the role of family as the primary community for laypeople, and recognizing the need for the parish to assist where the family ideal is not reached or is breached, the bishops point out that laypeople expect a similar "intimacy, support, acceptance and availability" in their Christian communities. The implications for parish organization and revitalization are clear to the bishops, and "such trends are welcome in the Church."[22] In the remarkably open and fresh spirit in which the entire document is penned, the bishops conclude:

> We are convinced that the laity are making an indispensable contribution to the experience of the People of God and that the full import of their contribution is still in a beginning form in the post-Vatican II church. We have spoken in order to listen. It is not our intention rigidly to define or to control, to sketch misleading dreams, or to bestow false praise. We bishops wish simply to take our place and exercise our role among the People of God. We now await the next word.[23]

What a wonderful thing it would have been if the authors of the parallel Roman documents had managed to achieve the same tone! Unfortunately, even at their best, the products of the Curia exude a very different aroma and convey a very different understanding of their role.

Fifteen years after *Called and Gifted,* the U.S. Catholic bishops produced a follow-up set of reflections, *Called and Gifted for the Third Millennium*.[24] A somewhat longer document, some twenty-five pages as compared with the earlier document's total of nine pages, this letter covers much the same ground. It reflects the ecclesial situation of its own time, different in two notable ways. The first, referred to by the bishops, is that at this later time they can see better the enormous scope of lay involvement in the work of the church. They suggest that one in two parishes has some form of paid lay minister. The second way, not commented on by the bishops, is that this letter is of course written after John Paul's *Christifideles Laici*, though before the quite negative 1997 Vatican "Instruction," which we examined earlier in this chapter. It is not accidental that although this document still breathes an openness to the work of laypeople, it devotes only one and a half of its twenty-five pages to lay ministry, whereas the earlier text spent three and a half of its nine pages on the same topic. It is also not a surprise to find the bishops much more sparing in their use of the term "ministry." While they retain the term in this brief section, they use it nowhere else in the document, using instead the language of "mission," the pope's preferred term. And their discussion of ministry is itself reserved to work within the church. All talk of "Christian service ministry in the world" has disappeared. The document seems to reflect the views of the pope, who had spoken on this very subject in April 1994, at a symposium entitled "The Participation of the Lay Faithful in the Priestly Ministry." Quoted at length in the 1997 Vatican "Instruction," the pope's address strictly limits the use of the word "ministry" to describe the apostolic activity of laypeople. While he is comfortable in a highly qualified way with the use of the word "ministry" to describe the roles of laypeople in supplying "functions more proper to clerics" which "do not require the character of Orders," he is of the mind that the term can be used only in this way. Laypeople exercise "ministry" when they are officially deputed to roles "temporarily entrusted to them."[25] The implication is clear. When they exercise their right and responsibility as laypeople to do what the U.S. bishops in 1980 called "Christian service ministry in the world," which they do in light of baptism and explicitly not through some deputation by the church, the pope would insist that this is not ministry, though it is mission. Perhaps the U.S. bishops in 1995 preferred to drop the whole topic rather than be forced to unsay what they had so confidently asserted only fifteen years previously.

THE THEOLOGICAL DEBATE ON THE LAITY

During the almost forty years since Vatican II ended, there has been an enormous expansion in the role of the laity in ministry within the church. "Christian service ministry in the world" or "mission to the world," call it what you will, is far more difficult to quantify, since you cannot count the positions held. While some of it is conducted in organizations, most of it by its nature is the work of individual Catholic laypeople, on their own initiative, living openly their religious convictions. But the anomaly is clear; while the official concerns of the church, both in Rome and in the United States, have been more closely focused on internal ministry, the consistent (and correct) emphasis of theological reflection has been to stress the secular character of the laity. Of course, a stress on secularity can be used in two ways. It can, on the one hand, fuel an effort to stimulate the laity to engage the world in dialogue, to begin to get *Gaudium et Spes* off the page and into reality. On the other hand, the focus on the secularity of the laity is important to those who want to stress the extraordinary character of lay involvement in internal mission, and particularly of lay involvement in those forms of ministry previously the exclusive possession of the ordained.

To develop a balanced understanding of the role of the laity internally and externally, as we shall see in the next chapter, we have to confront squarely the question, What does the "secularity" of the laity actually mean? For now, as we draw this chapter and this part of the book to a close, it will be helpful to look at some of the issues raised by more recent theological reflection. Limited as our investigation must be, we shall focus our attention on writings that cluster around the question, What does it mean to be a layperson? In other words, we shall insist on precisely the issue that we have seen that the church, at least since the work of Yves Congar, has failed to address, if not avoided. The authors we shall refer to come from all points on the theological spectrum, conservative, moderate, and radical.

The writings of Ramiro Pellitero reflect his Opus Dei background by representing the layperson as a kind of Christian soldier in the world.[26] He or she is engaged in the sanctification of the world through the practice of the Christian life within the world. But the world is itself entirely secular, while the church is entirely other. The layperson thus comes to be seen as a kind of frontier soldier at work in territory that is not bad, since it is created by God, but is alien to the gospel. Pellitero's study of the laity is primarily a critical review of Congar's ideas, and his discussions of both Congar and the council are on the whole fair. It is noticeable, however, that he avoids consideration of the texts of the council on the importance of reciprocity between clergy and laity. The council documents are eloquent on the need for a new understanding of the relationship of ordained and lay, one in which laypeople have not only legitimate autonomy in their worldly existence but also rights and responsibilities of giving voice to their concerns within the church. It is also quite significant that this particular conservative voice is clear that the church is not itself part of the secular world. Thus, purely secular activities conducted purely secularly are not part of the process of the sanctification of the world that is the primary work of the laity.

The point of view presented here by Pellitero, not dissimilar to that of official Vatican treatments of the laity, envisages a church held firm in the grasp of a centrist authority. Laypeople are surely understood to have an indispensable role in the evangelization of the world, but definitely as foot soldiers in what will be an eschatologically protracted campaign. Strategy and tactics will continue to be determined by the hierarchical leadership. It seems clear that this approach to the problem does not take the secularity of the laity sufficiently seriously, perhaps because it does not allow for a secular dimension to the church. Church and world are quite separate entities, destined to be joined only in the kingdom of God. Laypeople are properly present in the secular world, but one cannot avoid the feeling that their true home is, in Pellitero's view, the church. But what does this mean for the greater part of the life of the layperson and—let us face it squarely— for much of the life of the clergy? Are ordinary, everyday pursuits simply theologically neutral? Is the world simply that which is to be transformed through the evangelizing and sanctifying role of the church?

The great but mysterious and eccentric theologian Hans Urs von Balthasar has something similar to say in his various writings on the laity.[27] Von Balthasar's attitude to Vatican II is quirky, to say the least. He starts from the conviction that the clergy and religious failed to understand the council and thus caused confusion for the laity. The "opening to the world" was not something that fazed the laity, but the clergy understood it to require "the secularization of the theology, catechesis and preaching that they practiced," and led to many innovations that "were most unworthy of belief and which the laity quickly recognized as unecclesial."[28] While it is true that some laypeople reacted negatively to the council, the most negative of reactions were reserved, in fact, for the liturgical changes that truly in many places did confuse the laity. The confusion was indeed often a product of clerical clumsiness. But this apart, it is difficult if not impossible to justify von Balthasar's generalization.

Von Balthasar's theological discussion of the laity has some surprising elements, however. For one thing, he understands the calling of the disciples to Jesus as the establishment of the community of faith, not as the creation of a hierarchy. The disciples are called to leave everything and follow Jesus, are given power to face the evil spirit, and have the message of the kingdom put into their mouths, even before the Sermon on the Mount. Before there is hierarchy, he says, we have the demand of radical discipleship and the sending forth to proclaim the kingdom. Obviously, therefore, these two calls belong to the laity as much as to the ordained ministry. This view is clearly contrary to that of Congar in the 1950s, whom we saw writing that the structure of the church, including its hierarchical structure, came into existence before the church itself. That position was untenable, and von Balthasar's is much more promising. In particular, it links all the faithful, including the laity, to Jesus' call to work for the kingdom, which is the call inherent in the gathering of the community. The proclamation of the kingdom becomes, on this understanding, the raison d'être of the church. "The idea that mission is above all an affair of the clergy and not equally an affair of the laity," writes von Balthasar, "must be quite seriously relativized." The pastoral office is "primarily a function within the church" to serve the whole people, and only through serving the whole does it actually become "a Christian witness to the world outside."[29]

If there is a drawback to von Balthasar's vision, it may be that the layperson is drawn too fully into the apostolic mission. Just as in the case of Pellitero, we find that merely living out one's secular life in the secular world is diminished in theological importance, compared to active involvement in the process of evangelization construed more narrowly. Von Balthasar writes, for example, that the closest approximation we might get today to something like the original community would be one that would try "to live the radicalism of the counsels but unseparated from the world, and in which the members can be priests as well as non-priests."[30] This is a little too close to a description of Opus Dei or Communion and Liberation for comfort, and those organizations cannot be the norm for the lay life, however valuable they may be to their own members called in this way, or even to the church as a whole. Indeed, von Balthasar and Pellitero are quite close in their view of the questions. There are also potential problems with von Balthasar's discussion of Christian witness as "witness to the world outside." Leaven, it should be remembered, is only effective when it is within the dough. The Vatican Constitution *Gaudium et Spes* is rightly known as "The Church *in* the Modern World," not "The Church *and* the Modern World." But his fundamental insight is sound, that the ordained ministry serves the church, and that if "Christians as a whole do not give witness," then "this function exists in vain."[31] To put it a little more trenchantly than he does, "No witness, no mission. No mission, no Church."

A more moderate thinker, Bonaventure Kloppenburg, takes a view of things that is rather different from Pellitero and von Balthasar. Indeed, what is striking about his work is that while it is little more than a very clear and competent survey of the council teachings, it is quite refreshing to read.[32] No radical, Kloppenburg seems quite liberal nevertheless, in his faithfulness to the texts of a council that has been largely sidelined in the last quarter-century, for all the protestations to the contrary. While he would have been described as a centrist at best at one time, the center has now moved so far to the right that his very moderation seems quite progressive. In the discussion of sanctification, for example, he confesses that he thinks it will not be long before a father or mother may exercise their priesthood "by officially and solemnly blessing the food before meals, the labor before the harvest, the tools of their work, their home and children. . . ."[33] "Official and solemn" blessings seem unlikely to be licensed for laypeople anytime in the near future, and this is thirty years after his book!

Kloppenburg presents a very clear summary of the council's position on the meaning of lay existence, looking at it under three headings: there is a generic positive element, a negative element, and a specific and functional element. We have seen these three before. The first is the unity and radical equality of all Christians through baptism. The second is the way in which the laity are often defined by what they are not, such as "not ordained," which Kloppenburg rightly says has been rendered unacceptable by the stress on equality through baptism. The third is the secular character of lay life, which he divides into the apostolate of sanctification, of evangelization, and of involvement. For Kloppenburg it is this third element that is "the layman's special vocation in the Church."[34] The "apostolate of involvement" is an intentional living out of the Christian life, including all their secular activities, though, as *Lumen Gentium* said, "even in secular affairs there is no human activity which can be withdrawn from God's dominion" (*LG* 36).

Kloppenburg's more moderate approach, one perhaps more faithful to the entire breadth of the council teachings, seems to open the door to giving theological value to secular activity unconnected to any intentional work of evangelization. If we say with Kloppenburg that "there is no human activity that can be withdrawn from God's dominion," then we have shifted subtly from the position that secular activity must be sanctified through some extra sanctifying work of the layperson (closer to Pellitero's view). Carrying Kloppenburg a little further than perhaps he would want to go, we can say that secular activity is already holy in virtue of the fact that it lies within God's dominion. The default, we might say these days, is "holy." God has both created and redeemed the world. So the burden of lay life in the world is to respect the character of God's holy creation. Disrespect or abuse of secular reality is "withdrawing from God's dominion." This obviously does not replace or sideline the more conscious process of sanctification and evangelization that may go on at times in lay ministry to the world. "Preaching the gospel" may sometimes be the direct responsibility of the laity. But the more common and more specifically lay responsibility is to cooperate in and further God's design for the world, as it is written within the world itself. And perhaps the most challenging dimension of this task relates to the church as "written within the world itself."

Among the more influential theological voices at the council, that of Edward Schillebeeckx has been one of the more creative in the years since, at least on the topic of ecclesiology. Schillebeeckx has concentrated on what he sees as a lack in the council documents themselves. As we have already seen, he believes they had too much of a focus on the lay apostolate and paid insufficient attention to elaborating a theological reflection on what it means to be a layperson, with all that this would imply for ecclesiology in general. In two substantial works he has scrutinized the relationship of priest and layperson, and the resistance to the ecclesiological vision of Vatican II.[35] The first book, *Ministry: Leadership in the Community of Jesus Christ*, examines closely the structure of ministry in the church of the first two centuries. It turns in the final chapter to a highly critical view of the 1971 Rome synod's failure to look courageously at the structure of ministry and concludes with a vision of the church of the future as "a community of brothers and sisters in which the power structures which prevail in the world are gradually broken down."[36] The second book, *Church: The Human Story of God*, takes up the same set of issues and, in its fourth chapter, tackles head-on the issue of an ideological as opposed to a historically sophisticated understanding of the church. For Schillebeeckx, what is most depressing about the Roman efforts to return to preconciliar attitudes is the refusal to take seriously the historicity of the church. An abstract and ideological understanding divorced from historical realities is used to justify exaggerated claims for the present-day structures of the church. But these came into existence in Constantinian Rome. They were confronted by the growth of bourgeois, more democratic values in the late Middle Ages and by the ideas of the Protestant Reformers. These historical currents caused greater intransigence and more extravagant claims, leading to the highly monarchical papacy of the nineteenth and twentieth centuries. But in today's world it is preposterous to think of the church over against the world. The message of Vatican II is that there needs to be solidarity with the world—indeed, for Schillebeeckx as he sounds one of his most characteristic notes, a solidarity with suffering humanity. It is in the context of a dynamic, historically conditioned church that Schillebeeckx looks at the role of the laity. Clearly, as we have had occasion to say more than once already, a particular ecclesiology implies a particular theology of the laity (and of the clergy, of course).

Then a Franciscan priest, the Brazilian theologian Leonardo Boff achieved considerable notoriety in church circles with his 1985 book *Church, Charism and Power: Liberation Theology and the Institutional Church*.[37] An outspoken defense of liberation theology's preferential option for the poor, the book criticizes all previous ecclesiologies, even those of Vatican II, as inadequate to the historical reality of the day. The laity must be involved in everyday reality, especially in its political manifestations, siding with the oppressed and favoring "integral liberation." "The activity of the laity," says Boff, "is not an extension of the hierarchy." Laypeople are not secular, but rather the individual layperson "is a member of the Church in the secular world and has a direct mandate from Jesus Christ."[38]

The bulk of Boff's book is a critique of the pathologies of the church that prevent it from operating as it should, with a preferential attention to the oppressed and with a full internal commitment to human rights, genuine participation, consultation, and so on. Toward the end of the book he turns to the primarily Latin American phenomenon of "base Christian communities," which are grass-roots Catholic communities, stressing attention to scripture and to social change and most commonly led by laypeople, often women.[39] It is difficult to determine what exactly it has been that has concerned the Vatican most about the phenomenon of liberation theology. On the surface, it complained primarily of the uncritical use of Marxist concepts and of "historicist immanentism," which seems to be Vatican-speak for a reduction of the church to its sociohistorical role in human liberation at the expense of a more transcendent salvation. But the root of the unease is far more likely to be the specter of an alternative ecclesiology in which laypeople play a profoundly important animating role in the local community. Spurred originally by the terrible shortage of priests in Latin America, the base communities became of necessity the primary experience of church for very many people. Rome seems to have been deeply worried about the long-term effects of a noneucharistic, lay-led scripture service "replacing" the mass. But the attempt to undermine the effectiveness of liberation theology, which began around 1980, was surely wrongheaded if the alternative was to be only the occasional access to sacramental worship. It may also have played into the hands of the Pentecostal missionaries, who have made such remarkable inroads into the Catholic population during the last twenty years.

The phenomenon of base Christian communities offers the church at large a model for lay ministry that needs to be taken seriously. For one thing, the church as a whole is becoming more and more like the Latin American church in its dire shortage of ordained ministers. But more importantly, the base communities working at their best show a serious degree of lay involvement in the worship and leadership of the local community, coupled with an equally vigorous outreach to the world. The social and political realities of life in the secular world come to be seen as genuine concerns of the church. They are also obviously the primary task of laypeople. This emphasis explains the charges often levied against liberation theology, that it "reduces" salvation to a political liberation. But a look at the life of the base community shows this charge to be a falsehood. Liturgical life and the struggle for justice become intertwined in liberation theology in a way that has not occurred elsewhere in the Catholic world.

American Catholic feminist theologians pose another set of issues that bear on our topic. One challenge to the church that is more obviously true than most is that its fine words on human rights are intended for export only, that it preaches human freedom but does not extend these freedoms to its own members. Nowhere is this more obviously true than in the long misogynistic history of the institutional church. Leave aside for the moment the sensitive question of the exclusion of women from ordained ministry in the church. It is, after all, only the tip of the iceberg. Throughout the history of the church women have been held subordinate to men. The gospel has never been allowed to subvert this shame of European culture and has often been used to shore it up. At the same time, women have always been the more fervent gender, and to this day are the ones who support the work of the local church in a thousand, often-unrecognized ways. They have been offered the spirituality of *agapē* as a hegemonic discourse and have been led to embrace their own oppression. But at least since Vatican II, if not before, they have begun to shake off these shackles.

The particular challenge for feminists writing on laypeople in the church is clearly illustrated in the work of Rosemary Radford Ruether.[40] For Ruether, the experience of church needs to be of "intentional communities of faith and worship," of communities of nurture.[41] This, she would say, is the way that church ought to be for all Christians, and is not. In *Women-Church* Ruether is writing for women who find that the existing institutional churches are counterproductive for women, that "their words are so ambivalent, their power so negative, that attending at their fonts poisons our souls."[42] If we wish to consider this group to be unrepresentative of Catholic lay women as a whole, then we need also to bear in mind that the hegemonic character of the discourse of the institutional church has blinded the vast majority to consider even the possibility that Ruether is correct. Ruether is certainly right that communities of nurture are necessary and that it is far harder for women to find such support in the existing institutional structure.

Ruether moves from impeccable first principles to challenging conclusions. She maintains correctly that the many aspects of the church, including repentance, Eucharist, and ministry, "are simply expressions of entering and developing a true human community of mutual love." To identify the church with an ecclesiastical superstructure, she goes on, is "the greatest possible distortion . . . . The whole concept of ministry as an ordained caste, possessing powers ontologically above nature and beyond the reach of the people, must be rejected." Because we must understand clericalism as "the expropriation of ministry, sacramental life and theological education from the people," so all base communities "are engaged in a revolutionary act of reappropriating to the people what has been falsely expropriated from us."[43] She is not opposed to "authentic leadership based on function and skills." When the community has determined what it needs, "it then becomes fairly easy to delegate various tasks to people who have the readiness to undertake these tasks."[44]

Ruether's constructive position challenges the lay/ordained distinction in quite radical ways. While her critique of the church's ideological sexism has a great deal to recommend it, her alternative proposals will raise questions for many and pose challenges for the subsequent development of our argument. In particular, we shall need to consider the claim that leadership can be based on community delegation according to function and skills. The easy dismissal of this is to call it a Protestant notion of ministry. But that is just too facile. The harder question to be asked is whether or not it is possible to get beyond the model of an ordained priestly caste while still adhering to some distinction between ordained priesthood and the priesthood of the laity. Ruether would obviously not believe this to be possible or desirable. But it seems just possible that she is led to this conclusion by the common assumption that if we peel away the gender bias, mandatory celibacy, and other caste-specific accoutrements of ministerial priesthood at the present day, there is nothing left. If at least we stay within the Christian tradition, it is appropriate to ask what scripture's account of the calling of the Twelve is supposed to mean.

No brief survey of postconciliar theological reflection on the laity would be complete without reference to Hans Küng, the doyen of dissidents. Küng was a very young *peritus* at Vatican II. Although he is the author of about fifty books, including two major works on the church,[45] here we shall focus on a more recent collection of his occasional writings, *Reforming the Church Today: Keeping Hope Alive.*[46] In a crucial central chapter, "Shared Decision-Making by the Laity," Küng points out that the Vatican documents are careful to see the laity as the church, not merely belonging to it. Moreover, all the members of the church share in the apostolic succession. Unlike Ruether, Küng continues to see a place for "the special apostolic succession of the diverse pastoral service," but rightly points out that it is a *ministerium*, not a *dominium*.[47] From a biblical perspective, Küng argues, "the shepherds are not the masters but the servants of the Church." If so, then how can it "in practice be possible to exclude the Church or the congregation from joint decision-making?"[48] Opposing both an unbiblical democratization, which would render clergy the delegates of the congregation, or an unbiblical clericalization, which would do the opposite, Küng calls for a shared responsibility that will give laypeople genuine involvement in decision making. First, the principle of collegiality must be extended to all members of the church and to the church at all levels. Collegiality is not just for bishops (this was Suenens's point). Second, presiding officers should be elected freely by "a representation of the pertinent churches" ("presiding officers" means pastors, bishops, and pope).[49] Both positions, by the way, show how strongly Congar influenced Küng, not least in the checks and balances he suggests as counters to mob rule.[50]

Küng's book moves us into a most important area of lay involvement in the church to which we have not previously paid much attention. The question of the extent of lay participation in decision making is intrinsically connected to any ecclesiology. One frequently hears discussion of such topics countered by the bald statement, "the Church is not a democracy." Cardinal Suenens, the reader will remember, had his own response to this, arguing that there was a democratic principle at work in the church (laity), just as there was an oligarchic (bishops) dimension and a monarchic (pope) dimension. Küng is a little more radical. For him, the church cannot be tied endlessly to one sociological model of governance. Those who think the church is a monarchy should be open to the possibility that it might be or become a democracy. One sociological model can give way to another. In truth, of course, Küng believes that the church is neither democracy nor monarchy. Those who lead the church do so as servant leaders. Those who are served, thinks Küng, should have a role in the selection of their servants. And Küng's arguments for this are drawn from scripture and from the teachings of the council on the equality of all the baptized. It is hard to argue with his point that if you are not allowed to be involved in decision making, you are not a full and equal member.

The theological debates upon which we have merely touched here offer us a few directions in which to pursue our investigation into a lay ecclesiology. Standing out clearly from all the others is the question of how to balance the life of the layperson, placed as she or he is between involvement in the liturgical life of the worshiping community and involvement in the secular world, with responsibilities to family, culture, society, and the polis. How is a layperson at one and the same time a fully involved member of the church and a fully secular citizen of the world? How should we correctly conceive of the balance of sacred and secular? We shall turn to these questions and more in the remaining chapters of the book.

Part Two

Where We Go from Here

5

Secularity

TALKING ABOUT "THE SECULAR" from a religious standpoint means considering the world, dependent on God for its existence and suffused with divine presence through Christ and the Spirit, but not in such a way that the presence of God changes or suspends the natural laws of the universe. This, of course, is not the usual meaning of "secular." "Secular" is most often contrasted with "sacred," so that God is in the latter realm and not in the former. Thus, modern "secular" human beings do not need God, at least not for their secular activity. Such an understanding would obviously make sense for those with no religion, and this is often what is meant by "secular." But it also describes the worldview of those many believers for whom "God" and "the world" are radically distinct realities. When God and world are separated into the different realms of sacred and secular, then the tendency is also to see church and world as similarly distinct. The church, in an obvious sense, is "in" the world but not "of" the world. It is that perfect society here on earth beloved of Robert Bellarmine and the fathers of Vatican I. Congar himself was perilously close to this fallacious picture of church and world when, trying to identify the particular charism of layfolk, he wrote in the early pages of *Lay People in the Church* that "the layman then is one for whom . . . the substance of things in themselves is real and interesting."[1] The contrast is with the clergy, of course, and as we have already seen, Congar repented of this dichotomizing. It is probably not helpful, in the end, to suggest that the ordained minister does not find the things of this world real and interesting in themselves, any more than it is correct to think of the layperson as living outside the Christian story, within the world. Rather, the Christian story must be seen as one that lets the world be the world. The clergy may perhaps be the keepers of the story in a way that laypersons are not, but all—lay and ordained alike—live within the story, as they live within the world.

The understanding of the secular that we wish to propose here is quite other than a sacred/secular duality. Catholic theology is both creationist and incarnational. These two principles, stressing the world as God's work and the enfleshment of God in earthly reality, cannot but lead to a positive evaluation of the world. The danger in such a view, of course, is that the sacred overwhelms the world, that the world becomes a *mere* symbol of the love of God, a sign that is exhausted in its signification. On the other hand, we can avoid that conclusion by deeper thinking about creation and incarnation. Creation is not an instrument of God's love but an expression of God's love. Its distinctiveness is its gratuity. It is a free gift of love without strings attached; with strings, it would be imperfect love. Incarnation is not a ruse to subvert the deplorable effects of human freedom gone awry, but rather a demonstration of how human freedom is to be lived out. The cross is a consequence of a free and loving embrace of the world; and resurrection is not a ticket out of the world, but rather the transformation of life itself.

In what follows in this chapter, we shall have a lot to say about the secular and about its "unconditionality." This simply means that God gave the world to itself, with its own autonomy, as the place in which human beings live out their destiny to be—human beings. When the believer says that we are "made in the image and likeness of God," she means only that we have the potential to love as God loves and that this potential is to be brought to fulfillment within the world, within the limitations of earthly, secular reality. Like our unbelieving brothers and sisters, we have one task: to make the world a more and more truly human reality. Like them, we can fail through fear or greed. Like us, they can succeed through courage and generosity. And we all, believers and unbelievers alike, fail or succeed by the same standards, those of true humanity.

The relationship between secular and sacred, then, is much like that between nature and grace expressed most memorably by Henri de Lubac and discussed in chapter one.[2] To the neoscholastic worldview that marked the persecutors of the "new theology," the sacred is something God superimposes, whether it is sacred history on top of secular history, the church on top of the world, or grace producing a supernatural dimension of the human person grafted upon a basically (or basely) secular original. To the new theology of Chenu, Congar, de Lubac, and Daniélou, to Karl Rahner and the "transcendental Thomists," and to postconciliar theology in general, there is one history, the church is a worldly reality, and the desire for God is not grafted onto the secular base, but is a natural expression of the human being as created by God. To speak, then, of the secular is not to speak of a godless reality which requires some special divine act to open it up to an awareness of the holy. Just as we can speak of a graced nature, so we can also talk of a secular that is always already sacred. Nature is graced, even for those with no knowledge of God, and the world is always already sacred, whether or not we know it to be so. Moreover, because nature is in itself already graced, the "natural" order within which we live needs no special rules or awareness for it to ascend to the order of grace. "Grace," as Georges Bernanos so famously said, "is everywhere."[3] The world and the human beings who inhabit it are always already open to the infinite, even and perhaps especially when they follow the order of nature. Thus, we are led to the conclusion that the humanization of the world, whether conducted by a Christian or undertaken by a Buddhist or an atheist, is the world growing into the plan of God. While we are left quite certainly with questions about what the special role of the church might be (which we shall address later in this chapter and in chapter 7), the world's own struggle toward a fuller humanity *is* "salvation history."

We are secular beings. We live and breathe the world, as the world lives and breathes in us. We are people in a human world, and we are organisms in a material universe. We live simultaneously in a world of meanings and a universe of causes and effects. There is human intentionality and the blind chance of physical reality. Both the struggle for meaning and the experience of chaos are inescapably part of the secular. Any religious discourse that would suggest that the world is not our home would be a serious misreading of an incarnational theology.

We are born, live, and die within the secular world. Whatever it may mean to be religious, it cannot be something that relativizes the secularity that is so much a part of our very existence.

At the same time that we are secular beings and live out our lives within the secular world, as Christians we also tell a story about this secular reality. Our Christian story is one that expresses the conviction that the world is the creation of God, that God in Jesus Christ was as intimately involved in the world as it is possible to be, and that God remains present in the world in the work of the Spirit. As Catholics we also assign a particular role in our story to the church, the community of faith that remembers Jesus and continues, through the power of the Spirit, to proclaim him to be the Christ, the Son of God. But none of this obliges us to think of the world as anything other than our God-given home, the place in which grace is poured out upon us and in which the gift of salvation is offered to us. And nothing here encourages us to think of the church as a kind of outpost of the sacred, whence the cavalry make occasional christianizing forays upon the local population. The church is the community of those who cherish the story and accept the human consequences of believing that the world, in all its secularity, is the free gift of God. But we are called to the same worldly commitment as our unbelieving brothers and sisters take upon themselves. While all Christians live in hope of resurrection and look forward to the fullness of the reign of God, they cannot do so in any way that undermines the commitment of Christian praxis to this world.

While the secular world is complete, sufficient if not self-sufficient, it is also profoundly mysterious. This is not the same as saying that it is full of mysteries, which is of course also true. There are clearly many things in our world that are mysterious, as mythmaking and storytelling, science and the arts only go to show. All of them, in their different ways, make it possible to live with mystery. Many things that were mysteries to our ancestors have been cleared up; many mysteries remain, but we live in confident expectation that they too, in their time and turn, will be explained. Perhaps our confidence in the powers of explanation is overweening or unjustified. We do not always notice that new mysteries sometimes replace old ones. The mysteries of the atom and DNA are fast disappearing. But the mysteries of why we do not harness this knowledge to good rather than evil purposes proliferate. As the mysteries of the character of our universe begin to succumb to science, the mysteries of its scale continue to confound the powers of the human imagination.

The mystery of the secular is not the mysteries of its details, but the mystery of the whole. "Mystery" is of course a human category, and humans are meaning-endowing beings. But if to be secular is to act within the capacities of human possibility, then "the meaning of the whole" is something that exceeds the potential of meaning-endowing beings. In some ways, Christianity would deny this. Catholic theology has always argued that there is such a thing as a natural human capacity to know the infinite. Inspection of the characteristics of the secular world or reflection upon the capacities of the human mind can lead the human being to posit the existence of God. This is that "natural theology" that the Catholic tradition at least has firmly adhered to. But this apparent difference cannot hold up. The same Catholic tradition has also always imagined natural theology to work only as an exercise in "faith seeking understanding." If you are already a person of faith, having encountered the God who comes to you in revelation, then the world itself in all its secularity is the gift that constantly reminds you of the divine giver. The meaning of the world is its gift character, but the gift is itself no differently experienced than is the world for one who is not a believer. If you are not a believer, however, then to posit a meaning of the whole is to exceed the limits of the human. The world cannot be a gift if there is no giver. Outside the act of faith, which is itself an elicited response rather than a spontaneous impulse, the meaning of the whole eludes us.

The secular desires a meaning with which it cannot endow itself. When Paul writes in the Letter to the Romans that "the whole creation has been groaning in travail together until now" (8:22), he is writing of the thirst for ultimate explanation that is demonstrated in the finite explicability of the parts that make up the whole. But the desire does not endow the desired end with reality. Wish fulfillment is always a danger, especially when so much is at stake. Working purely within the limits of human possibility as meaning-endowing beings, all that can be determined is that the secular exhibits a dynamism toward interpretability, but that the ultimate explanation that it so longs for, if it exists at all, lies beyond the capacities of the secular itself. Here, of course, the question is left open of whether or not the longing for explanation is the innate dynamism toward fuller explanation of a rational universe or simply neurotic behavior. Without benefit of revelation, the world can only be divided into the yearners after "God" and the nihilists.

If the meaning of the whole escapes the capacity of the whole to determine it, this must not be allowed to turn into a reductionism in which life in the world is really about something else. Religious meanings often exhibit such a character, and they do not do justice to a creator God or an incarnate Lord. To say, for example, that secular reality can only really be understood in a transcendent frame of reference is inevitably to reduce secularity, to compromise its graced character, in the name of something supposedly more fundamental. The history of Christian spirituality is replete with examples of this world-hating attitude. In the words of Thomas à Kempis in *The Imitation of Christ*, "the more I go out among men, the less I come back a man." The good life comes to be about avoiding the world, and all too often the complexity of secular reality becomes an obstacle course that will determine an outcome to which it is only accidentally related.

The problem for ecclesiology in general and for theology of the laity in particular is to develop a language for the secular that will grant the secular its full autonomy, will not reduce it to a means to a greater end, but will at the same time allow for the act of faith. Historically, this has been the discourse of revelation. Unfortunately, however, revelation has been too often misinterpreted as a kind of "message from another planet." In this picture, God speaks across a great divide, into human history where human beings gratefully receive a message that they otherwise could not ever have encountered. The act of faith becomes an assent to a whole lot of information and advice about living, and often to an overall subordination of human history to a higher or deeper layer of "salvation history" in which our true destinies are revealed to us. Heaven obliterates history. Of course, this kind of understanding of revelation is consistent with neither Hebrew nor Christian scripture. In the former, we see an account of God's dealings with Israel in which the medium of God's relationship is the warp and woof of history itself. Historical process is the self-communication of God with Israel, to such a degree that the pagan Cyrus, king of Persia, can be seen as an agent of God's covenant. And to such a degree that Elie Wiesel can hint, in his autobiographical novel *Night*, that Adolf Hitler could teach God a thing or two about historical faithfulness.[4] The same focus on historical process is continued and intensified in the Christian New Testament. For Christians, God's perfect self-communication occurs in the life, death, and resurrection of a single historical individual, Jesus of Nazareth. For Christians, the message of the Bible is oriented to and distilled in one human being. What Jesus demonstrates in his concrete historical choices, and what God does in and through Jesus, as demonstrated in the details of his actual life, is the culmination of divine revelation. The message is not from another planet, but in the encounter with a human being.

The language of revelation speaks to our world and in fact discourages the understandable human tendency to want to flee the tragedy of the historical process into a heavenly Shangri-La. The covenantal promises to Abraham are fulfilled in the earthly reality of the promised land. The Hebrew prophets excoriate pious words if they are not validated by a historical commitment to justice. Jesus' proclamation of the kingdom is faithful to the historical covenant faith. The kingdom is "at hand," and repentance for sin is the order of the day. The first major adjustment that the early Christian community has to make involves recognizing that it misunderstood Jesus' message as otherworldly. The world was not coming to an end, and community building, not apocalypse, was to be the order of the day. Jesus, the presence of God in history, was the affirmation of the goodness of the secular; and Christians see the Spirit of God, which persists in the world, wherever human goodness and creativity are encountered. That the Spirit is particularly present in the church, a truth we will address later in the chapter, is evidence of the importance of the faith community to secular history.

The Christian makes an act of faith not in some usurpation of secular, worldly reality but in the one who affirms the goodness of the world. Consequently, the person of faith lives in and deals daily with a secular reality that is in no way different from that of the nonbeliever. The world we encounter is exactly the same. The courses of action we take in the world, the priorities we set and the plans we make may be indistinguishable from those of at least the more thoughtful of our agnostic or atheistic fellow citizens. Nor do we have a secret plan or are we possessed of privileged information, so that we live in the world like undercover agents. The scriptures certainly give us ethical guidance, though it is sometimes ambiguous and often no better or worse than what we might encounter in Lao-Tzu or the *Qur'an*. In the end, our difference is in the story we tell about the world, one that stresses that we are affirmed by God and that we in turn affirm the goodness of the human and the natural world. Our task in the world is to keep alive the goodness that is real before, and even without, Jesus but that is finally affirmed in his life, death, and resurrection. This is a secular project in the sense that we share the project—if not the story we tell about it—with people of other faiths and people of no faith at all.

We can now return to Congar's description of the layperson as "one for whom . . . the substance of things in themselves is real and interesting," and qualify it still further. As we noted earlier, this seems to be one of the forays Congar made into depicting the laity that he later came to regret as suggesting too dramatic a separation between layperson and ordained minister. He continues by suggesting that the cleric, or even more the monk, is interested in things not for themselves "but for something other than themselves, namely, their relation to God."[5] To elucidate this point he quotes St. Thomas on the point of view of the philosopher and the "*fidelis*," the person of faith. The former "is interested in a thing's own nature, the *fidelis* in its transcendent reference." Congar does not want to suggest that the person of faith is identical to the cleric, but that the distinction between worldly concerns and the things of religion is parallel. At this time in his development, Congar did not see the sacredness of the autonomy of the secular. The transcendent reference of things is of course an altogether acceptable mystical preoccupation, as we go to God through contemplation of worldliness. But mysticism is not a clerical preserve any more than the world belongs to laypeople alone. Congar's early distinction between lay and cleric suggests either that there is something deficient in the layperson's attitude to the secular, one of involvement, or something superior in the cleric's relativization of the merely mundane.

Congar, as we saw in chapter 2, later came to think that the distinction between lay and cleric was better expressed in the category of different ministries. His point can be illustrated through reflecting on postconciliar changes in the understanding of vocation. We are all born laypeople. As we mature as Christians, if we are reflective people and women and men of prayer, we are surely moved by the Spirit to consider our roles in the faith community. Before the council, certainly before mid-century, a "vocation" was a sense of being called to the priesthood or the religious life. You could test that vocation and proceed to ordination or religious vows. If you or your superiors determined this way of life was not for you, you "didn't have a vocation" and you returned home and got on with your life as a layperson. Your family were probably disappointed that they had not been blessed with a priest or a nun, but they accepted it with good grace. At least you hadn't gone through with the whole thing, only to change your mind later and "come out" as a spoiled priest or ex-religious. So mom shifted the focus of her hopes to that "nice boy" or "nice girl" you would meet and marry. Maybe a grandson might be a priest . . . .

All that the council had to say about the importance of the lay apostolate changed the understanding of vocation, if not always its estimation on the street. Christian maturation still surely leads to serious discernment of the way of life to which God is calling us, but today there is much more evenhandedness in the evaluation of the paths of ordained ministry, religious life, or the life of the lay Christian. If - anything, the pendulum has swung a little too far in the opposite direction, though that has probably got a lot more to do with the contemporary distaste for celibacy than with any appreciable diminution in generosity or apostolic zeal. In any case, the life of the layperson is a calling, a vocation to life in the world. It is now understood to be different from, not worse or better than, the life of the ordained minister. Moreover, they are both seen as ministry. A better word to convey the point here might be "service." Priest and layperson serve in different ways, but they serve the same reality, namely, the People of God, to which, as the council taught, all people of good will are somehow connected. If the ordained minister has particular responsibilities toward the life of the faith community and the layperson has particular responsibilities toward the life of the human community, they are both collaborating in the identical mission. They both affirm the world as good, for the sake of the one whose life and death confirmed this goodness, just as in the worship of the community both collaborate in remembering, praising, and blessing that same Jesus of Nazareth.

Secular reality, then, is the only reality we can experience. The church is not another reality, but a particular reality within the secular. The church may exist to proclaim the affirmation of the goodness of the world in the life of Jesus, to protect the story that Christians tell about history, but it does so as a community within history. Its role does not call for any interference in the unconditional freedom of the secular to unfold as the human reality that it is. It may certainly exercise a prophetic role in history, but this is no more and no less than recalling secular reality to its responsibility to unfold in faithfulness to its human character. While the world may be challenged for its failures to live up to its secular freedoms, and celebrated when it succeeds, it cannot be called to be anything other than fully human. If Jesus' life and death affirmed the world, the church follows in his footsteps— and the laity are in the vanguard.

RESOURCES FOR
A THEOLOGY OF SECULAR REALITY

Our task of constructing a theological understanding of the secular is not something we have to shoulder alone. In the twentieth century many Christian thinkers and not a few post-Christians have made the attempt. Here we shall look at what we can learn from four distinguished figures, a Lutheran, a Jesuit, an agnostic, and a Baptist.

Dietrich Bonhoeffer

The *locus classicus* for all discussions of the secular character of Christian life must be the brief notes that the Lutheran pastor Dietrich Bonhoeffer penned to his friend Eberhard Bethge, which appear in a few pages toward the end of *Letters and Papers from Prison.*[6] The particular circumstances in which they were written, awaiting his fate at the hands of the Gestapo, and the extraordinary courage and saintly intelligence of their author have certainly led to their having an impact altogether disproportionate to their status in Bonhoeffer's mind. They are little more than jottings, and the prisoner passes them along to Bethge in the most tentative and qualified fashion. The ideas make their first appearance in a letter of April 30, 1944, prefaced by an obviously heartfelt wish that Bethge were there with him, "because I don't know anyone else with whom I could so well discuss them to have my thinking clarified." What concerned Bonhoeffer is not dissimilar to what had been bothering Abbé Godin just a couple of years earlier in France. Human beings are becoming "radically religionless," and so the question arises of what role, if any, the church can play in a world that exhibits a complete absence of religion. "If religion is only a garment of Christianity," writes Bonhoeffer, "then what is a religionless Christianity?" (*Letters and Papers*, 247).

Bonhoeffer's notion of "religion" owes much to Karl Barth, like Bonhoeffer a leading opponent of Nazism and a signer of the Barmen declaration. This established the Confessing Church, which grew out of the need of its members to distance themselves from the accommodating stance of the Lutheran Church. For both Bonhoeffer and Barth, "religion" was a human category in which God was all too easily fashioned in a human image. For much of its existence, the Christian church had been a spectacular example of the close association between religion and culture that made it nearly impossible for Christians to hear the Word of God as it challenged them to look beyond cultural stereotypes and human images of God. Bonhoeffer certainly did not go all the way with Barth, accusing him of a "positivism of revelation" which was of no more use to the ordinary person in the street than was the culture Christianity of the liberal church. Barth had failed to make any effort to translate dogmatic concepts into religionless terminology. Instead, wrote Bonhoeffer, we have to ask ourselves how we are "'religionless-secular' Christians, in what way we are the *ekklēsia*, those who are called forth, not regarding ourselves from a religious point of view as specially favored, but rather as belonging wholly to the world" (p. 248).

There is a remarkable intellectual ferment in the writings of Bonhoeffer's last months, all the more extraordinary because of the terrible circumstances in which it was going on. In letter after letter, he shows himself occupied with the problems of living the Christian life in the modern world, not at all with his own fate. But the thoughts are scattered and incomplete, if not random, and he would surely have been the first to say that they were not ready to see the light of day. They are remarkably good examples of that essential step in the thought processes of the theologian, thinking aloud without concern for tradition or heresy or the ears of the pious or the ignorant. Writing from one theologian to another, Bonhoeffer is in the thralls of the creative process and should not be held accountable for the orthodoxy or even good sense of every word. That having been said, his ideas clearly have struck a chord with successive generations of theologians, not all of them simply employing Bonhoeffer's vision to justify their own secular theology.[7] It is certainly possible to extract a number of ideas from his writings that will help us to refine our own notion of the secular, and even to talk of the secular dimension of the church.

In the first instance, Bonhoeffer is insistent on overcoming notions of God as a *deus ex machina* or a "God of the gaps." So, of course, are most of us, in the sense that we recognize the autonomy of scientific investigation and explanation and do not try to intrude God into their conclusions. But the withdrawal of God from such a role usually means that God is invoked instead to handle so-called limit questions, those of suffering and death in particular. This tactic is equally unacceptable to Bonhoeffer, because it still uses God as the *deus ex machina*. In fact, he writes that resurrection is not the solution to the problem of death. The transcendence of God is not the transcendence of human philosophical thought. Indeed, "God is the beyond in the midst of our life" (p. 249). God's transcendence means that God is as close to us as we are to ourselves. God is not a stopgap. Rather, "[w]e are to find God in what we know, not in what we don't know" (p. 276). This is at one and the same time the rejection of the God out there in favor of a God known in the here and now and yet a caution against a sacramental understanding of God. In the sacramental approach typical of Catholic thought, the world as created constantly talks to us of God, refers us to God, reminds us of God. But Bonhoeffer would think of this, I believe, as an instrumental reading of the secular, in which its value is proportionate to its sacramental significance. Its value rather is in itself, certainly created by God but possessed of a freedom and autonomy that a sacramental significance could only belittle. Perhaps we might challenge him with the *Baltimore Catechism* and point out that a sacrament is not a mere sign. If the world were just a sign that pointed to God, it would be devalued. But a sacrament makes real that which it signifies. Just as Bonhoeffer suggests, the world seen as sacrament must be filled with God, or it is not a sacrament.

Bonhoeffer is also convinced of the this-worldly message of the

Bible. It is not about redemption, if redemption is to mean eventual translation into another order of being in another place. It is also not taken up with individualistic notions of salvation, but rather with "righteousness and the Kingdom of God on earth as the form of everything" (p. 252). Old Testament faith was in a historical redemption, while Christian hope in the resurrection must send us back to life. Like Christ, we must "drink the earthly cup to its dregs" (p. 299). If so, then we are not concerned with the beyond but "with this world as created and preserved, subjected to laws, reconciled and restored" (p. 253). Indeed, "our being Christians today will be limited to two things: prayer and righteous action among men." We stand at a point where the Christian message must be reconstructed, after the demise of religion. So, "all Christian thinking, speaking, organizing must be born anew out of this prayer and action" (p. 265).

While some of Bonhoeffer's more radical statements may seem at first sight to go beyond usefulness to our purpose, a closer inspection may reveal more of value. For example, he says that we have to live in the world "as if God did not exist." "God would have us know," he writes, "that we must live as men who manage our lives without him" (p. 322). He thinks that we only learn to have faith by living completely in this world. "By this-worldliness," he writes, "I mean living unreservedly in life's duties, problems, successes and failures, experiences and perplexities" (pp. 327–28). The transcendental is not to be found in "infinite and unattainable tasks" but in "the neighbor who is in reach in any given situation" (p. 338).

Statements such as these may seem to hover on the verge of denying the otherness of God, but in fact they only explore the secular in just the way that the Catholic layperson should explore the secular. They recognize that the world is our given and that God is encountered in Christ in the midst of historical process. Jesus' being for others, thinks Bonhoeffer, is the experience of transcendence, and genuine experience of God is encounter with Jesus Christ. Scripture has very little to say about another world, and the marks of discipleship are exactly those which Bonhoeffer stresses. If Jesus' being is being for others, then "our relation to God is a new life in existence for others through participation in the being of Jesus" (p. 338). The church "is the Church only when it exists for others" (p. 339).

The challenge of Bonhoeffer for our project is not so much theological as ecclesiological. His thoughts on the secularity of the contemporary world carry conviction, and his attitude to revelation as encounter with Christ and the discipleship that must follow is both orthodox and profoundly helpful for considering the lay calling. But to Bonhoeffer the problem with Catholics is their closeness to the church. "We cannot, like the Roman Catholics, simply identify ourselves with the Church" (p. 339). Of course, he understands the church here to mean the institution, which all too often in his experience has accommodated itself to society, most tragically and recently in the craven appeasement of Nazism espoused by the Lutheran Church in Germany. But Catholics need to take his words seriously. The institution is always in danger of being too cozy with the powers of this world. Perhaps if Bonhoeffer had lived to see Vatican II and its preference for the image of People of God over institution, he might have seen some hope for the Catholics!

William F. Lynch

The work of William F. Lynch, S.J., is contained in a short series of slim books in which he explored various dimensions of the human imagination, drawing upon his extensive knowledge of philosophy and classical literature and delving at times into a theology of mental illness. One of his later books, *Christ and Prometheus*, speaks directly to our concerns.[8] About the task of the religious imagination Lynch is clear. It must, as it encounters the secular, allow for its autonomy, but at the same time it must never betray its long-term vocation to bring "total unity to the universe under God and total internal unity to its own imaginings." But the challenge of the secular is different from what it once was. For a long time, the secular seemed "an occasional thrust outside a basically religious image of the world." Now it is "an overwhelming presence in which the religious imagination must learn to exist" (p. 7). So we must construct a new image of the secular.

The secular is marked by a series of internal tensions. The first of these is that it is at one and the same time a confident love of energy and power but also a deep distrust of that same power. The energy and power, the "building strains" in secularity, are something great, the foundation of so many of the achievements of secularity. But they are accompanied by guilt at the immensity of the power, which shows itself at times in irony, pastiche, and parody, at times in a wary concern for "the frequent inhumanity of the project" (p. 20). Lynch's analysis seems not only to uncover the "dialectic of the Enlightenment," to which many others have referred, but also to be an early recognition of the role of the "postmodern," both countering and commenting on the potential of modernity to become inhuman. If Prometheus is the figure who symbolizes the extent and greatness of the achievement of the secular human being, then Prometheanism is the label for the distortions that can occur when the power and energy become separated from their human source. True secularity "is meeting its worst contemporary crisis" in "these areas of life that have become self-enclosed and independent of the human" (p. 54).

These thoughts lead us to Lynch's central concern for the secular, that it not become merely "technique," which he associates with the cosmocentric impulses, but that it remain permanently linked to human unconditionality, the anthropocentric impulse. If technique is allowed to go unchecked by the human, then it becomes "a universal, interacting, self-escalating creator of a worldwide spirituality of efficient means independent of ends" (p. 54). In words that bear a remarkable convergence with those of Bonhoeffer, Lynch suggests that the problem for the religious imagination is also to become less cosmocentric and more anthropocentric. In a cosmocentric world-view, the religious imagination sees the human being as some kind of point in the cosmos, moving through it "in order to get somewhere," as a means to an end. This is the "religious world or point of view," and if we stick to it we will limit the imagination. Of course, says Lynch, we cannot abandon the cosmos or God as the center, but the imagination "also possesses enormous resources to help the world construct that which religion unnecessarily fears, an anthropocentric world, with man and the human also as center and measure of all things" (p. 55). So the religious imagination, when it sees the world as a means to an end beyond it, is guilty of some of the same dehumanizing impulses that secular modernity itself has exhibited. For the secular to be truly whole, to be truly human, the religious imagination must allow it its head.

Writing in the heyday of "secular theology," Lynch is proposing something quite different. The challenge of secularity, he insists, is not a struggle between the human being and "God." At the center of the secular we find not the object but the human being. So, for Lynch, secularity is not a journey through the cosmos (Prometheanism) but through the human (Prometheus). The "unconditionality" or utter freedom of the human is what is at issue. Everything in the secular is subordinated to the unconditionality of the human. This is what it means to see the human as "the measure of all things," than which there is no better definition of secularity. But it must be the whole human, the fully human, in all its dynamism.

This is the time of passage to a new image of secularity. The religious and secular imaginations have a common logic. Lynch's image of the secular is that "everything should have or should come into its own life" (the unconditioned development of its own identity). There is a place for the sacred, but not one of control. The new image of the sacred is as "ground and creator, model and origin, of secularity thus conceived" (p. 133).

The religious imagination needs to pass into a more realistic period "accepting things as they are and can be, without the perpetual concern that something is missing from the picture" (p. 135). We need to forge a new dialectical relationship between religious and secular that will not just be metaphorical, but will issue in "a common action and a common life" (p. 137). "This inwardness of secularity," thinks Lynch, "comes from the outside and is all the more inward and autonomous for doing so. It is a creation of the outside and stands in a continuous relation to an outside. This means that the inwardness of secularity is a creation of God and the sacred" (p. 138).

Lynch's view of the secular is certainly theological, but is founded in a theology of creation rather than one of incarnation. In fact, like Bonhoeffer before him, he thinks that the sacramental imagination of the Catholic tradition can be a hindrance in allowing for the unconditionality of the secular. Religious symbols cannot be imposed upon the secular without compromising its unconditionality. So the split that Protestantism has always seen between the sacred and the secular actually gives it an advantage. Lynch quotes the Protestant scholar William O. Fennell that a sacramental view of nature "seems to do justice neither to the nature of God, nor to the nature of the world." Scripture reveals "a gracious will to create and to redeem, not for his own but for the being and good of another than himself." God, says

Fennell, "sets [the world] free from himself to be itself."[9] While Lynch is suspicious of the dialectical character of much Protestant thought, which posits absolute separation between God and the world, he wants "to get to the same non-sacramental and unconditional goal." Religious explanations cannot be allowed to replace the unconditionality of the secular, above all that of the human, to which all other secular unconditionality is referred. But, in a typically Catholic transcendental move that must owe at least something to Karl Rahner, God is understood as the ground of that very unconditionality.

A vision like Lynch's raises some interesting questions for the secular character of lay life. Above all, there is the question of the role of the layperson as evangelist, and of the church as spreading the message of salvation. If the world is to be allowed to proceed in all its secular unconditionality, how is redemption or salvation to be conceived? Both sin and redemption, it would seem, must be confined within the secular. The sin of the secular can be seen clearly as the failure to exercise the fullness of human unconditionality, which will always turn out to be some kind of accommodation to the world of things and to the power of the will. The stress of the gospel message must be on the freedom of the children of God, on the truth that sets us free, on freedom from law, sin, and death. What we need to be saved from is our failure to be fully, freely human, and to insist on the centrality of the human person and community in the secular world. Perhaps the positive connotations of the synonymous notion of liberation would be helpful here. Human beings are often complicitous in their own structural oppression by the forces of objects and things, power and the strength of will. Equally often, they are held captive by powers that they are unable to control. Liberation/salvation is then to be found both in the struggle for a more human world and in the struggle to deal with our own internal weaknesses, which limit our willingness to exercise fully our freedom. Structural sin and personal sin are thus revealed to be two faces of the same coin.

Lynch's book does not include a developed theology to accompany these views on secularity, though clearly one is implicit in all he has to say. But if there is a serious lacuna, it seems to be in ecclesiology. How should we conceive of the role of the church in Lynch's vision of secularity? Obviously, the church is an entity within the secular world, but most theologians and surely Lynch himself would want to say that it is something more than that, though Lynch would presumably not be happy with a sacramental ecclesiology. This much is clear. The church must respect the unconditionality of the secular, and of the human within it, imposing no set of religious symbols to interpret the world in terms of some other, more fundamental reality. The lay person is for this reason quite clearly in the vanguard of the church's worldly persona. The ordained ministry's role will be to make sure that the church is more and more what it is supposed to be, for the world and not for itself. Lynch's model surely moves us toward some version of the servant model for understanding the church, and to a "high" theology of the laity.

Jürgen Habermas

In the writings of Jürgen Habermas we find a secular analogue to Lynch's vision of the religious imagination. Habermas, a man who, by his own admission, has no feel for religion, has constructed a vision of life in the contemporary world that speaks in more detail than Lynch's of the character of the actions that human beings must undertake, if their world is to be one marked by the free play of human unconditionality. We cannot do justice here to Habermas's enormous corpus of writings, but two texts in particular invite our closer inspection. One is the two-volume *Theory of Communicative Action*, which appeared in the early 1980s. The second is a volume of essays compiled from a conference at the University of Chicago Divinity School in 1988, *Habermas and Religion*, to which Habermas graciously responded at length.[10]

Habermas is committed to the unconditionality of the human and is one of the loudest voices warning contemporary society of its drift into what Lynch refers to as Prometheanism. As an atheist, he is also a good test case for the compatibility of religious and atheistic worldliness. To Habermas, human behavior is grounded in communicative action, which means the free, open, and undistorted communication between two or more human beings, with the intention that understanding should occur. This is the mark of all essentially human activity, from interpersonal relationships of all kinds to the workings of a truly democratic society. Alongside the communicative action that is typical of the human is a realm of instrumental rationality that governs the way in which human beings manipulate the inanimate social system within which they live, and which also internally controls the myriad impersonal interactions within the system itself. The "lifeworld," to use the phenomenological term that Habermas prefers, exists alongside the system. Both are good and necessary. The lifeworld is the world conceived of as a human environment governed by linguistic interactions. The system is the world of means/ends rationality that exists alongside of and interpenetrates the lifeworld. But for all kinds of complicated reasons connected to the rise of modernity, the system has become increasingly powerful and has come to "colonize" the lifeworld. In other words, while the essentially human character of society ought to mean that the system operates within human constraints as a servant of the lifeworld, the system has spun progressively out of control, and the human has often been instrumentalized to the system. In Lynch's terms, Prometheanism has overwhelmed Prometheus.

Habermas's prescription for dealing with this sorry but undeniable state of affairs is to shore up the democratic ordering of society. It is in free and open communication oriented to consensus upon norms for action, or "discourse-ethics," that society can be wrested from the control of systems imperatives. Whether truly democratic action will triumph is an open question in Habermas's view. The signs of hope that exist are the various progressive movements that struggle against the power of the system—ecological movements, antiglobalization movements, and above all the feminist movement, which has the advantage, in his view, of possessing not only a critique of society but a plan for an alternative.

It is not difficult to see the parallels between Lynch and Habermas. Both of them recognize that the good ordering of society depends on the free movement of human unconditionality. For both, the best hope of the world is that it become more and more fully human. This anthropocentric view does not deny the value of either systems or of the cosmos, but sees the only truly rational course of action to be the referencing of everything nonhuman to the human. Habermas's emphasis on human communication may seem—and is—drier than Lynch's call for the free exercise of the human imagination, but neither would have any serious differences with the other's central claims.

Not, at least, until it came to the matter of religion. For Lynch, the recognition of the autonomy of the secular follows from the exercise of the religious imagination, affirming the world as created by God to be free to be itself. To Habermas, for whom the religious imagination, if it is anything at all, is a mythologizing faculty, we live within the secular, without warrant for any wider perspective. For this reason, if for no other, Habermas does not even consider the Christian churches as exemplars of groups struggling to preserve the lifeworld. But if he could be persuaded that the church's secular role is to foster the unconditionality of the human—admittedly a daunting task—he might just be willing to revise that judgment. Curiously enough, there may be more ecclesiological potential here than Lynch can provide.

Harvey Cox

Few theological writings have had such an immediate impact as did Harvey Cox's *Secular City*.[11] Few if any works of religious reflection from the 1960s are still the subject of such intense discussion.[12] The book is not particularly original, as Cox has himself noted on numerous occasions, but it was very timely. It brought together a series of reflections on the phenomena of secularization and urbanization with much of the then new "secular theology." It spoke to the emerging feeling of the times that metaphysics was no longer the way in which to imagine the divine reality, and it offered a concrete philosophical anthropology, an ethics, and a spirituality for Christian life in an era of rapid social change. The book begins with an argument for the biblical basis of secularization. The account of creation in Genesis, writes Cox, is "a form of atheistic propaganda" (*Secular City*, 20), persuading its hearers that nature itself is not a mysterious spirit-realm but a matter-of-fact reality created by a specific being who stands outside it. Yahweh's decisive act for Israel is the event of the exodus, in which politics is desacralized. It is revolutionary, an "act of insurrection" (p. 22) through which space is made for social change and by means of which the separation of the religious and the political is established. Finally, the historical sensibilities of the Bible deconsecrate human values, recognizing their time-bound mutability. This "healthy relativism provides the philosophical basis for a pluralist society" (pp. 27–28).

Cox's work is a sustained application of Bonhoeffer's insights on religionless Christianity. Cox looks at what he sees to be the two principal characteristics of modern urban life, its anonymity and mobility, and defends them as necessary for living in such a space. Then, more interestingly, he takes up Bonhoeffer's challenge to find a "nonreligious interpretation of the gospel" for secular human beings and argues that "pragmatism and profanity enable urban man to discern certain elements of the gospel which were hidden from his more religious forebears" (p. 54). Pragmatism for Cox is a mark of the present age of technopolis, as magic was of the age of myth, and metaphysics of the "age of the town." Modern pragmatic human beings are more interested in process than in substantive questions and find truth in action rather than in the lifeless systems of ontology. In this, says Cox, they are more faithful to the biblical witness, since "the Jews had no gift for ontology at all" and preferred to talk of the acts of God rather than of the divine nature. God's actions are paramount to the Hebrews, and for Jesus truth is revealed in doing the truth, not in words. So the pragmatist's refusal to think in religious categories may itself open her to "that effective truth which is found both in the Bible and in the emerging functional era" (p. 58). Of course, like Lynch, Cox warns against the reduction of pragmatism (Prometheus) to functionalism (Prometheanism) and stresses the human origin of meaning and purpose.

Cox mounts a similarly aggressive defense of profanity. "Profanity" or what we have thus far encountered as "secularity" is the insistence on the human character of the sources of meaning and value by which we live our lives in the world. It is the same thought that Lynch had when he argued that the world must not be interpreted in religious categories. To put it as strongly as Proudhon or Camus, Cox's favored interlocutors, "God" is the enemy of human freedom. But in Cox's theology of creation, "God" is the biblical giver of the world to human beings, to continue the work of creation begun, not ended, in the divine act. "God" is not the timeless metaphysical entity whom Cox rightly thinks that Camus and other atheistic commentators have in mind. But they are absolutely correct that the metaphysical God is the enemy of human freedom, subsuming all reality under itself in some watertight philosophical system that delimits human possibility. Here the existentialists were right. God must not circumscribe the human project. But as Cox sees, again correctly, the biblical God gives secular reality to the human in order to pursue that unconditionally human project.

If a theology of creation marks the first half of Cox's book, a theology of the world delineates the second. Here Cox is focused on the phenomenon of social change and on how to interpret traditional religious categories in terms of social change. He sees the world in crisis and calls for a revolutionary theology. In many respects, this portion of his argument is the most socially conditioned, the most marked by the frazzled thinking of the sixties. Yet he is accurate in his assessment that a political world is beginning to give way to a technological world and in his claim that the Christian has to find a way to move forward boldly into that world and to discard the outmoded ways of the past. The God-given secularity of the human being entails both freedom *and* responsibility, and the responsibility shows in conversion to "a willingness to participate in the constant improvisation of social and cultural arrangements which will be changed again and again in the future" (p. 105).

Given the need for pragmatism and profanity in the secular world marked by anonymity and mobility, what of the church? In conformity to his pragmatism, Cox is more concerned with the ministry of the church than with its nature. It is a people before it is an institution, and it is a secondary reality, needing a clarification of the idea of the kingdom before it can be talked about at all. Its ministry is simply the continuation of Jesus' ministry, which was marked by a threefold task, namely, "to announce the arrival of the new regime," to "personify its meaning," and "to begin distributing its benefits" (pp. 109–10). Following Jesus, the church must proclaim (*kerygma*), must reconcile (*diakonia*), and must demonstrate the character of the new society (*koinōnia*). The church, says Cox, "is the avant-garde of the new regime." The kerygmatic function is traditionally described as proclaiming that through Jesus God has defeated the principalities and powers. Now we must name them anew as "all the forces in culture which cripple and corrupt human freedom." To preach is now to "broadcast the seizure of power." The function of *diakonia*, or service, is exercised in "healing the urban fractures," and that of *koinōnia* is to make visible in technopolis what the signs are of the kingdom, understood as "a reality that is breaking into history not from the past but from the future" (p. 127).

We are now positioned to pursue two questions in the remaining

part of this chapter. First, in the light of the riches of Lynch, Bonhoeffer, Habermas, and Cox, how can we envisage the role of the
church in the world? We saw in earlier chapters that Vatican II provided us with all sorts of resources for examining this question, but
not the extended meditation on the nature of the secular that Lynch
and the others have now afforded us. Nevertheless, *Gaudium et Spes*
does go some way in that direction, and we shall need to consider its
picture of the world. The second question follows upon the first.
Given the ecclesial reality in its secular form, how shall we live as lay
Christians in a secular world? A secular ecclesiology will thus spill over
into a spirituality of the secular.

THE SECULARITY OF THE CHURCH

The single biggest problem bedeviling both ecclesiology in general
and theological reflection on the lay state in particular is the mystifi-
cation of the church. Throughout history, all kinds of images have
arisen from time to time to describe the ecclesial reality. The best of
them have been biblically based, and most of them are given respectful attention in the very first chapter of *Lumen Gentium* (*LG*).[13] But
it is equally true that many of them have had their day and survive
today as part of an honorable tradition, without speaking effectively
to the contemporary moment. To how many people does the image
of "sheepfold" really reveal something valuable about the nature of
the church, still less about the role of laypeople within it? Worse, while
no one will turn a hair to hear that God is the shepherd of the ecclesial flock, the council pressed the image too far for the present age
when it referred to the people as "sheep" and the bishops as "human
shepherds." *Lumen Gentium* also recalls the images of the "tillage of
God," the vineyard, the new Jerusalem, "our mother," and "the spotless spouse of the spotless lamb." These are images true to the biblical witness, true in themselves, but silent or even counterproductive
in today's church. The image of the spouse is a good case in point. If
we have learned something in these last decades about the notion of
spouse, it is that there always should be and sometimes is a fundamental reciprocity and genuine equality in the relationship of spouses
to each other. A marriage is a community of equals in which not only

love but also leadership are shared and in which strength and dependence are mutually expressed. It is very hard to interpret the Christ–church relationship on the model of husband–wife without either doing violence to what marriage is or engaging in a subtle form of ecclesiolatry. When the council fathers expand on the image of the bride of Christ, they speak the wisdom of the tradition but reveal its hopeless inadequacy to convey meaning today. For them, Christ the bridegroom not only nourishes and cherishes the church as bride, after having united her to himself by an unbreakable alliance. But, "once purified," Christ willed the church "to be joined to himself, subject in love and fidelity" (*LG* 6). This is simply not the way we understand marriage today, not even in sacramental theology. Passivity and deference do not mark the contemporary experience of marriage. The image doesn't work any more, in part because the experience of Christians in the secular world has outgrown this and other images of the church, though the church has evidently not yet caught up to the fact.

If these variously anachronistic images of the church are no longer helpful, some biblical images fortunately have escaped the depredations of history. Some of them the council fathers do little more than list: the church is a building, the "house of God in which his family dwells," "the dwelling-place of God among men," "the holy temple." The image that they have wisely favored for our times, however, is the much-discussed image of the church as the People of God, a people to whom everyone in the world of whatever faith or lack of it is somehow related (see *LG* 13). This image has the wonderful advantage of a certain ambiguity. It means, on the one hand and in the first place, the people who constitute the worshiping community, the community of revelation. These are the ones who know through faith of the wonderful saving love of God for the whole of creation, and in a special way for the human race. But it also refers to the entirety of that same human race throughout history, including those who lived before Christ, those who have no knowledge or love of him, and those yet to be born, the community of redemption. Putting the two together in our world, the People of God is the human family, the secular world within which is hidden the leaven of the community of faith. The image of People of God in this wider sense opens the church to the secular, as it incorporates it within the secular.

The church is a secular reality. To say this is not just to make the obvious point that the church is in part a historical institution, like the United Nations or the League of Women Voters. Rather, it is to make the much more far-reaching claim that the meaning of the church is to be uncovered through dwelling upon the secular reality within which we live and die. This seems a strange notion only because we have lived for so many centuries with the sacred/secular dichotomy, with the notion that there is a divine "out-there" which is the extrinsic possessor of a meaning for the worldly "in-here." The church is then understood as partially or temporarily "in-here" but for the sake of an eventual consummation in the "out-there," a fulfillment that would of course overwhelm whatever meaning the church in history might possess in itself. But we have learned from Lynch's response to Bonhoeffer's challenge to speak in a secular fashion of God, that the secularity of the world is its sacredness, in the sense that this is what it was created by God to be. God does not have a plan for the world that goes beyond the unconditional freedom of the human as God created it. The secularity of the world *is* the divine plan. In this light, it seems clear that the Jewish vision of God's relationship to the world is much healthier than the dualistic obsessions that Christianity later grafted onto the worldview of Jesus and the early church. Salvation history *is* secular history.

Theological reflection is a human response to the divine gift, but one frequently not exercised with appropriate humility. What God has given us is only discernible to us by examining what we have around us. God gave us a world, a history, Jesus and the church. That, from the Christian perspective, is the material upon which theological reflection works. Theological reflection is not gifted with a privileged insight into the mind of God. Scripture, tradition, and the history of theology do not know more than is revealed, and what is revealed is the gift of a world, a history, Jesus and the church. Beyond this revelation, one supposes, there is a mysterious supplement that far exceeds in its riches anything that we could imagine, and since it is from there that the gift comes, we name the giver of this gift "God." But we cannot really reflect further on what this God is like. Attempts to do so have left us wrapped up in the kind of metaphysical aridities that Harvey Cox excoriates. Here is where his theological pragmatics is so important. We know God only by knowing how God acts. And God

acts in history, in and through the secular processes that God has created in all their unconditionality and absolute freedom. Theological
reflection must practice a certain chastity of the intellect. To borrow
Wittgenstein's formulation in the closing line of his *Tractatus*, "what
we cannot speak about we must pass over in silence." As far as ecclesiology is concerned, this means eschewing all efforts to relativize the
historical reality of the church to some "mystery" of the church hidden in the mind of God. It is the historical and hence secular reality of
the church that must be our focus.

If Lynch is right that God is best understood as the ground of the
freedom of the world, then the church is that segment within secular
reality that lives in that conviction. As I have suggested earlier, the language of affirmation is perhaps a less arid way of expressing the same
insight. The church is that part of secular reality that is convinced that
it is affirmed in the free unconditionality of the secular. In plain
English that breaks some of these theological rules but perhaps makes
the point more clearly, the church knows that God made the world
out of love, to be its own free self. Now if this is what the church is,
there arises the question, What is the church *for?* And the answer must
surely be that the church exists to live in the secular world, to live out
the free unconditionality of the secular, in the way in which people
would who believe that the world is affirmed (by God) in its secularity, and—taking up that second most important insight from Lynch—
that the unconditionality of the secular is summed up in human
freedom. The role of a community that knows it is affirmed in its
human unconditionality is to proclaim and cherish the unconditional
freedom of the human. This has to be what it means to evangelize.
This is not merely what theologians have always referred to as "a
preparation for the gospel" (*praeparatio evangelica*). This is the
gospel. The good news is that God loves the world and that in Jesus,
the presence of God in the world, the reign of God is here and now.
The "not-yet" of the reign of God, the fullness that is to come, can
only be sought through the exercise of human freedom to make a
more human world.

Many theologians, among them Bonhoeffer and Lynch, have
declared that the church exists not for its own sake but for the sake of
the world. Lengthy lists of the responsibilities of the church to the
world often succeed such a statement, while in practice the tasks of the

community of faith are few, if complex. The church must be fully engaged in the secular, with all the confidence in the goodness of the secular that must come from the conviction that God has affirmed the secular in all its unconditionality. The church must not be afraid to proclaim the unconditional affirmation of the secular. That is what it means to say, as the church must, that "God loves the world." The church has to go beyond affirmation to cash it in through a relentless and self-sacrificing engagement in the secular, struggling constantly to promote any and every initiative that recognizes the *human* unconditionality of the secular. The church must affirm and support Prometheus, while it cautions against the tendency toward Prometheanism. The church must be on the side of the lifeworld, the world structured by language, not on the side of the system, the world structured by objects and their manipulation. And, of course, the church can do none of these things unless it is itself a community committed to the human freedom of its members.

While it is quite correct to say that the church exists for the sake of the world, this does not mean that its value is exhausted in its involvement in the furtherance of human unconditionality. The church is also oriented to God. It has the responsibility to keep alive in itself that vibrant faith in the affirmation of the secular that God has given it. Thus, the worship of the church is as important as in traditional understandings of the church, if not more so. Through their involvement in worship, the members of the church renew their sense of God's affirmation and strengthen themselves for the task of the further humanization of the world. Worship is a task of the church, but not *the* task of the church. It is not even the most important task of the church. As the prophet Amos made so abundantly clear, the worship of the community is valuable to the extent that it is a reflection of the struggle for justice that God demanded of Israel. If the church is not engaged in the world, in all its secularity, maintaining its human unconditionality, rejoicing in the secular, then its worship will be empty, because its worship is praise and thanksgiving to the one who created the world to be secular and free.

If this is in outline how the church must be in the world today, then how are we to envisage the relationship between the roles of ordained ministers and the laity? Yves Congar, we remember, came in later life to see that it was not that the layperson's role needed to be defined relative to that of the priest, but rather that the priest's role must now be clarified relative to that of the layperson. Such an insight can only follow upon a radical rethinking of the reality of the church, in which its life in the world is its primary raison d'être, and hence its layperson is its primary "minister." This is also clearly a consequence of a prophetic reading of the relationship between worship and ministry. Worship is justified only when ministry is taken seriously. Worship is instrumental to ministry, not the other way around. Thus, the particular responsibilities of the ordained minister are exercised in the context of affirming a reality that has been validated elsewhere, in the work of the church in the secular world, hence in the work of laypeople.

This model of the clergy–lay relationship raises many questions about the day-to-day functioning of the church and the ways in which offices and responsibilities are exercised. It is certainly a head-on challenge to the idea that "ministry" is something that pertains primarily to the clerical state. It, of course, refutes the conservative insistence on the separation of church and world, and it forces deep thinking on the nature of leadership and authority in the church. In particular, we shall be forced to ask how we should conceive of leadership within the church, and how that should be related, if at all, to church leadership in the secular world. If the ministry of the church is primarily in the humanization of secular reality, and if this is principally the work of laypeople, then how does the present structure of leadership and authority in the church, vested as it is entirely in the hands of a clergy whose primary responsibility is not this work of humanization, actually serve the mission of the church? Might it not be the case that alongside the new forms of ministry that must emerge if the ecclesial reality of a secular church is to be respected, new forms of leadership must also be conceived? There is an important principle to be insisted upon here. Structures of leadership and authority in the church exist to serve the mission of the church. The church's mission cannot be defined with the intention that it fit in with hierarchical structures and patterns of authority. Mission cannot be subordinated to structure. To do so would be to create an ecclesial version of Habermas's "colonization of the lifeworld by the system." The system, the ecclesial structure, is good insofar as it supports and is under the authority of the lifeworld. But when it becomes uncoupled, it dominates and preys upon the lifeworld. Applying this analogy to church life can illuminate many of the present-day pathologies of church life. Similarly, John Paul II's recipe for the humanization of the economic order, which he offered in his 1981 encyclical letter *On Human Work*, works here too. In that letter John Paul insisted on the "priority of labor over capital," that is, on the need to preserve the right relationship between structures and the human community they exist to support. Capital is good if it serves labor. Too often, says the pope, capitalism allows the relationship to be reversed. Too often, we would have to say, the same is true in the church. Too often the system becomes self-justifying and the human reality of the church is made subservient to it. But such a distorted relationship cannot stand in face of a theology of the secular. God "so loved *the world*," not the church.

A LAY SPIRITUALITY OF SECULARITY

"Spirituality" is a vague word and too often is assumed to relate solely to the life of prayer and devotion that the faithful Christian possesses alongside his or her secular life. This is a serious misconception. "Spirituality" refers to the entire life of the Christian as it is intentionally related to God. My "spirituality" is the framework for my believing life in the world. Daily life in the world can no more be divorced from spirituality than can prayer and worship from daily life. Like the life of faith in general, spirituality is anchored in and validated by the way in which we live. Our commitment to this way of life and the concrete choices it entails is celebrated in prayer and worship and is offered to the God by whom, through faith, we are convinced that it is affirmed in all its richness. If we have determined that the focus of Christian life is on the secular, and on the promotion of the human unconditionality of secular life, then Christian spirituality will be indelibly marked and definitively shaped by these commitments. Lay spirituality in particular will enjoy this secular character in a particularly all-embracing manner. The clergy, of course, live in the secular world just as much as laypeople do, but they also have a primary responsibility for maintaining the worshiping community as a place where God's affirmation of the secular is celebrated. They are, consequently, not so much "set apart for sacred things" as redirected to a vitally important but less central role in the mission of the church. Their spirituality will have to reflect that, without denying or ignoring the centrality of human unconditionality to the church's self-understanding. What, then, will be the principal characteristics of a lay spirituality, of a lay being-in-the-world as committedly secular human beings?

The Lay Person as Prometheus: Freedom

The first and primary characteristic of secular lay spirituality is freedom. The human being is created by God to be unconditionally free in the world. In this gift God makes no distinctions between Christians and non-Christians, between believers and atheists. The baseline in Christian spirituality is then a kind of worldliness, not in the sense that it denies God but in the sense that being free in the world is that which is common to all human beings, and that which, as willed by God, is fundamental to our spirituality. We are made to be free in the world. But we are also made intelligent and possessed of the capacity of deep feelings. We are made to be aware of our world, of what it is and is not, of what it needs more of and what it needs less of. We have a human dynamism toward questioning, exploring, and understanding. We have human capacities for problem solving, system building, knowledge, and wisdom. As human beings in solidarity with all other human beings, what we share in the first instance is the sense that we alone are responsible for dealing with this worldly reality. The world is ours to maintain, to improve, even sometimes to save.

The responsibility to live within the world, to seek to deal with it through the exercise of our own human capacities, is the commitment of Prometheus. Prometheus resists any expectation that help will come somehow from beyond the world, or that there are solutions to the problems of the world to be found outside the world, to break in and absolve us of our responsibility for the world. But by far the dominant characteristic of Prometheus is confidence in the capacity of human beings to engage and indeed to conquer the world.

The Promethean posture of our Christian spirituality, then, has two dimensions. In the first place, it needs an absolute commitment to worldly resources and limitations. In taking responsibility for the future of the world, it shoulders the entire responsibility. Second, and as a consequence of the first, it rejects the gods. Prometheus is beyond needing to depend on the gods. The ancient Prometheus was tortured by Zeus for stealing fire from the gods and giving it to human beings. His crime was to render the gods unnecessary to human life. The modern Prometheus lives at some intellectual distance from those ancient Greek gods, but daily steals fire from the gods as he or she engages in the struggle for human control of the world, within the limitations of the human. Prometheus does not pray for God to do what we cannot do for ourselves, because God has put us here precisely to do for ourselves. Our freedom is our greatest gift, even if it comes at a terrible price. The price of our freedom is that God will not intrude upon it. Like a parent watching a baby learn to walk or a child struggling for the first time with a bicycle, God may be cheering us on, moved by the pathos of learning, but cannot do it for us. It is up to us.

We are Prometheus, yes, but we are also Adam and Eve. The first parents in the Garden of Eden are Promethean figures. Like Prometheus, they steal something from God. God, in a typically Zeus-like move, has warned them against eating of the fruit of the tree, lest "they become like gods." But there is something in them that drives them toward knowing more, even at the cost of disobedience, even at the price of the loss of paradise. The "happy fault" Augustine speaks of is not so much that they sinned and therefore made necessary our salvation in Christ but that, having been created free, they could not limit their own drive to know and be more. The fall is the true creation of the human world. One might even say that the fall must have been in God's plan. Paradise is for infants, not for human beings. When God ushers Adam and Eve from the garden and stations sentries to bar their return, God gives them the world. God inaugurates their Promethean task. Only then do they realize what God had meant, when he told Adam to "rule the world and have dominion over it." God planned the whole thing. But what God planned was that the human race should be excluded from innocence and challenged by the gift of total freedom to work in the world with all its joys and its sufferings. When Adam and Eve are thrust from the garden, God takes leave of them—but with a light rather than a heavy heart. Now creation can *really* begin!

In practical terms, the baseline for Christian spirituality is a worldly orientation. The project of a Christian life is a worldly project. We are taken up with the world, fully engaged in the world, interested in the things of the world, as Congar would say, for their own sake, not for the sake of some "higher" value. While Christians will certainly affirm the higher reality of God, the creator of all that is, there is no higher value for the Christian life than the value with which the world has been endowed. We live lives of integrity, we love our families and friends, we help build our communities, we work hard to make the world a better place to be, all because these things are good in themselves and need no reference to some higher value in order to justify our commitments.

The Lay Person as Human Prometheus: Limitation

The second fundamental of lay spirituality is limitation. William Lynch was very clear that the danger of the Promethean vision is that it becomes Prometheanism. That is to say, we can forget that the human subject is at the center of the Promethean vision and substitute a coldly calculated manipulative relationship to the world, in which means-ends rationality has come to occupy the ground that rightfully belongs to the human community. In Habermas's terms, we can become slaves of the system, rather than its controllers. Rather than having dominion over the world, the world becomes lord over us. Which of us would not agree that exactly this terrible fate is one that we are currently staring in the face? The great ills of the modern world, from drugs to terrorism, are the result of forgetfulness of the centrality of the human. The personal alienation that leads to drug dependency and the alienation of whole peoples, which seems to stimulate acts of violence, are responses to the feeling of helplessness in the face of a dehumanized world. Islam's critique of the West includes both an envy of its achievements and a telling and accurate critique of its potential for cultural destructiveness. The addict is the product of an uncaring society.

In order to avoid the drift into Prometheanism, we have to recognize that the unconditionality of the secular is a limited unconditionality. As Lynch so clearly maintained, it is a human rather than a cosmic unconditionality. What secular freedom entails is the full development of the unconditionality of the human. We are free, but free to be more and more what we are. Our project is to make a world that is increasingly centered on the specifically, richly, and fully human.

Clearly, such a picture requires a philosophical anthropology of sorts, a clear articulation of what it is to be human. But in the construction of such a picture of the human, we are constrained by our secular condition. As Lynch would say, no religious symbols may be employed in determining this picture.

The great nineteenth-century atheistic critics of religion knew the truth of human unconditionality. They were united in their view that religious belief makes for weak people. Religion is the alienation of the human, said Feuerbach and Marx and Nietzsche and Freud, each in his own way. Of course, they were convinced of this and largely accurate on their own terms, because the God they were envisaging was a God who demanded that humans relativize the human and the human world to the realities of the beyond. They were also criticizing a Christianity that had accepted such an impoverished understanding of God. Consequently, all human achievement was belittled and all sin was sin against God. For Nietzsche's Zarathustra, "the sin against the earth" was the great trespass. Zarathustra's advice, "be faithful to the earth," points religious believers in the direction of secularity. Given the kind of God they envisaged, and it was a God that many religious believers followed then and follow now, the atheists saw the consequences accurately. Marx knew that such a religious belief (of course he envisaged the possibility of no other kind) meant a yearning for a heavenly beyond that undercut any and all attentiveness to the human project. Freud saw accurately that this God, this cosmic daddy in the sky, was attractive to the neurotic individual who would not and could not face up to the genuine character of earthly existence as finite, mysterious, and often unjust. Before them all and perhaps most perceptive of all, Ludwig Feuerbach analyzed religious language to show that its very character is alienating, constantly measuring human achievement as a pale shadow of the divine perfection.

Just as we are not allowed in the pursuit of human unconditionality to import religious hermeneutics, so we are not obliged to the atheistic vision of religious faith. Both false steps are undercut by the conviction that God is the ground of human unconditionality. The second task of Christian spirituality, then, is to determine what limitations are imposed upon the unconditionality by the adjective "human." It certainly cannot mean an inattention to the cosmos or to the nonhuman natural world around us, for these constitute our home and we must "be faithful to the earth." But it also cannot be understood as crudely anthropocentric, licensing an exploitation of the nonhuman, despoiling rather than having dominion over the natural world. It must in the end be a matter of recognizing the symbiotic union of human and nonhuman. What is truly human is the loving incorporation of the human and nonhuman in one world. The truly human is limited by the God-given freedom to be co-creative and co-preservative. Of course the human is "free" to deny this, free to exploit, and free to seek to dominate both the human and the nonhuman world. But this act of "freedom" would distort human unconditionality by introducing means-ends rationality into human discourse. The one who acted "freely" in such a way would treat others as objects, thus effectively denying the distinction between instrumental and communicative reason and asserting, in the end, that only this "I" is the center of all things. The options are clear: symbiosis, with all that this will mean for human life, or a reductive anthropocentrism that reveals itself to be a naïve but ruthless egocentrism.

The practicalities of a spirituality of limitation mean that to be fully human we must live in the world as part of the world, in close interconnection with the nonhuman world and in exactly correct relationship to the system that we have created, but which always threatens to turn us into its subjects. The project of developing a social ethics that corresponds to this theological principle will owe nothing more to religious symbolism, since it too is a secular project. This makes social ethics and eventually public policy a fully pluralistic undertaking among human beings whose common humanity is the ultimate solidarity. Christians bring no extra information to the table at which the discourse (theoretically) takes place. The fact that Christians possess an enlivening conviction that God has affirmed them in their secular unconditionality brings them to the table of a discourse ethics and keeps them at the table for the endless, asymptotic approach to an ideally human world. Belief in God is the basis for the stamina that is needed to fashion an ethic that is faithful to human freedom, but it is not the source of ethical principles by which the discussion should be delimited or, still worse, foreclosed. In this sense, if in no other, the Catholic inclination to an ethic derived from natural law conforms better to a pluralistic world order than does one that filters ethical principle through biblical narrative.

The unconditionality of the human, and the faithful conviction that God is its ground, implies a commitment to true democracy. If the fully human world must be shaped through human choices and a discourse based on respect for the search for what is the fully human, and if it must eschew the easy route of importing ethical principles from the biblical narrative, then it can only flourish in a public forum that is without constraint. This statement is not a commercial for American or European styles of government, at least not as they have worked out in practice. In fact, the pathology of American public life at the present time is very much a matter of "the colonization of the lifeworld by the system." The political should be a matter of free debate about options within a consensus about the objective of a fully human world. Today the space for such debate is almost completely obliterated by the power of special interests and the money that is deemed necessary to the democratic process. But a democracy purged of these aberrations is the only political form in which the theological project of human unconditionality can be pursued. Autocracy, including that special form that loves to call itself theocracy, is precisely unacceptable because it occludes human freedom. If God is truly the ground of the unconditionality of the secular, then religion must bow before it.

The Layperson as Christian Prometheus: Responsibility

The fact that we have established that the Christian brings no privileged information to the process of constructing a truly human society does not mean that there is nothing distinctive about the Christian way of being involved in the enterprise. For the Christian, revelation is the story of God's ongoing affirmation of the human people, and the special role that the community of believers in Jesus must play in God's plan. It is through Jesus that the plan of God for the world is made fully manifest, Christians believe. But that plan is about the world, not about Jesus or God. The death and resurrection of Jesus are for the world, not for God, and most certainly not for himself. Jesus' life and death are secular events, occurring in the world and explicable in terms of the forces of good and evil. That is, Jesus is the focus of conflict between the struggle for full human freedom and the struggle of worldly powers to control and constrain that freedom.

The Christian, as the believer in Jesus, is then the one who is confident in the need for the struggle, assured of its eventual outcome, and sober both about the price that individuals may have to pay and about the time that may pass before the reign of God begun in Jesus is fully realized in the world. The lay Christian, not the cleric, is the one who must take the heat in the day-to-day work of co-creation. The lay Christian is the one upon whom the burden and honor of working for a more fully human world have been placed. These characteristics do not make the lay Christian any more likely than the non-Christian to further the discourse of the human community toward its ends, because they provide no special insights about the particular steps that need to be taken. But they should keep the lay Christian at the table longer. Discouragement is simply not in the cards. Responsible commitment to the process can only be encouraged by the overwhelming sense that we are accountable to God for the exercise of our human freedom, since God is its ground. Jesus, of course, is the exemplar of "responsible commitment to the process," though we usually call it his "faithfulness to his Father's calling." And so we can say that the lay vocation is responsible commitment to the process of unfolding human freedom.

A NOTE ON ORDAINED MINISTRY

As we saw in the first half of this book, laypeople have been a theological afterthought throughout the history of the church. They are "not clergy." It may seem that the picture I have begun to present here of a secularized ecclesiology may be making the opposite mistake of obliterating the importance of the ordained ministry to the church. This is certainly not my intent, though I am convinced that the church must face up to the fact that Congar and Schillebeeckx were right when they both separately said that today it is the clergy relative to the laity, not the laity relative to the clergy, that is in need of explanation. Of course, all that has been said above about involvement in the struggle for human freedom applies to the ordained ministry as well. They are citizens of the world; they vote, and they participate in human unconditionality. But their distinctiveness is that they must take a back seat in the struggle for human unconditionality. Their role is to preserve the community of faith as the place of the Spirit par excellence, the place where God's affirmation of human freedom is constantly celebrated and where God, the ground of secular unconditionality, is praised and blessed. Their work is instrumental to that of the laity, who are in the vanguard of the church's mission. But it may be that, as we rethink the structures of ministry, a different understanding of the respective responsibilities may emerge.

6

The Liberation of the Laity, the Liberation of the Church

IN CHAPTER 5 WE ENGAGED in a prolonged theological reflection on the secularity of the laity and the secularity of the church. This lay and secular ecclesiology will be worked out in more detail in the final two chapters of the book. For now, we have to turn away from strictly theological reflection for a time to an examination of the existential condition of laypeople in the church. The test case will be laypeople in the North American Catholic Church. Among the so-called developed countries of the world, the church in the United States retains the highest level of practice and is the church in which the laity have come to assume increasingly visible roles in the day-to-day work. It may well be that the future of the church lies in the Southern Hemisphere, but for now the American church remains vibrant and shows signs of offering one workable model for the future.

If the vocation of the laity is to human freedom, their existential predicament in today's church is that they are in chains. The freedom of the children of God, proclaimed by the gospel and in many ways the goal of Christian mission to the world, is transgressed within the community of the faithful itself. It may seem odd to be making such a dramatic statement. After all, we have used so much space pointing out the great advances the church has made in understanding the laity theologically, and we have had frequent occasion to emphasize how much apostolic activity the laity are engaged in at the present time. But it is not at all the same thing to be active and to be free. The slaves who maintained the economy of the southern states for so many years were active, talented, creative individuals, but they were not free. The Catholic laity, for the most part, do not know of their oppressed condition and would deny it if it were argued in their presence. There are, of course, many forms of oppression. Perhaps the worst, spiritually if not physically, is the one in which the captives have been induced to embrace their own oppression. It is just such a condition of "structural oppression" that I believe is the present condition of the laity in the church. Because the laity are oppressed, the church itself is oppressed. The same ecclesial ideology that has come to exercise hegemonic control limits the freedom of the entire faith community, including those in positions of leadership. In fact, perhaps they are the most oppressed of all, since it is hardest for them to "think outside the box." They have too much invested in the status quo.

The leadership crisis that has rocked the American church in the first few years of the new century has provided the church with a *kairos*, a moment of opportunity, to recognize and respond to the structural problems of which it is a very good illustration. However, recognition of the problem did not need to wait for such a deplorable example of its effects, any more than dealing with this particular problem will necessarily remove the underlying causes. In this chapter we need to paint a picture of the crisis of leadership in the life in the church and of the squandering of lay experience that it reveals. Second, we shall examine in detail the idea of structural oppression, which will shed light on the condition of the laity. Finally, we shall talk of how this oppression is to be overcome, of how the laity need to rise up and rescue the church. For it is the church's future that is at stake here, not just the freedom of the laity. This is not about laity versus church leadership, still less about laity versus clergy. We all live together in a faith community that is dysfunctional in some important respects and needs significant structural change. These kinds of changes come best from below, from those who are least invested in the maintenance of the present structure. But this can happen only when they have found it possible to name and face their own oppression. To name and face the oppression is the task of the current chapter.

THE CRISIS OF LEADERSHIP
IN THE CHURCH TODAY

There is a crisis of leadership in the church, and the laity need to come to the rescue. In so many ways, the promise of Vatican II has been unfulfilled, none more so than on the issue of coresponsibility about which Cardinal Suenens wrote so presciently some thirty years ago. The last thirty years have shown a consistent return to a highly centralized authority structure in which even the bishops are frequently reduced to advisory roles. Some find Roman intrusiveness extending to extraordinary levels—witness Archbishop Rembert Weakland's forceful rebuttal of efforts to deny his authority to make architectural modifications in the cathedral in Milwaukee.[1] If at least some of the bishops feel unduly harassed, then what of the priests, and still more the laity? Consider some examples. Large numbers of the laity feel that the time is right for the ordination of married men to the priesthood. Many have no objection to the ordination of women. Many believe that homosexual Christians should not be expected to live celibate lives. The church's teaching on "artificial" contraception is dead letter. What the people want is sound preaching on the scripture, help in living holy lives in the midst of the challenges of our world, and leadership that has some sense of the priorities of Christians today. What we have is an episcopate of men selected more for their commitment to the party line on outmoded ideas about contraception, ordination, and homosexuality, more for their administrative capabilities than for their stature as spiritual leaders. Often fearful and disengaged from ordinary life, for the most part unimpressive rather than evil or Machiavellian, they do not carry conviction. The capable minority, especially if they are willing to show any independence of judgment (which in most cases means they were made bishops before the present pope took office), are stuck in small dioceses or hidden away in assistant bishop positions. The major metropolitan sees tend to be occupied by people who are made in the image of John Paul II, though not of the same stuff. Often bright, frequently personally holy, usually extremely hard-working, they are there to block change and to shore up the present system.

While the crisis of leadership is manifested in many ways, there is no clearer example than in the appallingly poor response both of Rome and of the American bishops to the problem of priestly pedophilia. In my own home diocese the previous bishop tried to protect the church from expensive damage awards against pedophile priests by arguing that the priest was an "independent contractor" and not legally an employee of the diocese and therefore that the diocese was not liable! This particular bishop has now moved on to higher responsibilities. The total inadequacy of the institutional response to the problem of sexual abuse of minors highlights a structural weakness in the church whose ramifications go far beyond this single issue. At root, the ordained ministry, which includes within it the entire structure of leadership in the church, is a self-policing system. We all know what happens in such a system, whether it is the CIA, the local police force, or the church. The leadership closes ranks to protect itself and to make sure that no change occurs. The system fights hard to prevent "outsiders" from being involved in oversight. It is human nature, though whether it is how a church should behave is another matter.

Among the many distinguished Catholic laypeople to address this problem is Lisa Sowle Cahill.[2] Writing directly about the problem of pedophilia, she accuses the church of hypocrisy in its double standards. Divorced and remarried Catholics or openly gay Catholics, she writes, "cannot participate fully in the rites of the church." But "priests who have committed a worse offense against Catholic teaching can administer those same rites." She also sees that the problem at the heart of this scandal is not celibacy, as some have rushed to conclude. Rather, we should blame the closed society "largely insulated from the realities and values of ordinary people" within which the crisis has occurred, and the culture of control, complacency, and authoritarianism that "reaches all the way to Rome." Cahill's remedy is "a more open and collaborative model of governance—including women and lay men at the highest levels." Not wishing to pit priests against people, Cahill adds that "many pastors are allies in [the] struggle" and "lasting institutional change will require the equal participation of the laity, priests, bishops and the Vatican itself."

The crisis of leadership in the church is not attributable to the fact that all the bishops are celibate, or that they are all men. Male celibates are perfectly capable of leading communities and of living fruitful lives. The crisis is linked much more to the fact that leadership is the province of an enclosed elite caste, two of whose characteristics happen to be celibacy and maleness. Looking at the church as a system, we can see clearly that the greater the authority the individual possesses in the structure of the church, the further divorced the individual is from the ordinary life of the people he is supposed to lead. Remember when President George Bush, back around 1990, visited a supermarket and marveled at the technological miracle of the scanning machine at the checkout? Friend or foe of Bush, after that weren't you just that little bit less confident in his ability as commander-in-chief? How often do you think curial cardinals can be seen in the checkout line at the grocery store?

If one dimension of current church leadership is its divorce from ordinary life, a second is that narrowness of outlook that inevitably marks any self-perpetuating enclosed group. Here celibacy and gender do have a role to play. There is nothing wrong with being a male celibate, but the restriction of leadership to celibates impoverishes the institution by the exclusion of so much experience that the celibate cannot access. The restriction of leadership to those of the male gender impoverishes leadership still further. Imagine if only women were allowed to play baseball, or if only men were permitted on the basketball court. Think how much we would be missing!

A third element, inevitably interwoven with the first two, is that the elite male celibate caste, which exercises all leadership in the church, just happens to be the very same group to whom priesthood is reserved. It is a good question to ask, whether if the ordained included both women and married people, and if the church continued to locate leadership exclusively among the ordained, the leadership crisis would still be there. Obviously, the ordained would have richer experience on which to draw. But the ranks of ordained ministers would continue not to include lay experience, and—perhaps to a lesser degree—they would still flirt with that narrowness of viewpoint that bedevils professional leaders. In particular, it would exclude secular people from leadership in the church, and that would be a problem, both humanly and theologically speaking. So it would seem that the leadership crisis will not be solved merely by broadening the ranks of the ordained, but necessitates inclusion of the voice of the laity. Since there is no immediate likelihood of a change in the law of celibacy or the inclusion of women in the ranks of the ordained, opening church leadership to the laity seems even more urgent.

The laity came to the rescue of the church once before, if John Henry Newman is to be believed, in the dark days of the Arian crisis, which threatened the future of the fourth-century Christians. Newman's well-known essay *On Consulting the Faithful,* published anonymously in *The Rambler* in 1859, mounts a defense of brief remarks made in the previous issue, also anonymously by Newman in his role as editor.[3] There he had written to the effect that "in the preparation of a dogmatic definition, the faithful are consulted, as lately in the instance of the Immaculate Conception." It is a matter of rather surprising historical record that Pius IX, usually considered (rightly) a cautious and fearful conservative, required the bishops to investigate the views of the laity before proceeding to the dogmatic definition of the Immaculate Conception. Though the occasion for Newman's original remarks had been an editorial encouraging the bishops to "consult" the Catholic laity on the eminently practical issue of representation on a proposed Royal Commission on elementary education, Newman's essay dealt much more directly with theological questions. His principal concern was to explicate an understanding of the *consensus fidelium* or *sensus fidelium,* terms that he used interchangeably. He concluded that "the voice of tradition may in certain cases express itself, not by Councils, nor Fathers, nor Bishops, but by the *'communis fidelium sensus'* " (the common agreement of the faithful as a whole). Newman illustrated his point at length by consideration of the Arian crisis in the sixty years after the Council of Nicaea (323 C.E.), years in which, he wrote, "the body of the Bishops failed in their confession of the faith." It was the laity who took up the slack and preserved that faith. The governing body of the church fell short and "the governed were pre-eminent in faith, zeal, courage and constancy." "It was mainly by the faithful people," said Newman, "that Paganism was overthrown."[4]

Although what was at stake in the church of the fourth century was the central doctrine of the divinity of Christ, and what is at stake now in the church is not the same, both moments in history are marked by a moral failure in leadership. Newman was not saying that all bishops were failures—Athanasius was a shining exception—or that all the laity were heroes, and he had kind words to say for the "parish priests." But he argued that "on the whole" and as a whole the bishops failed in their responsibility to teach the truth. It was the heroic constancy of the laity that supplied for their lapse, for more than sixty years, despite the genuine physical violence frequently done against them by the Arian bishops.

Newman's discussion makes very clear that what rescues the church is the laity's courageous insistence on what is right, even when their own leaders seem at times to be deserting them and when some would even do violence against them. Theologically, this truth is founded in the teaching of Vatican II, which Newman himself influenced on this point, namely, that the whole body of the faithful shares in the Spirit-guaranteed infallibility of the church. In Newman's formulation, "their consensus through Christendom is the voice of the infallible Church." The whole faithful possess a kind of intuition or instinct for the truth, a "jealousy of error, which it at once feels as a scandal." While there are understandably many lay Catholics who are deeply discouraged both by the scope of clerical sexual abuse and by the failure of episcopal leadership, and whose attachment to the church is weakened, it would not be correct to describe this as a crisis of faith. Doctrine is not at issue here. But we face a crisis of confidence in church leadership and a crisis within that leadership itself. This crisis was there even without a single pedophile priest. They have only alerted us to the urgency of the problem. So there is indeed an important agenda to inspire the laity to rescue the church once again. The leadership of the church is just as trapped in structural oppression as is the laity, but the laity are more psychologically free to bring it to public attention and to insist on change. However, the changes that will make a difference are not the relatively simple matters of changing laws on celibacy or gender in the ministry, effective and necessary as those might be. At root, the problem is one of a need for patterns of ministry to match the postconciliar understanding of the church as a communion rather than as an institution. The affective reality of a communion is solidarity among the members. The juridical necessity is accountability. Fellowship and accountability are a good recipe for a mature community of faith.

THE LIBERATION OF THE LAITY

It is difficult to avoid the conclusion that the Catholic tradition currently squanders lay experience, and that this is directly connected to the degree of the church's dysfunctionality. This is most tragically apparent in the effective absence of lay experience from the formation of teaching on personal, and particularly on sexual, morality. In the Catholic tradition, of course, laypeople have neither active nor passive voice. They cannot be elected to office in the church, and they are not allowed to participate in the election of others. There are clear and understandable historic reasons for this split between a clergy who teach, preach, and exercise jurisdiction, and a laity who do not. For most of the last two thousand years, to be clergy was to be educated, to be lay was to be uneducated. While that has been a long time changing, it has certainly changed now, and it is no disrespect to the ranks of the Catholic clergy to say that most educated Catholics will now be found outside the clerical ranks. Indeed, in the United States, thanks to the vigor of Catholic colleges and universities, one could probably make the more remarkable claim that most theologically educated Catholics are not clergy.

One of the most striking characteristics of much contemporary theology is the attention paid to the context of the theologian or the community engaged in theological reflection. Attention to context is a direct result of the turn to experience as normative for theology which marks the entire development of Latin American theology of liberation and those other theologies sharing a family resemblance—especially in feminist, womanist, and *mujerista* thought[5]—the concrete circumstances of the doer of theology come into prominence. In the past, they were not merely in the background; they were invisible. Increasingly today the theologian is expected to be open about her or his social location and identity, because factors such as class, race, gender, age, and sexual orientation are considered germane to understanding the conclusions at which a particular thinker might arrive.

While issues of gender or sexual orientation are definitely out in the open among theologians today, few, if any, authors in the Catholic (or any other) tradition have reflected upon the particularity of *lay* experience as a starting point for theology, or have recognized the context of lay Catholics as being just as distinctive as that of *mujeristas* or gay and lesbian Christians.[6] One obvious reason for this oversight is the fact that lay Catholics include many people who are already self-identified as members of more obviously distinct groups. There are many Hispanic women lay Catholics, lots of gay and lesbian Catholics, and not a few African-American Catholics. In the liberation theologies that emanate from these groups, their being members of the laity never seems to emerge as worth comment. A second and perhaps less obvious reason for the lack of a sense of the laity as a distinct group is that the very notion of being "lay" includes within it connotations of passive acceptance of one's place as recipient of grace, of the Spirit, of the sacraments. Rarely, if ever, at least in the popular imagination, does being "lay" seem to imply a particular activity or ministry within the community. At the same time, no one questions the fact of the exclusion of lay voice from formal participation in ecclesial leadership. Differences between passive and involved laity, or between liberal and conservative lay Catholics, on the question of lay voice in the church do certainly occur. But these largely have to do with whether laypeople *ought* to be accorded leadership roles, not with whether they as a matter of fact possess them at the present time. While conservatives would be content with lay levels of participation and leadership, and liberals would not, all would agree that laity are juridically excluded from leadership positions in the church.

Given the fact of lay exclusion from voice in the church, why is it that there is little or no organized attempt to change this? There certainly exist groups such as Call to Action which stress the democratization of church structures, but they involve a tiny minority of laypeople and—much more importantly—only a small fraction of those who are dissatisfied with the current role of the laity. Why, if the problem of lack of lay voice exists, is resistance so spotty? Is it that most people do not see a problem, and those who do are just constitutionally indignant, or is there some other explanation?

The low level of lay protest at the role of laypeople in the church is a product of the systemic or structural oppression of the laity. The concept of structural oppression was developed in religious reflection first of all in the Latin American theology of liberation, but is now a commonplace in all liberation theologies. It is particularly important to understand the precise character of this notion of oppression. The concept draws attention to actual structures within a particular society, in this case the Catholic Church, which result in oppression, while they may or may not have been set up with the intention of oppression. It also leaves open the question whether or not those who benefit from the oppressive structures do so consciously, accidentally, or by default. Certain oppressive social structures, such as chattel slavery or *apartheid*, are consciously intended systemic oppressions. Others, such as societies that are *de facto* rather than *de jure* racist, or which demonstrate elements of patriarchy, reveal systemic oppression that may not be so consciously intended, at least in its origins, but which is not necessarily any less oppressive. Thus systemic oppression by no means requires that we understand the individuals occupying positions of power within the system to be consciously engaged in the physical or emotional abuse of those victimized by the structures.

The accusation of systemic or structural oppression of the laity in the Catholic Church does not, then, require the claim that clergy consciously oppress or abuse non-clergy. Indeed, as we shall discover, there are good reasons to see the oppressors in this particular structure as themselves oppressed, to a degree, by the very same divisions. The claim is only that the division between clergy and laity, as understood in the Catholic tradition, systematically subordinates and undervalues the lay lifestyle, lay talent, lay leadership, lay experience, and lay spirituality. While the patterns cannot be equated to those of slavery, they certainly reproduce in striking ways the structures of racism and sexism. Racism, sexism, and clericalism all at root are moved by a belief, however inchoate, in the lesser humanity or lesser intelligence of the oppressed group, thus justifying the subordinate position in which the underclass is then to be maintained. But the conviction of the inferiority of the oppressed race, gender, or class is often clearly a rhetorical move intended more to shore up the status, prestige, and power of the oppressor class than based on anything objective at all. To take an obvious example: white supremacists are themselves usually the poorest evidence for the supremacy of the white race. Just take a look sometime at the kinds of individuals who attend the rallies, or listen to the arguments their leaders make.

It may seem to be a serious exaggeration to argue that the Catholic clergy believe the Catholic laity to be less human or less intelligent than priests and bishops. Of course, none of them would ever say that, and perhaps none of them would ever think that. But the patterns of behavior and the structures of the lay/clerical divide within the Catholic Church suggest that in fact the laity are systematically treated *as if* they have lesser talents and are of lesser account. Laypeople are of course not ordained to celebrate the Eucharist, and there is no good reason to take seriously any lay demand that they be permitted under normal circumstances to do so. Of course, it is a far different claim to want patterns of ministry and ordination to be transformed so that the lay/clerical distinction is no longer problematic. What is not in dispute here is that at least at the present time some are ordained to celebrate the Eucharist and lead the community at worship, and some are not. The problem lies much more in the historical accretion to this segment of the clergy of *all* formal manifestations of leadership, power, and authority in the church.

The issue under consideration here is more fundamental than a mere call for a better attitude on the part of the clergy to the laity, or for the laity to be allowed to exercise more nonsacramental functions in the daily life of the church. On the one hand, the "clergy" in the clergy/lay distinction simply indicates those members of the church who happen as a matter of fact to have been singled out in the community to lead it in its sacramental worship, while the "laity" are those who do not feel called to this particular ministry. This in itself is not oppressive. The problem lies much more in the fact that "clergy" in the clergy/lay distinction is also a designation for a group of people who hold all authority and exercise all leadership in the church, by virtue of possessing a calling to preside at worship, which is by no means the same thing. Moreover, the problem is greatly exacerbated by the fact that for purely historical reasons a series of entirely extrinsic factors (maleness, willingness to commit to a celibate lifestyle) delimits not only those whom the church considers to be truly called to ordained ministry but also those who can lead the church, preach the homily, teach with authority, or even be formally incorporated in the communal discernment of the gospel.

The problem endemic to the lay/clergy distinction is not solely an administrative or attitudinal one, though there are elements of both of these at work. It is at root a theological problem inherent in the notion of the relationship between ordained ministry and various forms of leadership, though one that becomes as apparent as it does only because of the purely accidental exclusion of women and married men from the ranks of (ordained) leaders. In other words, any questionable or even negative elements in the historical association in the Catholic tradition between ordained ministry and authority are masked just so long as the restriction of ordination to celibates and men goes unquestioned. When such restrictions are scrutinized, and particularly when their connection to leadership is examined, and the essentially ideological argument for their continuance is uncovered, a theological argument against them is the more likely to be mounted. While a theological argument for the ordination of women is by now unremarkable in the Catholic tradition, the less common but arguably more necessary theological challenge is the one to be mounted against the traditional connection between ordained ministry, on the one hand, and positions of leadership and authority, on the other. While it would undoubtedly be beneficial to the church to have many more laypeople in visible leadership positions, and while their exclusion is symptomatic of their subordination, it is not there that we should locate the principal battleground of systemic oppression. Much more troubling is the crippling effect on lay consciousness of lack of voice and its concomitant marginalization, a phenomenon that as a matter of fact has as one of its consequences the decreased probability that many laypeople would be qualified to put themselves forward for just the sorts of positions of leadership in the church that are listed above. In her great book on the origins of liberation theology, *Cry of the People,* the late Penny Lernoux made an important sociological distinction between "poor cultures" and "cultures of poverty."[7] The former are not problematic. Though distinguished by lack of material means, they are communities with a rich cultural life in which the dignity of their members is not in question. However, a culture of poverty is one in which the poverty has become so overwhelming that its psychological effects are such as to deprive the community of hope and to substitute a climate of demoralization and decay. Clearly, for Lernoux, structural oppression is what turns a poor culture into a culture of poverty. A similar distinction may be instructive in plumbing the depths of lay oppression; while the notion of "the laity" is not in itself degrading or inappropriate, the impoverishment of lay culture and lay expectation resulting from systemic oppression is deeply problematic. Like the denizens of a culture of poverty, the laity are depressed. And because they are depressed, they are less likely to be aware that they are oppressed.

The first step in emergence from structural oppression is for the laity to move from depression to a recognition of their oppression, and the prerequisite for this is to be able to name their own oppression. In liberation theology, such a step is called "conscientization," and it is the primary awakening of a community, through which it begins the struggle to pass from being object or victim of history, as defined by someone else, to subject of its own history. Through conscientization, people begin to take charge. In whatever context, it represents achieving or reclaiming adulthood from those who have reinforced the infantilization of the victims. In whatever context, it is the moment at which the patriarchs, patronizers, or "parents" are challenged to abandon their stranglehold on power, and, all too frequently, the moment at which they often redouble the strength of their hold.

The conscientization of large segments of the Catholic laity, at least in Massachusetts, took place in the full glare of the media spotlight during the early months of 2002 and was symbolized in the extraordinary growth of Voice of the Faithful (VOTF) from a few hundred members to about sixteen thousand during the first half of the year.[8] Over and over again, we saw hordes of ordinary faithful churchgoing Catholics standing up to protest against the behavior of the church in general, and their archbishop in particular. Beginning with protests over Cardinal Law's poor handling of the sex-abuse crisis, the movement quickly broadened its attention to structural reform of the church in general, accurately seeing that the cardinal's behavior only hinted at a much larger problem. But while Catholic laity all over the country mirrored Boston's protest, and while some of them joined VOTF, the voices continued to be heard most loudly in Boston. The catalyst for conscientization was so much more flagrantly evident in Massachusetts. Where the catalyst was not obvious, the move out of depression into conscientization did not take place to the same degree.

Infantilization. Conscientization. Self-definition. These are the Egypt, Sinai, and promised land of lay liberation. While Latin American liberation theology has been able to make more direct links to the exodus narrative of how a non-people is chosen by God to become a people, and indeed to become God's people, the American Catholic laity *as* laity must do a lot of tacking to get to the same point on the other shore. But the fundamental predicament is structurally identical in the two groups. Historically, their reality has always been defined by their particular structural oppressor, and their objectification and

alienation have been reinforced by all kinds of social sanctions and cultural codes. Indeed, the parallels are very striking.

The poor of Latin America, according to the vision of liberation
theology, are submerged in their culture of poverty, until awakened
through encounter with the scriptures in a context in which they are
encouraged to vocalize their sense of the relationship between their
own oppressed condition and the voice of God in the Bible, singling
out the marginalized as God's special object of concern. Strengthened
by their new awareness of the preferential option for the poor in the
God of the Hebrew Bible and the Jesus of the Gospels, they can take
simple, humble, but nonetheless courageous steps to change the structural oppression under which they live. For the most part, this is less
a matter of a direct challenge to political authority than the attempt to
take charge of their own lives in their own communities and to insist
on the right to a dignified human life in which their basic needs are
met. Such "agitation" was most frequently identified as subversive
and was struck down in often violent ways. Often the local church
sided with the poor, but sometimes not; sometimes the national and
international church sided with the poor, more often not.

These basic historical moments in the story of liberation theology
may well be paralleled directly in the story we shall one day be able to
tell about lay Catholic experience and the emergence of a lay theology
of liberation. In the local parish situation at the present day most of
the laity are relatively passive and uncomplaining, at least in public.
Some parishes allow for considerable lay involvement in the conduct
of worship and the organization of the parish community, but the
majority do relatively little of this, sometimes because the laity willing
to involve themselves do not exist, in itself a further sign of the reality
of the culture of oppression/depression. But even where lay involvement is encouraged, perhaps beyond what is strictly permitted by
higher authority (in preaching, for example), although there is some
erosion of the lay/clerical distinction, there is no possibility of real
change in that formal relationship. Structural change is out of the
hands of parochial clergy, however far-sighted they may be, though
interesting developments can occur when one of the braver bishops
feigns blindness and deafness.

A major element in intensifying divisions between laity and clergy
is the issue of clerical lifestyle (celibate, male), which creates a class

division as pronounced as that between rich and poor in Latin America. The division is of course not largely along economic lines, except in the poorer parishes, where the pastor is often living at a level of material comfort unknown to his parishioners. More important than economics, the characteristics of the lay and clerical lifestyles represent two different worlds. This is not only or even principally a matter of celibacy; it is much more the different forms of security, responsibility, and accountability that mark the two ways of life.

Catholic clergy have the most secure lifestyles of anyone in the community, except perhaps for the fabulously wealthy. While not highly paid, their material circumstances are never under threat, and downsizing, outsourcing, and the other manifestations of the new social barbarism that render even the upper middle classes anxious today are unknown to the clergy. Frequently managing parishes with doubtful financial solvency, they have few if any such worries for themselves. As celibate individuals, they do not know many of the more demanding forms of personal responsibility; and as essentially private, bachelor individuals, their ethical accountability in small matters and large is entirely located in their own consciences. The laity, on the other hand, typically live with those who hold them accountable and to whom and for whom they are responsible.

The lifestyle divide between clergy and laity is not the source of the problem of lay oppression, though it is undoubtedly symptomatic. The real problem is that all forms of authority, influence, leadership, and power in the church are reserved to a small minority of Catholic Christians distinguished from the others only by their possession of a radically different lifestyle. What we see is a true caste system, by vocation if not by birth. The laity are defined by the clergy. The respective rights and responsibilities are defined by the clergy. Laity, however well qualified or with whatever virtues and talents, are children in the house of the Lord. Attempts at real resistance to this, sporadic as they are, are interpreted as trouble-making, grumbling "dissent" that is not to be tolerated.

If real change in the church is to occur, there must be a mechanism and an agenda. There is a clear need for mass conscientization that, while it may only ever affect a minority, will at least be sufficiently widespread that it will be taken seriously. If the laity are ever to be given voice in the church, we must speak out. We must take voice, but we must also have something to say—we need an agenda. If we can find a way to raise consciousness but then have nothing serious to say, the charge of needlessly polarizing people might stick. If, on the other hand, we have an agenda but no mechanism—the condition of the church now, at least in my estimation—there is a danger of the church falling further and further into ineptitude, if not irrelevancy. To be irrelevant is to have nothing important to say, and the Catholic Church cannot be accused of this, even in its present wounded condition. But to be inept is to be dysfunctional in discharging its responsibilities to history, and it is here that the problem of lay voice becomes crucial. If for no other reason, this is why organizations like VOTF are so vital.

The agenda of a lay theology of liberation must then be to achieve voice in the church, that is, to be taken seriously on a par with clerical voices, priestly or episcopal, according to the degree of expertise one can claim or according to the measure of good in what we have to say. Of their nature, the majority of laypeople are not likely to be specialists in academic theology or in philosophical or theological ethics, and while some will (and do) contribute to the scholarly dialogue on such matters, most do not, cannot, and do not want to. But there is an enormous reservoir of lay practical wisdom on the challenges of living life according to the gospel, both theologically and ethically, that remains untapped because the clerical teachers in the church draw upon it little if at all, and because those whose experience it is are hobbled.

Most of what is wrong with the church today is to be found in precisely those arenas where lay experience would be crucial if it were attended to at all. There is the attempt to stifle debate by invoking authority over the exclusion of most married men and all women from ordination to the priesthood. There is the continued insistence on "banning" so-called artificial means of birth control, the voice of the Vatican in international debate on population policies and the rights of women, patterns and practices for the appointment of bishops, church teaching on homosexuality. There is the scandal of clerical sexual abuse of minors. Lay experience has an impact on each of these pathologies, either by shedding light on the problem, by rejecting the notion that there is a problem at all, or perhaps by cutting down to size some of the issues that seem blown out of all proportion by the seemingly unhealthy level of interest the teaching church appears to display in sexual sin. But the items on a lay agenda are less important than determining the means of lay conscientization.

If conscientization is demanded and the "culture of poverty" makes such an event unlikely to be spontaneously generated, the need for a historical catalyst becomes apparent. In this context one more parallel to liberation theology is helpful. While liberation theology certainly emerges in the encounter between the faithful people and the Word of God in scripture, the turn to scripture itself needs to be explained. The truth, in Latin America, is that it was in some sense occasioned by a growing desperation. As Jon Sobrino once said, "true theology begins in indignation."[9] The indignation of the Latin American people and the institutional church itself was aroused by the experience of the assault on human rights conducted by the many governments of national security that flourished in Latin America in the 1960s and 1970s and are by no means absent today.

The catalyst for the emergence of lay conscientization may well lie in the experience of living within what we may perhaps call, with some poetic license, "a church of national security." In other words, there are definite and important resemblances between the prevailing ideology of the Catholic Church at the present time and the ideologies of the governments of national security experienced in Latin America over the past three decades. Governments of national security invoke higher ideals of the constitution in order to justify (temporary) suspensions of constitutional rights. The church is deeply suspicious of dissent and—where it can—outlaws dissenters in the name of fidelity to the gospel. It invokes the example of Christ and the representative status of the priest to exclude women from any leadership role in the worshiping community. It rests its exclusion of (almost all) married people from priestly ministry on the traditional connection between such ministry and celibacy. While the church has no prisons in which to incarcerate people and no dungeons in which to torture them, the judicial processes to which it has subjected and continues to subject dissenters do not stand comparison with those of civilized society, and its sanctions on the guilty (principally deprivation of employment or right to teach) can have devastating economic and psychological consequences.[10]

The level of suppression of debate, voice, and freedom of the children of God has intensified in recent decades, perhaps for no more sinister reason than that the amount of dissent has itself grown considerably. But it seems unlikely that the attempt to stifle legitimate criticism that grows out of love of the church will succeed, at least in the long term. The scandal of pedophilia has certainly been the straw that breaks the camel's back for many American Catholics. For others, their rising to subjecthood will be a product of the controversy over women's ordination; for still others it will be celibacy or church teaching on some issue of sexual ethics—most likely on homosexuality or sterilization or one of the many irrational avenues down which traditional "physicalist" understandings of natural law carry the official moral teaching of the church. For very many, it will, above all, be a matter of recognizing the real oppression of women in the church. But whatever the particular occasion, this may be the spark that will ignite the intensely combustible mixture already present: deep love of God and the church, concern for the world, higher education, and distaste for cant from whatever kind of politician it emerges. How are lay Catholics to be conscientized, even given the necessary historical catalyst in the experience of each individual? It is axiomatic that the conscientization must come from within the lay community. Clerics, however well-meaning, cannot do this any more than whites can raise the consciousness of African Americans to their oppression, or men can lead the women's movement. Beyond the symbolic inappropriateness lies the fact that only one who shares the context and experience of the oppressed group is capable of stimulating the process of conscientization within the group. Thus, in the case of lay Catholics, there is a need to identify a vanguard of "intellectual workers" from within lay ranks to stimulate the process of conscientization.

Ada María Isasi-Díaz's concept of the theologian as professional insider, worked out in her book *En La Lucha (In the Struggle)*, takes the neo-Marxist sting out of Antonio Gramsci's term, "organic intellectual," but is explicitly indebted to that earlier concept.[11] Gramsci distinguished between the traditional and the organic intellectual. The former is a representative of the dominant hegemony and always argues against the claim that ideological interests are at work in intellectual life. The latter is distinguished by a critical awareness of ideology and seeks to overcome it through a dialogue between intellectuals and the masses. While it would be overly simplistic to suggest that Catholic theologians divide into traditional, clerical theologians and organic, lay theologians, it would be true that those theologians, clerical or lay, involved in liberation theologies fall clearly into the ranks of organic intellectuals.[12] Isasi-Díaz's professional insider, moreover, is a textbook example of such a person—from the community, entering into a dialogue with individuals in the community through the ethnographic interview, and working with and in the community to loosen the ideological and hegemonic chains that bind it.

Isasi-Díaz elaborates the notion of the ethnographic interview as a means to capture the directness of the experience of individual Hispanic women. But she adds the meta-ethnographic concern that these experiences not then be reduced to data, when their directness would be lost. A similar practice was carried on in Ernesto Cardenal's volumes of *The Gospel in Solentiname,* in which word-for-word transcriptions of debates on the meaning of scripture passages were preserved intact, not simply used as a basis for theorizing. In their concern for immediacy and in their involvement both of the people and the professional insiders, these examples suggest the way that lay conscientization might proceed. It requires the direct stimulation of the professional insider, but it relies for its efficacy on hearing and sharing the direct experiences of the nonprofessional. In the ensuing dialogue, both partners come to name more exactly the true character of their oppression. Indeed, Isasi-Díaz in particular is absolutely adamant that the "grassroots Latinas" *are* as much *mujerista* theologians as their professionally trained sisters (*In the Struggle,* 176–79).

In one final important respect, Isasi-Díaz's *mujerista* theology has a lesson for lay liberation theology. Throughout this chapter I have stressed the role of experience, and specifically lay experience, as a resource for theology. Isasi-Díaz points out that the experience that is valuable is not merely everyday experience, but "lived experience," namely, "those experiences in our lives about which we are intentional" (p. 173). This lived experience of oppression and domination is for *mujeristas* both the site and the source of their theology. In much the same way, we have to say that not just any experience is relevant to the situation of lay Catholics in the doing of a liberation theology. Indeed, for many of them their everyday experience is anything but oppressive—the white males among them, in particular, experience their secular and their ecclesial reality very differently. So in the doing of lay liberation theology it will be the intentional experience of being *lay within the church* that will be both site and source of the religious reflection. To tie this together to my earlier argument, the intentional experience of an oppressive church will be the catalyst in the process of conscientization.

A NOTE ON LAY THEOLOGIANS

Some years ago I wrote an article for a British journal on the ecclesial role of the lay theologian.[13] At that time, I envisaged the importance of lay theologians in the Catholic tradition principally in terms of their greater freedom from ecclesiastical censure and therefore as those who could "lead the charge" or "take the heat" in the inbred world of Catholic ecclesial controversy. That role still remains important, but I now believe it to be overshadowed by the requirement that these same lay theologians engage in the process of the conscientization of the Catholic laity. Helping the laity to name their oppression is probably the most important thing the theologian can currently do for the church, and the lot falls upon lay theologians because only they share the experience of being lay that is a prerequisite for the effective solidarity that must emerge.

The principal benefit to the church of this new work of the lay theologian is, of course, the conscientization of the laity. But there are some additional values of some consequence. For example, characteristic of the reciprocal enlightenment of both partners in the ethnographic interview, there is the conscientization of the lay theologian herself or himself. While the professional insider is an insider, sharing the lay condition, he or she is a professional, and to that degree less oppressed. (Indeed, the secular world's parallel to clergy/lay is precisely professional/lay.) It has always struck me forcibly how much of the oppression of Catholic laypeople, including many of my undergraduate students, is partially a self-oppression occasioned by ignorance of the history and theology of the tradition.

A second ancillary value to the church is the reinsertion of the lay theologian into the ordinary worshiping community. Again, I speak from my own experience. I am far less likely than my lay counterparts to imagine my soul or salvation endangered by absences, sometimes prolonged, from participation in a parish, and I am far more likely to shop around for a parish in which the levels of lay oppression are less than in most parishes. In these habits, I am representative, I believe, of most lay theologians. If this suspicion is correct, the result will be a separation of lay theologians from exactly those contexts in which lay oppression is most evident, namely, in the vast majority of Catholic parishes. Life on little islands of liberal sanity is comfortable, but it is not the vocation of the lay theologian. It does not stimulate liberation and the emergence of the voice of the laity.

What role might we then envisage for the lay theologian in parish life that will be at once more productive and—sadly but inevitably— more turbulent? We have already said plenty in the preceding pages about the theologian as professional insider and about the paramount importance of being a catalyst in the process of lay conscientization. To identify such activities seems to be rather easier than to find a forum in which these goings-on can take place, for, of course, an official space within the structure of parish life would indicate official approval of whatever officialdom imagines would transpire there. On the other hand, courses or talks on "New Structures for the Church" or "The End of Traditional Clerical Power," useful as they may occasionally be, are not what the lay theologian ought to focus on. The professional insider, let it be remembered, helps to create a space within which individuals can articulate and name their own experience in the church. The role of the lay theologian in the pastoral context, then, as opposed to her or his professional career as teacher, scholar, and so on seems to take on more of the character of therapist. The therapist orchestrates a process of self-discovery and self-healing, but the important work is done precisely by those who are not the therapist. And the ultimate test of the therapy is what goes on outside the therapist's office after the talking is over.

A final value I perceive to such a move toward lay liberation relates to a wider context than the Catholic Church. Having taught liberation theology now for the past twenty years, I have become quite accustomed every semester to the question of the relationship that white, male, heterosexual, relatively affluent people can have to the movements for liberation among the poor, women, African Americans, Hispanics, gays and lesbians, and so on. I have frequently asked myself the same question. While there are things to be said about support and empathy and so on, the truth of the matter is that, without the experience of structural oppression, not much real solidarity is possible. But once we recognize that lay Catholics need to come to an awareness that their own religious tradition structurally oppresses laypeople *as* laypeople, then even white, male, heterosexual, middle- and upper-class men—at least the Catholics—can find a way to become a group in solidarity with these other oppressed groups. Their conscientization as laity in the face of an oppression that is *not* death-dealing can be a first real but modest step in expanding the solidarity of oppressed groups. Of course, they will have to be aware of the many experiences of oppression and of how many of them are much more challenging than their own, and they will have to learn about the double, triple, and even quadruple oppression of some of their fellow citizens and indeed of some of those in the next pew. But the chances that this will happen are greater when the starting point is the experience of lay oppression and the next step is to recognize that among these laity are many who are articulate about the multiple layers of oppression in their own lives. Just as white feminists grew to appreciate the class and race analysis of their black sister womanists, and Latin American male liberation theologians were made aware of their own sexism, so there is hope for the white middle class, just as far as their openness to their own structural oppression is authentic.

HOW DEMOCRATIC
SHOULD THE CHURCH BECOME?

What, finally, of the consequences to the church? I have to confess that I am not much interested myself in novelties like universal suffrage in papal elections or plebiscites on proposed new doctrines. These may or may not come and may or may not be valuable. The first and most important development from laypeople rejecting their oppression will be to release the experience of 99 percent of the people of the church as a resource for religious reflection on the doctrinal and ethical issues of our time. The validity and representative character of one's experience and the quality of one's reflection upon it, rather than membership in a particular caste or even in a professional society of theologians, become the experiential basis for a religious reflection that will feed into the formation of authoritative teaching.

Lay liberation will not occur in the substitution of the Catholic Theological Society of America for the U.S. Catholic Conference, but will
occur only when the conditions exist in which the people can and will
speak for themselves and can and will be heard.

While universal suffrage in papal elections may not be the answer,
there is no doubt that it is time for the church to begin to democra-
tize many of its processes. The focus should in the first instance be on
what happens at the grass roots, in the parochial or base community
structures of the church. The parish is where almost all lay Catholics
are most closely tied in to the church and where what happens affects
them the most closely. A papal encyclical, for good or ill, is not going
to have the impact of a letter from the bishop, and the bishop's letter
is dwarfed in importance by the inspiring or challenging words of the
ordained minister. But perhaps more importantly, grass-roots change
should come first because it is only through this kind of incremental
transformation that the structures of the church at the higher levels
will be forced to bend to pressure. Self-policing systems always close
ranks to protect themselves, and the church is no exception to this
rule, based as it is on observations of human behavior. Even when, by
some miraculous intervention of the Holy Spirit, a John XXIII is
elected to the highest office, the system will do all that it can to
smother the genuine *aggiornamento* that he inspires. In the final
chapter of the book, I will lay out one model of how such changes
might take place in the church.

Thinking about how to effect real change in the church, first at the
grass-roots level and then later at higher levels, brings us back to Yves
Congar. Congar was always attentive to the need to think of the
church as a community of life, and he had some trenchant observations to make on the importance of the democratization of church
structures. In particular, he wrote of the need to revisit past practices
in the church in which the people enjoyed much greater participation
in the day-to-day management of the church. Congar went into great
detail on these questions in a lengthy chapter of *Lay People in the
Church* entitled "The Laity and the Church's Kingly Function."[14] He
rejected the argument that, since kings and princes used to exercise
considerable authority over ecclesiastical affairs, that authority can be
smoothly transferred to the laity today, since they are in our democratic world the modern equivalent of monarchs. But, says Congar,

"the historical bases invoked cannot be denied" (p. 243). This issue is especially important at a time in the church when we can trace many of the ills that affect the ministry to the career structure that is fostered within the clerical culture, and we need to look closely at Congar's conclusions.

Congar examines lay involvement in ecclesiastical affairs under five headings. First he looks at the part laypeople played in the election of bishops. While they did at times exercise some prerogatives "through usurpation," the whole thing led to such corruption that the church was careful to stamp out all lay connections with episcopal elections. Congar is quite clear that there has never been any "power of ecclesiastical rule" among the laity, but his regret is that false claims made for such power have overshadowed a different and important principle, that "of consent, as a principle, not of structure but of life, as a concrete law of all the great acts of ecclesial life, beginning with that of designation to the highest offices" (p. 247). The correspondence of St. Cyprian in the mid-third century, for example, makes clear that the "suffrage of the people" is a constitutive element in the selection of a bishop, along with the consent of other bishops, good recommendations by the clergy, and the judgment of God. Indeed, the consent of the laity is "the preferred principle of pontifical and canonical tradition," lying behind such statements as that of Pope Celestine I (d. 432) that "a bishop must not be imposed on the people against their will" (p. 245). While it has always been the case, Congar explains, that the actual *ordination* of the bishop is undertaken by the bishops alone, the *designation* of the best-suited candidate is a work in which the collaboration of the people is deemed essential.

Congar comes to similar conclusions in considering, in the second place, the role of laity in the councils of the church. While there have been fluctuations in that role, from lay signatories to conciliar decrees at one extreme (Council of Orange [529]) to absolutely no lay involvement of any kind whatsoever at the other (Vatican I [1869–70]), the general rule has been that laypeople would be involved in councils in a number of different capacities. This practice is licensed by the very first council of Jerusalem (51), where the nonordained had roles of welcoming, consultation, and the dissemination of the council's conclusions. In subsequent history, while the people were not always consulted about everything, they were frequently consulted where their expertise suggested it (in the early church, decisions about the lapsed; at the Council of Siena in 1423, on questions of marriage). In addition to the consultation, laypeople consistently had important roles of consent and publicity. As St. Cyprian wrote to his priests and deacons, "I have made it a rule from the beginning of my episcopate to decide nothing without your advice and the people's agreement" (p. 248). Congar's conclusions are that laypeople, once more, have no role in voting on doctrinal issues, but their consent and cooperation are vital to the living efficacy of what has been decided.

The third issue that Congar discusses is the very real power that kings and emperors have exercised in the history of the church, at times—like Charlemagne—truly ruling the church and often acting like popes within their own countries. Of course, as Congar points out, this role for rulers was a product of Christendom, of that real or attempted symbiosis of temporal and spiritual powers. And the emphasis was most definitely on power. But the Protestant Reformation and the autonomy of the secular that has followed it have meant that the symbiosis has been destroyed. The consequence of this is wholly positive, says Congar. The church is thrown back on her own spiritual resources, power and force are laid aside in favor of "effective action . . . through devotedness." This is an exercise of spiritual kingship (we might say "servant leadership") and not one of power. Although Congar does not mention it at this point in his argument, we might add that it was precisely in the overcoming of the symbiosis of temporal and spiritual, in the rebirth of the secular, that the modern theological idea of the laity is born.

Fourth, Congar looks at the role of the laity in determining the life of the community. He isolates two important functions, that of custom and of "initiative from below." But his conclusions are disappointingly negative. Though the laity do indeed shape the community through the force of custom, Congar bows to the 1917 Code of Canon Law's determination that "all the obligatory or legal worth of custom comes from above, from the approval given by lawful superiors . . . . *Properly speaking, there is no law-from-below in the Church.*" Congar warns against too close an analogy between custom in the body politic and in the church. In the Middle Ages, he says, there was recognized in custom "a product of that sovereignty which in the first place resides in the body politic itself," but the ecclesial order doesn't work like this. The secular pattern is for the body politic to give itself an order by which it organizes itself, but in the church authority is given, logically anterior to the fact. In other words, the hierarchical principle precedes the community (p. 257).

Much earlier in this book we had occasion to take issue with Congar over the weakness of arguing from the anteriority of apostleship over the community to which it is related. We also saw Congar himself coming to some realization that such a separation was unwise. Here we see a clear consequence of that kind of thinking, one that equates the church with a given order of governance. So Congar can conclude that "to have applied materially to the Church what is favourable to the community in old Roman law or in Aristotle would have been to dissolve the Catholic order" (p. 257). Perhaps. But here it may be salutary to recall Suenens's preference for thinking of the church's order as having three interrelated components, one of which is democratic. While apostolic authority is never to be rejected, there is no doubt that the ways in which it has been seen operative throughout history have always shown some relationship to the changing approaches to secular governance (Suenens's point again). The church cannot be considered exempt from the impact of the consistent drive toward democracy that has marked the last three hundred years. The weakness of Congar's position at this point is evident in his conclusions. Attempting to soften the subordination of initiative from below to canon law, he suggests that the kind of authority that ought to intervene in the management of custom is not legislative but "fatherly" authority. If there is one kind of authority that church leaders should refrain from invoking today, one understanding of authority that has had its day in ecclesial leadership, it is the fatherly, paternal, or paternalistic kind. The infantilization of the laity is the subtlest form of oppression.

Finally, Congar turns to the church's executive power. Here again he is forceful in asserting that "the Church's constitution is fundamentally hierarchical, not democratic" (p. 260). But this does not mean that laypeople cannot exercise real authority within the church, as in the example he offers of the role of advocate in ecclesiastical trials, or as we might adduce with our more recent knowledge, of the extensive role of laypeople in diocesan tribunals, as chancellors of dioceses, pastoral associates, and so on. He even mentions the interesting

questions that emerge from the fact that canon law envisages the possibility of a layman being elected pope. While this goes beyond the
issue of lay role in the church, since the elected person would proceed
almost immediately to ordination and consecration as a bishop, there
is one challenge for theologians. How do we explain the supreme
jurisdiction that the individual would possess from the moment of
election, before any ordination? Would this not in principle disconnect jurisdiction from ordination? Congar sidesteps the question,
however, to make some important concluding remarks on the general
question.

In sum, Congar addresses the real but limited role of lay "power"
in the church by returning to his beloved distinction between structure and life. The structure of the church is hierarchical, while the life
of the church is communitarian. Although in this particular book he
is handicapped by his commitment to the notion that apostolicity precedes community—and we have already said enough in criticism of
that particular weakness—the later healthier turn to an understanding
of the church as always a structured community fits smoothly with the
same distinction. It only precludes thinking of the church as possessed
of two orders, a clerical structure and a lay community. Everyone is
part of the community, and everyone belongs to the same structured
community. From the earliest days of the church all the texts are "at
the same time both resolutely hierarchical and indefeasibly communitarian" (p. 263). There can be no church without apostolic authority,
a legitimate bishop who is responsible for preaching, celebration, and
decisions. But the same texts, says Congar, also cannot envisage the
church without the consent of the community. The robust active consent and cooperation of the laypeople are essential to the life of the
church. In this way, the laity are effective in the church without actually possessing "any powers properly speaking." For Congar, the lay
role in "kingly power" lies in the force of public opinion, which in the
church is a Spirit-guided activity. Public opinion, of course, when not
directed toward trivialities, is nothing other than the *sensus ecclesiae*
that Vatican II was to declare to be one of the three forms of infallibility of the church. It lies behind the whole theology of reception and
the canonical notion of dead letter. When it is the overwhelming sense
of the church that a teaching is unacceptable, then it does not possess
the force of teaching. The Spirit-led *sensus ecclesiae* cannot come into

conflict with another Spirit-led authority. The Spirit cannot be at war with itself. Here lies the theological necessity for magisterial teaching to take account of the belief of the church. Here is the explanation for why any exercise of papal infallibility is a declaration of what the faith of the church has been and is, and can never be an attempt to move the church to a position that it has not previously occupied. Here is the role of consent. Teaching may be legitimately proclaimed by the institution but is not the voice of the Spirit if not incorporated into the life of the community through its consent (p. 264).

If consent is important, so is the withholding of consent or the removal of consent previously given. While one can jump too readily to conclusions that one favors, there is little doubt that such withholding and removal of consent play a large part in the life of the church. To take an uncontroversial example, it seems very likely that the consent of the community to the acceptability of slavery was withdrawn before the formal prohibition of slavery. Here the community challenged not only ecclesial teaching but also the words of St. Paul. In today's world, there seems every reason to believe that the community does not consent to the continued institutional insistence on the immorality of contraception. While it is perhaps less sure, there is some evidence to suggest that the institution and the community are at a standoff over the mandatory celibacy of the clergy and the exclusion of women from ordained ministry.

Congar had little to say about the withholding of consent, though it is surely implied in the lengthy discussion of the conditions for consent. His arguments for keeping the laity entirely out of "care of the Church's temporalities" also are not persuasive. He admits that lay involvement "could be a great help to the clergy" and that it would lead the laity to be better informed and more concerned for the maintenance of the church. But these values pale, he ends weakly, beside the "radical necessity that this task of the church should be, for its essential part, in the hands of the clergymen." At the same time, he is quite insistent on the importance of making use of lay ability and enthusiasm. Lay voice is essential, and it cannot always be polite. In words that predict much of the lay response to clerical abuse of minors, Congar paints a lively picture of lay zeal:

> There is always the possibility of their doing it from time to time, when, in a sudden access of enthusiasm, they jump the barriers of protocol,

and at their risk and peril cross the zone of silence and dignity behind which the priestly hierarchy too often isolates itself in order to protect the prestige of its authority and the stability of tradition. (p. 267)

A true democracy has far more to do with an interlocking pattern of consultation and consent than it does with an exclusive focus on the ballot box. We know full well that the very existence of elections does not of itself testify to the vibrancy of democratic life. To test for democracy it makes much more sense to ask about the health of the mediating structures in society that encourage citizens to participate in the formation of public opinion, to examine the quality of public discourse, and to scrutinize the accountability of leadership to the collective voice of those they serve. Some societies, like our own here in the United States, guarantee universal suffrage—even if they sometimes make it difficult in practice for certain sectors of society—while they place enormous pressure on the capacity of the electorate to make informed decisions. The rhetoric of public service is sometimes drowned out by the voice of special interests. Lip service to the democratic process is focused on the vote. A livelier and better-informed electorate is not in the interests of the corporate giants that increasingly control our destinies.

To make the church into a true democracy is not the same process as purifying any particular secular democracy. Congar is right that the church has always been a structured community and that given in its structure is a particular conception of leadership without which it would no longer be the church. Episcopal leadership is indispensable to the Catholic Church. But we are not necessarily tied to any particular understanding of the way in which episcopal oversight is conducted. Peter and James would not recognize the church of Rome. The rules for appointing bishops today bear little resemblance to those enunciated in the First Letter to Timothy. Bishops were expected to be married then, but may not be married now. Such differences are obviously inessential to the office of bishop. Some of us believe that the same may be true of gender. Similarly, the offices of priest and deacon have undergone innumerable modifications over the centuries, and there seems little reason to believe that no further changes will occur. Priests and deacons enable the better functioning of the episcopate, directed as it should be to the health of the community and not simply to the maintenance of particular historically

conditioned forms of the institution. The presbyterate and the diaconate ought to be almost endlessly flexible in form, provided that
they retain the central role of aides to episcopal oversight of the life of
the community. Unlike apostolicity, they cannot be traced to Jesus
himself.

While the church is not quite like a secular democracy, many of the
signs of health are common to both communities. To be specific, we
should test the health of the ecclesial community in ways analogous to
those we use to examine the health of the body politic. A healthy
church will possess lively mediating structures, a strong public forum
of ideas, and a clear conduit between those in positions of leadership
and the members of the community. This conduit must be a two-way
street. The community needs to have confidence in leadership's willingness to listen to its voice and incorporate that voice into decision
making. Contrariwise, leadership needs to be truly aware of its
accountability to the people it serves. While the church is not as open
to the depredations of the commercial interests that threaten secular
democracy, its leadership may be just as likely as the U.S. Congress to
protect the way of life it sees as its own and to close ranks against those
who would question elements of the system. It may not be as concerned about term limits or soft money, but it fights hard against
efforts at internal reform of ecclesial bureaucracy. Even popes struggle to manage the Curia!

RESCUING THE CHURCH

We can now see that the liberation of the laity from the systemic
oppression under which they suffer can be effected in the name of the
Spirit that gives life to the whole church. It is now clearly acceptable
to use the language of democratization. Moreover, as we outline some
of the steps that need to occur, it will become apparent, if it is not so
clear already, that the liberation of the laity is also the liberation of the
entire church. In Congar's terms, the liberation of the laity consists in
the reassertion of the pole of community, in the face of the excessive
focus on the institutional pole that still marks the life of the church,
forty years after Vatican II. A scholar as careful as Avery Dulles has
noted the unhealthy dominance of the model of institution over the

other ways of thinking of the church and the need for it to be put in its rightful place, as one dimension among others.[15] Managing this adjustment, however, is difficult. In the old insight of revolutionary theory, true structural change begins at the grass roots. In other words, do not look to the hierarchical element to restore the healthy symbiosis of structure and community. Look rather, in Congar's formulations, for the community to exercise its Spirit-given role of consent and withdrawal of consent, in the name of restoring balance. As Pius XII perhaps surprisingly wrote about the presence of public opinion in the church, "She is a living body, and something would be lacking to her life were there no public opinion in it, a want for which the blame would rest on pastors and faithful."[16] Thanks to the work of liberation theology over the past thirty years, we know something about how to proceed with the liberation of the laity. First, it will be necessary for the laity to take charge of their own liberation. It cannot be the work of bishops or priests, though they can certainly assist. The primary way they can help is by standing aside. If the laity have been marginalized in the church of the past, and they surely have, then they must claim the center of the stage for a time. Those who have occupied that center stage can stand aside willingly or be pushed aside. That is up to them. We also have to face the fact, however, that the extraordinarily long-lived culture of lay passivity will be difficult to overcome. Laypeople in large numbers will not want more responsibility or an opportunity for voice. Here, perhaps, ordained leadership has a role to play, insisting, as it stands aside, that passivity is not an option. Once again, the Vatican documents could be adduced in support of the need for a more active lay presence in the church.

If the time has come for the laity to claim center stage, we have to remember that center stage does not necessarily mean limelight. It is center stage at the grass-roots level. In Latin America the phenomenon of base Christian communities was born and nurtured in response to two needs. There were not enough priests to minister to the people in the regular structure of parishes, and there was a great need for a mostly passive people to find their voice. While the shortage of priests is not yet critical in this country, it is growing. And while the average Catholic American layperson is not the unlettered peasant of Guatemala or Brazil, she has not been accustomed to speaking out in the context of making responsible decisions for the future of the local church. It is one thing to criticize. We are good at that. It is quite another to construct an alternative vision of the way the church needs to move forward. But given the need to find voice in the context of the local church, the model of base Christian communities needs to be fostered. It may be in our American context that we need not turn to the kind of tiny groups that were characteristic of the Latin American church. Perhaps parish-sized forums would work, though only if they are partially subdivided into working groups within which everyone can indeed have voice. Within the communities, however they are structured, people can engage in processes of discernment, working out the way in which the scripture moves them to take action to change the church. Empowered by the word of God and the Holy Spirit, they can begin to take steps to move from being objects of ecclesial history to subjects of their own history.

In the process of communal discernment that needs to take place, there is a special role for the lay theologian. Ada María Isasi-Díaz, in her work on *mujerista* theology, has described the theologian as the "professional insider." This is particularly true of the theologian who is a layperson. He or she is at one and the same time a professionally trained theologian and a member of the oppressed class of laypersons. It is the theologian's right and responsibility, as a member of the oppressed class, to engage in the work of discernment on the same footing as any other member of the community. Being a theologian may make one much more aware of the dynamics and history of the present context, but it does not make one any less structurally oppressed. A lifetime's study and teaching never bring the lay theologian any closer to a formal role in the formulation of church teaching. But the lay theologian as theologian does have a particular service to perform for the discerning community. He or she is the guardian of the tradition. He or she is able to help keep the community honest to that tradition, not in a slavish repetition but in faithfulness to the dynamic unfolding of the Christian community's own self-understanding through time. While the base Christian community must discern the path the church must take into the future, the theologian needs to be ready to remind the community that it remains within the Catholic tradition.

The second emphasis of this raising of lay consciousness must be an orientation to action. The question for the community is never, What is the scripture or the Spirit calling us to think and feel? Our thinking and feeling are directed toward discerning what the scripture and the Spirit are calling us to do. Obviously, the decisions of the local community can only ever directly affect that same small number of believers, and some decisions lie beyond the authority of the local community. For example, it would seem to me that the local community could certainly determine things like the ways in which its finances are managed and the causes to which it is ready to contribute. It should certainly feel free to set up its own system of religious education in the way it sees fit. It should be empowered to determine who occupies its pulpit. It should definitely make decisions about the stands it will take in social-justice initiatives within the local community. But it does not belong to the community to ordain its own ministers or to determine how the doctrine of the real presence of Christ in the Eucharist will be understood within its own ranks. On the other hand, it may well have very pronounced views about ordination or real presence, and it certainly has the right to express those views. The logic of the base community structure is then that it will be smallest building block in a newly created church-wide pattern of consultative assemblies. This is what happened in Latin America, and it is the inevitable outcome of giving the people voice.

When such structures as we have been describing come into existence, there is always an encounter with leadership at every level. In the base community itself, classically understood, the leader emerges naturally from the group. But at the parish level there are ordained ministers to be taken into account; at the diocesan level there is the bishop; and at the level of the universal church, there is the pope himself. The question arises, then, of the precise relationship between the discerning community and the ordained ministers, who have traditionally been understood as the ones who lead the church, who make all its decisions, who govern in the name of Christ. As a more educated and more insistent laity emerges through this church-wide process, a potentially explosive situation is created. Neither lay demands nor ecclesiastical fiat can be the last word in the decisions of the community. How, then, do we proceed?

From the perspective of the bishops, the process must go something like this: listening/consultation, discernment, decision, listening for consent. The lay approach involves a similar set of activities in a somewhat different order: discernment, voice, listening to decisions, consent. Clearly, this two-way street demands restraint and respect on both sides for the mutual responsibility of both ordained ministers and laypeople for the life and the future of the church. Leadership in a democratic society is based on the principles of consent and account-ability. In our age, when all forms of governance, even in the church, will be colored by the clear human preference for democratic forms of social organization, consent and accountability will mark the life of the church.

Here in the first years of the twenty-first century in North America, the crisis of leadership in the church occasioned by clerical sexual abuse of children has highlighted in a particularly tragic manner the absence of consent and accountability in the day-to-day governance of the institution. Bishops have not thought of themselves as account-able to the people, or even to civil law. They have worked in secret to protect the system, and they have not sought the consent that they need from the community. As the problems became more obvious, and the behavior of some bishops came to be seen as scandalous, the laity effectively withheld consent. The changes that have occurred and will occur in the workings of the church that will prevent this kind of abuse of authority in the future will be directly attributable to the pressure of withheld consent, to what Pius XII rightly called the force of ecclesial public opinion.

It is a pity that it takes a crisis of this magnitude, with such suffer-ing for so many people, to remind us of how our church ought to behave. Vatican II was clear about relations between the ordained ministry and the laity, though its words still frequently fall on deaf ears. Let us hear them once more, as we look to our next chapter and a thorough examination of the collaboration of ordained ministers and laypeople in the mission of the church:

> Bishops, parish priests and other priests of the secular and religious clergy will remember that the right and duty of exercising the aposto-late are common to all the faithful, whether clerics or lay; and that in the building up of the church the laity too have parts of their own to play. For this reason they will work as brothers with the laity in the church and for the church, and will have a special concern for the laity in their apostolic activities. (*Apostolicam Actuositatem* 25)[17]

7

Mission in the (Post) Modern World

What the Church becomes in any age is never determined solely by the principles that constitute its distinctive life, but always by an interpretation and realization of them which actively engage the challenges of the larger society and culture.

—*Joseph A. Komonchak*

T HE CHURCH'S INNER LIFE and its external "missionary" face are two sides of the same coin. While the mission in a sense follows from what the church is deemed to be, mission as what the church is for has an impact on how the community understands itself. The mission is certainly the mission of this particular community, but the community is what it is in order to be faithful to this particular mission. Because there is such a close relationship between communion and mission, we have to treat them together, bearing in mind that in some ways communion precedes mission, and at times mission dictates the shape that communion must take. In the present chapter we shall have to move back and forth between the two realities, now focused on mission, now on communion. The reader will need to anticipate this approach.

COMMUNION ECCLESIOLOGY AND VATICAN II

We have to begin by returning to Vatican II once again, this time to look at its understanding of the church as communion. In reality, this is not such a difficult project. If there is one indubitable fact of con-

220

ciliar ecclesiology, it is that the ruling image is that of the People of God. This in a nutshell is communion ecclesiology. The church is a people; this is the horizontal dimension of communion, waiting to be unpacked. But it is not just any people. It is also a people *of God*. There lies the vertical dimension of communion with the divine, but it is clearly a vertical relationship between God and the whole church, and this is what keeps it Catholic and keeps it social. The individual's relationship to God takes place within the context of the community of the faithful, not in isolation from it; and the community is focused and centered through the celebration of the Eucharist, which is the moment in which the human–divine relationship is also most intensely realized. Thus, the horizontal and vertical dimensions of communion are both always present, always related to each other.

While there would seem to be no denying that the roots of communion ecclesiology lie in the image of the People of God, there is still plenty of work to do in drawing out the practical implications of this conviction. Here is where the various communion ecclesiologies go in their separate directions. They each offer slightly different answers to the same question: What does it take for fellowship among Christians and communion with God to be real in today's world? Building an ecclesiology today is then at least as much a matter of examining the world as it is of poring over scripture and tradition. Again, Vatican II says much the same thing in the insistence of *Gaudium et Spes* on "reading the signs of the times."[1] If we are not attuned to the way the Spirit is speaking to us through the events of the world and the people with whom we are surrounded, our religious reflection will be another exercise in abstraction.

Jewish thinkers will sometimes say things like, "All Jews agree that God spoke once on Mount Sinai, but Jews cannot agree about what God meant when God spoke on Mt. Sinai." Communion ecclesiology is a bit like this. All Catholic theologians agree that the vision of the church since Vatican II is one of the primacy of "communion." But there are almost as many interpretations of what this might mean as there are theologians to offer their views. In effect, the well-documented susceptibility of the text of Vatican II to the ideological preferences of its readers is at work once again. If everyone agrees that the church is a communion, and if that belief exercises little or no control over how the idea is cashed in in terms of the daily life of the church, what use is it? Wouldn't it be better just to skip the statement and get on with adjudicating the differences between competing ecclesiologies? Or is it perhaps the case that the commitment to the communion word helps it to act as a kind of glue to hold together the potentially fissiparous theological community?

Dennis Doyle's recent study of types of communion ecclesiology illustrates the problem very well.[2] A committed centrist, Doyle sees a gluelike value in the idea of communion ecclesiology and thinks, perhaps rightly, that it is the central organizing principle of the vision of the church in the documents of Vatican II. Early in the book, he comments that communion ecclesiology is "an attempt to move beyond the merely juridical and institutional understandings by emphasizing the mystical, sacramental, and historical dimensions of the Church."[3] Here too he is correct, and scholars as various as Avery Dulles, Joseph Ratzinger, and Leonardo Boff would concur in his judgment. But what follows does depend enormously on whether or not it is the mystical, sacramental, or historical dimension of the church that the theologian wishes to stress in preference to that of the institution. Of course, no worthwhile theologian would be willing to deny that all three elements need to find their place in a theology of the church. But the particular weight that is given to each of the three leads to different schools of thought and to the successive chapters of Doyle's very helpful book.[4] Furthermore, it is not simply the preference for mystical, sacramental, or historical that makes a difference. A historical approach can lead to the political commitments of liberation theology or to a reassertion of the historical primacy of the institution. A mystical approach can wrap the church in the life of the Trinity or focus on the institution as some vital lymph system of the mystical body. A sacramental approach can attend more closely to the liturgical realities or to the mission of the church in the world.

In general, communion ecclesiology sees the church as the community of disciples of Jesus, called into being by God and led by the Spirit. Who doesn't, one might ask, and therein lies much of the problem with the term. Who would deny discipleship, divine calling, or the Spirit? No one, of course. Yet the church has also meant other things in its history, and in a way communion ecclesiology is better identified by what it does not stress than by what it does. If we look again at the ecclesiology of *Lumen Gentium*, we note an emphasis on biblical models, on the idea of the People of God as the fundamental image of the church, on a tendency to be inclusive rather than exclusive, and on an instrumentalization rather than an idealization of the pyramidal model of the church. Communion ecclesiology in whatever hands locates the heart of the church in the life of the community and sees the structure as an instrument of the communion, not as its organizing principle. Thus the bishops of Vatican II chose to move away from a solely hierarchical exposition of the church, though the primacy of Peter, the collegiality of the bishops, and the *sensus fidelium* make clear that different responsibilities adhere to the various constituencies within the church.

Although there is a certain common enemy to the various manifestations of communion ecclesiology, namely, defining the church as an institution, the reality remains that some expositions of communion are better than others. In particular, we need to recognize that if communion is explicated in isolation from mission, then the particular mix of the mystical, the sacramental, the historical, and the social that appears in any given version of communion ecclesiology will simply be one theologian's favorite items from the theological buffet. What the church *is* is intimately connected to what the church *is for*. Just as a theologian cannot simply make things up in ignorance or defiance of the tradition, so she also cannot treat ecclesiology as a closed system within which we define the nature of the church in abstraction from the world in which it must live out its mission. Because communion is for mission, reading the signs of the times is a vitally important dimension of ecclesiology. And of course that the church is a product of the call of God to share in the divine life is a truth that no theologian can afford to undervalue. But how this vertical call is manifest in the horizontal realities depends not only on the precise mix of mystical, sacramental, historical, and social that we imagine the church to be, but also on our picture of the world, which should lead us to formulate that precise mix. In terms of Vatican II, we cannot treat *Lumen Gentium* in isolation from *Gaudium et Spes*.

Before we turn to our exercise in reading the signs of the times, let us conclude these reflections on communion ecclesiology with five modifying thoughts. In the first place, we need to think about institution relative to communion. It must be clearly understood that while the church in history will always have an institutional dimen-

sion, the precise form that the institution takes is subject to the vary-
ing fortunes of historical accident. The purpose of the institutional
element is to enable the daily life of the community of faith. So it does
not matter whether we are looking at the church mystically, historically, socially, or sacramentally; our focus will never be on the juridical
structures of church life. The meaning of the church lies in that which
is enabled, not that which—when it works as it should—enables the
daily life of grace. The irony—and often the tragedy, of course—is that
for so many it is the institutional element that is primarily envisaged
when "the Church" is called to mind. Still more unproductively, it is
often the particular contemporary and thus temporary historical form
of institution upon which we focus. But let us recall Congar's comment, which we touched upon in chapter 2, that the structural element of the church is destined to come to an end in the reign of God,
while the communion persists into all eternity. While this says nothing
about the historical necessity of the institution, it certainly implies a
priority to the element of communion. Structure is for life, and life is
not for structure.

The second point to make is that our perspective here is that of the
laity. Obviously, the laity exists in the same church as the ordained
ministry, but that does not mean that they always experience the
church in quite the same way. The clergy, intentionally or not, see the
church from the perspective of the institution that they represent and
will continue to do so at least for as long as they do not share the same
experience of life as the laity, with the same tensions, pressures, anxi-
eties, hopes, and joys. But although the laity often manifest an unhealthy dependence on the institution, laypeople's experience of the
church is primarily of the element of life, not of structure. In ways that
are not always healthy, even, the teaching authority of the church, its
canon law, its complex sets of sanctions and prohibitions, have much
less impact upon the Catholic in the pew than do the rhythms of worship. At the same time, where the institution does impinge on the life
of the laity, it is often in a negative way. Communion can come to
seem something that the institution often impedes, though clearly this
is not the purpose of the institution. In all probability, this is because
we think of community today as an important expression of human
freedom and equality. Just as we have abandoned any belief in the
rightness of class or hierarchy within the political community, so we

find it hard to continue to admit the hierarchical principle within our church community. While respect for office continues in both the secular and the church community, it is much less important than the respect which people earn. Laypeople in the church may want very much to admire and respect their leaders, but they are ready to withdraw this respect when circumstances require it. Bishops who have impeded the investigation of the sexual exploitation of young people by predatory members of the clergy are one ready example. They may remain in office for a time, but they are no longer leaders.

Third, the church must not be afraid to talk the language of the Spirit. Communion ecclesiology in its more vibrant manifestations is open to the power of the Spirit at work in its midst and sees the Spirit as that which calls and keeps the community in being. Any mention of the Spirit is alarming to the keepers of the institution, and always has been, since the Spirit of God is not susceptible of bureaucratic managing. It is also true that people can claim the Spirit's authority to validate their own point of view, so there is no doubt that discerning the Spirit is an important ecclesial function. But for too long the institution has reserved to itself the discernment of the Spirit, when in reality it is a work of the whole community. Vatican II's stress on the *sensus fidelium* draws attention to the role of the whole people empowered by the Spirit (*LG 12*). We have talked of this function earlier as the consent of the laity that brings life to the teaching of the magisterium. The Spirit is almost by definition impossible to contain within any bureaucratic structure, but fills the life of the church, animating it, challenging it to do more in God's name, and sometimes calling it to account. Though some wrote off Cardinal Suenens when he turned in the 1970s to the work of charismatic renewal, it has always seemed to me a logical step for him to take. The council's vision of the church, which he did so much to shape, is certainly one of Spirit-filled communion.

Fourth, we must reiterate the symbiosis of communion and mission. While communion can be a cozy notion upon which to meditate, the validity of the particular expression of communion in the church is to be found in the quality of that same community's commitment to its mission. The praxis of communion is visible in the church's faithfulness to its mission; the praxis of mission is directly connected to the understanding of communion. If what we mean by "communion" is an inward-looking, self-congratulatory, and fearful huddling together against the forces of modernity—the "communion" of the nineteenth-century church—then "mission" will mean little more than the periodic excoriation of the "outside" world. But if communion means a generous and loving association of free and faithful children of God, then the dynamic excess of love, without which it is not love at all, spills over into a mission to the whole human race, one marked by a generous sharing of the knowledge that God wills to save the world. There will be a consistency between the life of the community, the communion within which it lives, and the objectives sought in its fulfillment of God's call to proclaim the coming of the reign of God. On the one hand, the communion is that which strengthens God's faithful people to be the presence of God in the world. On the other hand, the public face of communion is a primary element in securing the respect of that secular world which is the place wherein the mission is carried out. We must feel and know that the community supports our mission, and our mission demands certain things of the community of which we are a part.

Finally, the relation of mission and communion must be complicated further by the introduction of the important idea of witness. While we have been at some pains to say that there must be a close relationship between the realization of communion and the commitment to mission, our perspective has been from within the community of faith. When we look at the church from the standpoint of the secular world, the importance of witness is immediately obvious. Traditionally, people talking of "witness to the gospel" have meant something theologically correct but pastorally unhelpful. Of course, there are times when it is important for the church to stand up for its values, most especially when it is sure of its ground and the values are unfashionable. But too often this kind of witness envisages an uncommunicative and even rigid stance. Better by far to think of the witness of the early church which according to Tertullian led onlookers to exclaim, "See how these Christians love one another!"[5]

Effective witness to the gospel in the world of today must be a praxis that draws both admiration and understanding from those who do not share the Christian story. Of course there will be times when witness will be to hard truths that the world will not want to hear. But precisely because we will want even those difficult stands to be received, the everyday witness cannot be of that character. Our world values integrity, courage, and participation, and rejects hypocrisy, weakness, and isolation. The point at which the world meets the church is in the church's mission, in its active presence in the world. It is important that the mission is seen as one that shares a common purpose with the rest of humanity. Only then will it lead to an appreciation for the form of communion out of which it emerges, and then only if the world can perceive a connectedness between what we preach and what we practice. Above all, then, effective witness lies in demonstrating that work in the world is an outgrowth of our faith, and that our life in communion leads naturally to the mission in which we are engaged. The world will rightly reject any lack of integrity here, and mission will consequently be ineffectual. Scandals (literally, stumbling blocks) in the public face of the church have much less to do with proclaiming values that may be unfashionable than with proclaiming values that we fail to live by. Few, I think, are turned away from the church because of the celibacy of the clergy, even if they are not persuaded of the value of celibacy, but many are turned away by public failures to live celibate lives. Few, I think, would reject the church because there are authoritarian bishops, but many are rightly turned off when church leaders who are supposed to proclaim a gospel of truth, love, and freedom are found to be moved far more by political imperatives to shore up the face of the institution. Effective witness, then, though it involves the specificity of gospel faith, must be built upon a base of ordinary human integrity.

READING THE SIGNS OF THE TIMES

None of us needs an expert to tell us what the world is like, but making sense of what we see is something with which we may need assistance. We experience the world every day—we read about it in newspapers and journals and we watch it on television, but we need help to interpret what we see. On the one hand, it is hard for us as individuals to know enough to make informed judgments based on our powers of perception alone. On the other, we may suffer from our own narrowness of viewpoint. It is human nature to interpret the world in ways that promote our own interests or maintain us in what we imagine to be our rightful place in the world. It is difficult for us to get enough critical distance from our own place in the world so that we can take a more objective view or try to view the world through the eyes of those so differently situated from ourselves.

As we try to read the signs of the times, we have to be careful not to focus on details that concern us, but to search out the underlying structures that shape history. We may and should be concerned about any of the following: drugs, world poverty, climate change, environmental collapse, terrorism, public health, and many other major problems of our world. But the mission of the church cannot be tied to any one of these concerns, and, indeed, the church is involved in one way or another in efforts to address all of them. They are all, too, signs of the times, but reading them is a matter of looking deeper, trying to isolate the common element to all and the primary common cause, if there is one. Obviously, they represent threats to our world and to the quality and even viability of human life on earth. They are evidences of antihuman elements in creation, of what might in earlier times have simply been called negativity or evil or sin. Identify the evil, find the sinners who cause it, and speak out against them—this might well have been the preferred course of action. It is not so simple any more.

One contribution that the secular world has made to the church's powers of analysis is the idea of structural or systemic oppression, which has been taken up in at least some sectors of the church in the notion of "structural sin." Call it oppression or call it sin, the term draws attention to the objective evil that is caused in the world by the existence of formal and informal structures for which no one individual or people is directly responsible. Slavery is a formal structure, gender discrimination is an informal structure (though it would be a formal structure in societies which legislate the subordination of women). But in both cases, while it is people who commit the acts of bias and oppression that realize slavery and the subordination of women, it is the existence of these structures that enable and even legitimate the oppression. Structures can be sinful, even if it is not possible always to identify the sinner. Even living unthinkingly within such structures can be sinful, although the individual may not consciously or directly engage in discrimination and may even proclaim that he or she is "not a racist" or "not sexist." It is among these structures of oppression that we will find the root causes of the antihuman element in our world. And it is the oppressive structures that lie so deep we do not see them, or those that actually present themselves to us as values, that our reading of the signs of the times must attempt to uncover.

The mission of the church is to proclaim the gospel. It is also to call the secular world to its own deepest selfhood as a human community. These are not competing goals. Indeed, the latter is contained within the former, as an indispensable component without which "proclaiming the gospel" is incomplete. This requires both the deepening of human solidarity and a concomitant growth in the sense of the whole, that is, of a common human purpose. Classically, the task of engaging in solidarity with all human beings in building a more human world has been referred to as a *praeparatio evangelica*, a sort of "softening-up" for the full gospel. Eschatologically, this is no doubt the case, but in a world of extraordinary pluralism, preaching the gospel means concentrating on justice, against what is antihuman. The mission of the church must be conducted in categories that can be received by those who are not immediately open to evangelization in the normal sense of the word. When we use the language of human solidarity and common human purpose, it is communion that we are talking about. Solidarity or fellowship among human beings is "horizontal" communion. Our mission is to promote human solidarity and to encourage the human community to look beyond short-term gains and narrow scales of values to the true well-being of the world that is our home. Success in this common purpose can only lead toward uncovering a "sense of the whole," something that requires recognition of some deeper value or standard to which the world must aspire. This is the relation of the whole to its ground, which we can express theologically as "vertical" communion. In theological parlance, solidarity among human beings leads to solidarity with God.

If the mission of the church is always "to call the world to its own deepest selfhood as a human community," in any given time and place this mission will be carried out in somewhat different ways. When the church did not speak out against but encouraged slavery, promoted anti-Semitism, and furthered the subjugation of women, it was failing catastrophically in its mission. While the gospel does not contain explicit condemnations of any of these social obscenities, the logic of the gospel commits Christians to struggle against everything that constricts that freedom to be human without which the full expression of God's loving creation is impeded. But the church, like other human institutions, learns the lessons of history and is bound up in the same growing human wisdom to which the secular world is subject. The Catholic notion of the development of doctrine is crucial here. While Christians believe in the fullness of revelation in the Bible, this certainly does not mean that the church of this or any other century has all the answers. The message of the gospel is unlocked at any particular time in the interaction between the word of God in scripture and the way the Spirit speaks to us through the signs of the times. Drawing out this relationship is the work of the theologian in the church; proclaiming it publicly is the work of the bishop. Living it is the mission of the whole community.

If the mission of the church is to call the world to its own deepest selfhood, this has concrete consequences for the shape of the community. It is quite impossible, for example, for a church that is still locked in a rigidly hierarchical framework to suggest anything convincing to the secular world about the true nature of freedom. A church that seems so often to prize secrecy over accountability and that maintains a premodern attitude to women, for all the theological language of complementarity in which it wraps it up, cannot carry conviction when it talks the language of human solidarity. If rights are to be promoted, the community that promotes them had better have evidence that it lives by them. If integral human solidarity, human autonomy, and a special concern for the weak and marginalized are proclaimed in church teaching, they need to be practiced within the institution. The religious community cannot be excused from the responsibility of abiding by the rules of the human community.

When we search our world today for the underlying causes of environmental damage and human misery, we find ourselves focusing on the same reality that is also responsible for much of our comfort and security and for much genuine human accomplishment. Today we have to confront directly the flawed picture of human fulfillment that is promoted by our current market-driven capitalist vision of reality. Because this vision is so powerful and so incomplete, the mission of the Christian community today will be deeply involved in challenging the largely unquestioned sway that the capitalist vision seems to have over the world. It is, in important respects, after the end of the cold war, the only remaining effective antihuman ideology.

It is obviously not sufficient simply to proclaim that global capitalism is the evil genius of the twenty-first century. Capitalism is certainly not the only source of evil in today's world. Moreover, to challenge it does not mean being opposed to progress or to wealth creation, still less to the technologies that at least offer the promise of a better life to all God's people. But we certainly have to recognize the extent to which our world is controlled by commercial powers of such magnitude that most political structures are impotent before them, and all human beings are their slaves. The economic powers that seem in many respects to rule our world today undermine so much of what it takes to be human, and they invite resistance in the name of humanity. But, and here is the point for Christians, the only effective opposition lies in the vision of an alternative life and worldview. The church as communion must show itself to be a workable model in miniature of what the church as mission is offering to the world, to counter the antihuman bias of global capitalism. Thus, we must give shape to the communion that the church is by reflecting on its mission, and we must ensure that the mission remains an expression of the underlying communion.

The particular challenge of capitalism becomes clearer in the larger context of "globalization."[6] The postmodern world has in a sense become miniaturized. Everything in today's world is so remarkably interconnected that no one is untouched by what happens on the other side of the world. Its one "overarching feature" is "integration."[7] Even an enthusiastic spokesperson for globalization such as Thomas L. Friedman, who clearly recognizes that "the driving idea behind globalization is free-market capitalism," is sensitive to the problems of the "powerful backlash from those brutalized or left behind by this new system." In Friedman's helpful terminology, the system of globalization must be able, if it is to succeed, to produce wealth (the "Lexus") while respecting indigenous cultures, communal identity, and a sense of "home" (the "olive tree"). "You cannot be a complete person alone," he writes. True, "[y]ou can be a rich person alone. You can be a smart person alone. But you cannot be a complete person alone. For that you must be a part of, and rooted in, an olive grove." The challenge facing both countries and individuals "is to find a healthy balance between preserving a sense of identity, home and community and doing what it takes to survive within the globalization system." "How will people start to react," asks Friedman, "if they find this system just too damn hard and too damn fast for too damn long?"[8]

In Friedman's vision, the challenge is to preserve a balance between the Lexus (economics) and the olive tree (culture). This for Friedman is both an ethical and a strategic challenge. It is ethical in the sense that the leaders in the conscious component of the globalization phenomenon, the manipulators of global capitalism, must recognize the need for our olive trees. And it is strategic in the sense that the system will fail if it asks too much of too many for too long. But globalization is in the end, he thinks, tapping into universal human desires. Dismissing "revolutionary theorists," he comments that "the 'wretched of the earth' want to go to Disney World—not to the barricades."[9] So, while the balance has to be preserved, it is the responsibility of the economic system to achieve that balance, in its own interests and for the (material) benefit of the human race.

If the challenge of globalization is rightly (and elegantly) expressed as the need to balance the economic and the cultural, it cannot be left up to economic interests to establish the balance. The balance between the Lexus and the olive tree is a *political* challenge. Friedman's mistake is similar to the one made throughout much of Catholic social teaching, which from Leo XIII to John XXIII argued, on the one hand, for the need for justice and, on the other, against political action to achieve it. Politics as the art and science of human community—which is, unfortunately, not the way it is mostly understood or practiced today—must always ask the larger question about the sense of the whole and will put important but subordinate issues in that context. In this respect, politics is quite like religion. Under the surface at least, it works with an overarching vision of the human and a commitment to a particular understanding of human fulfillment.[10] As a theologian might put it, politics is the refinement of mission in the service of communion.

Religious responses to globalization are not yet numerous; one important challenge can be found in the work of Daniel M. Bell.[11] Bell is not a liberal. He is part of the emerging and occasionally strident voice of "radical orthodoxy," whose leading figures could best be described as socialist in politics while theologically conservative. They owe something to Victorian High Anglicanism, a little to the radical Reformation, and a great deal to Augustine's vision of the City of

God.[12] If they have common convictions—and they do—they are those outlined in John Milbank's *Theology and Social Theory*. This long, complex, and brilliant work has two fundamental principles. The first is that there is a Christian failure of nerve in the valorization of Enlightenment and modern secular society, ceding the victory to an individualism that in the end substitutes the priority of violence for that of peace. The second is that only Christian theology has the capacity to overcome nihilism and reassert the primacy of "the absolute Christian vision of ontological peace."[13] Powerful and enterprising, radical orthodoxy also suffers from a tendency toward Christian exclusivism, if not outright totalitarianism. The pluralism of postmodernity is not construed as a value.[14]

Despite these reservations about radical orthodoxy, Bell's work is suggestive for understanding the task of the church today. He begins by analyzing the ways in which capitalism has created a scale of values which even those who cannot conceivably benefit from the capitalist system have been seduced into internalizing. Following French thinkers like Michel Foucault and Gilles Deleuze, Bell refers to this phenomenon as the "disciplining of desire."[15] The world is divided into those who have the means to access some of the consumer goods and creature comforts of capitalism and those who cannot but would if they could. More significant than the mere consumerism is the attitude to the world that accompanies it, one in which individualism and personal self-aggrandizement are the order of the day. This modern, "savage" capitalism, as it is named by the Latin American thinker Franz Hinkelammert, must be countered by the Christian community.[16] In the name of humanity, the church has to mount a counteroffensive.

Bell recognizes that in Latin America the church of liberation theology has been engaged in this struggle against savage capitalism for a number of decades. But he distinguishes between the poor choice of weapons made by liberation theologians and the promise of base Christian communities. The theologians—and indeed the universal teaching of the church—have tried to oppose the excesses of market economics by promoting the expansion of the idea of human rights. Catholic social teaching has gone way beyond the liberal understanding of human rights as various freedoms of the individual to incorporate a whole series of economic and social rights—the right to work, to education and health care, and so on. But, says Bell, to speak the language of rights is still to speak the language of the liberal tradition in political philosophy with which capitalism is so comfortable. Base your struggle on the espousal of rights and you will lose the battle, not because rights are bad things but because the capitalist system will outsmart you.

The way forward for the church in countering capitalism's discipline of desire is to offer an alternative model for the whole of life, one whose discipline of desire does not speak the same language as that of global capitalism. Thus, capitalism will be unable to handle it. Looking at the praxis of base Christian communities in Latin America, Bell identifies a discipline of forgiveness and repentance, a praxis of love of enemy that is apolitical in the usual sense of the term but offers a genuinely alternative, gospel vision of how life should be lived. For Bell, this is a true politics, not the reductive understanding of politics espoused by the secular world. Politics is located in the whole life of the community, not in the mechanism for policy making and elections. So, a political alternative to global capitalism must be one that offers an alternative way of viewing the whole of life. To Bell and the other radical orthodox theologians, this requires a return to a vision of the "peacable kingdom" of Augustine's *City of God*. For them, the Christian church in its premodern integrity is the "perfect society" that counters the antihuman realities of savage capitalism.

While Bell's book is extremely valuable for its articulation of capitalism's "discipline of desire," his countermodern standpoint needs correction in two directions if we are to find him ultimately helpful in articulating the mission of the church. We require a more nuanced approach to the complex legacy of modernity, which allows us not simply to jettison the Enlightenment. And we need to step back from the potentially totalitarian implications of radical orthodoxy's claim that it is Christian society that holds the key to history. Then and only then will any alternative we propose to the vision of global capitalism be open to reception in a pluralistic world.

Radical orthodoxy needs to be corrected by the work of those who do not share its unqualified suspicion of the Enlightenment. Important among these resources is the Vatican II Pastoral Constitution on the Church in the Modern World (*Gaudium et Spes*), which illustrates a more complex and dialectical approach to modernity than that of radical orthodoxy. The text of the document, indeed, paints a picture of reciprocity between church and world. Of course, it might be—as Bell and others think—that the church has become a pawn in the hands of modernity and needs to cleanse itself of such well-meaning but fruitless liaisons. A second valuable resource is the alternative reading of the relationship between Catholicism and modernity suggested by Charles Taylor in his 1966 Marianist lecture, "A Catholic Modernity?"[17] Taylor argues that the bifurcated legacy of modernity means that the church's response to it cannot be univocal. But it is in the postconciliar ecclesiology of Edward Schillebeeckx that we find the most thoughtful articulation of the axiomatic character of religious pluralism. For Schillebeeckx, what marks "the modern structure of religious personality" is that human beings see themselves as "beings with divergent possibilities." So, pluralism becomes "cognitive reality," part of our personality structure, and simply does not allow us to countenance the view, for example, that "outside the Church there is no salvation."[18] Bell's views, complemented by those of Vatican II, Charles Taylor, and Edward Schillebeeckx, will enable us to articulate a healthy understanding of mission.

THE CHURCH IN THE FACE OF MODERNITY

Since Theodor Adorno and Max Horkheimer's *Dialectic of Enlightenment*, it has become a commonplace to think of modernity as both a blessing and a curse.[19] It is, on the one hand, perceived as the source of our modern human rights, of the democratic ordering of society, and of scientific and technological progress, all stemming from the valorization of the individual and of human reason unaided by revelation. However, the same assertion of the autonomy of the human over against the divine and that of the individual over against ancient collectivities are identified as the twin sources of contemporary malaise. The anonymity of our world, its consumerism, its subordination to technological and corporate imperatives, its ordering according to the logic of inhuman if not antihuman systems, are all laid at the feet of a modernity left unchecked by a holistic vision of human society. In Habermas's terms, the "linguistification of the sacred" that makes possible our modern lifeworld comes to be threatened by the very system it created, like some postmodern Frankenstein myth.

Our own so-called postmodern age largely understands itself in relationship to that modernity of which it is a direct descendant. Different attitudes to modernity show up postmodernity as ungrateful child, rebellious adolescent, or willing heir to the business. Postmodernity, depending on its attitude to modernity, is *countermodern, radically postmodern,* or *late modern.*[20] The first looks to remaking the world according to a premodern template, usually though not always that of an idealized medieval world. Its dominant attitude is nostalgia, often mixed with a good dose of anger. The second is only too happy to throw off the discipline of humanism demanded by modernity and to frolic in the pleasures of a guiltless consumerism. Its dominant attitude is insouciance, a careless, carefree, and ultimately thoughtless rapture. The third is focused on the ambivalence of modernity, committed to the value of the Enlightenment legacy while only too aware of its destructive potential, and determined to find a way to continue to promote the former while reining in the latter. Its dominant attitude—and here I inevitably give away my own preferences—is a calm realism about the terrible plight of the world and an unshakable conviction that there is yet hope.

All three of these attitudes have their ecclesial corollaries and lead to dramatically different understandings of the character of Christian mission and the relation between mission and communion. The nostalgic or countermodern approach is to be found in many places in the Christian church, often associated with a high degree of comfort with some of the technologies of postmodernity,[21] and usually marked by an ahistoricism similar to that of the neoscholasticism we discussed in chapter 1. Here I would locate both Christian fundamentalism, which is clearly fueled by a fear of the Enlightenment, and the more conservative impulses of John Paul II's restorationist Rome. Strikingly, just as fundamentalism is largely a nineteenth-century creation born directly out of a fear of modernization,[22] so the historical perspective of present-day conservative Catholicism seems to imagine that the Rome born of precisely similar nineteenth-century fears of modernity is the eternal Rome of Peter and the apostolic age.

In the days of Vatican II, the conservative, curial, "minority" faction was a clear example of nostalgic countermodernity. Today we can see similar instincts at work in Christian theology, both inside and outside Catholicism. The Catholics have "movements" like Opus Dei and

Communion and Liberation, Episcopalians can claim radical ortho-doxy, and Protestantism can finds its version, to a degree, in the "postliberal" theological perspective usually associated with the work of Hans Frei and George Lindbeck.[23] These instincts clearly show themselves, closer to our own present concerns, in the way in which the Vatican works, in its obsession with secrecy and its clericalism, even when put to the service of admirable causes. They emerge above all in the defeatism of popes. They are evident in the Paul VI of *Humanae Vitae* (1968)' though spectacularly not in the Paul VI of the council and of *Populorum Progressio* (1967), his great social encyclical on the development of peoples. They are clearly present in the John Paul II of *Ordinatio Sacerdotalis* (1994; on reserving the priesthood to men alone) and *Veritatis Splendor* (1993; on moral relativism), though not in the John Paul II of *Laborem Exercens* (1981; on human work) or *Centesimus Annus* (1991; on economic freedom).[24] While institutional imperatives will always lead the church to err on the side of caution, too often the negativity that accompanies them seems to correlate with a loss of hope. It sometimes seems that the institutional vision is tied to a pneumatology of nostalgia, a sense that the work of the Spirit will always be to return us to past verities, instead of some-times carrying us confidently forward into new understandings of God's truth.

If the conservatism of countermodernity is all too plainly evident in the Christian churches, the radical form of postmodernity is also pres-ent, though neither so obvious nor so plentiful. Fundamentally, like countermodernity, it is unhistorical. For the countermodern idealiza-tion of the past it substitutes an equally indefensible rejection of the importance of tradition. This has had its theoretical forms, above all in the "death-of-God" theologies briefly prevalent in the 1960s,[25] but it is to the more popular cultural variant that we need to attend more closely. Human freedom as the hard-won achievement of the Enlight-enment is taken out of the context of the discipline of the Enlighten-ment and becomes a simple license for novelty. Theologically speaking, it means that the cherished practices and doctrines of the tradition are placed on level ground with the bright ideas of this morning's *Kaffeeklatsch*, and aromatherapy and prayer or the cross and human fulfillment are just so many options on the theological *smorgasbord*.

Within Catholicism there is no theological movement of radical postmodernity, but there are currents of thought and practice that owe allegiance to it. Curiously, one of them can be found in Vatican II itself. The Vatican Council was a creature of the 1960s, and reflected both the optimism and the lack of realism of that time. Its uncritical acceptance of the theme of development, matched to a high degree in John XXIII's *Mater et Magistra* and *Pacem in Terris*, and only modestly qualified in Paul VI's *Populorum Progressio*, shows a somewhat one-sided interpretation of modernity. This is, of course, corrected even to a fault in the social encyclicals of John Paul II. But the more common expression of this radical postmodernity is to be found in the uncritical embrace of the popular wisdom of the times. Thus, "bringing the Church up to date" is not seen as the need to maintain the dynamism of thought and action that goes by the name of "development of doctrine." Instead, it becomes an excuse for jettisoning things of value. John XXIII talked of "opening the windows to let in a little fresh air." But he did not envisage using these same open windows to discard venerable but dusty items for the bulk trash.

A more balanced approach to the relationship between Catholicism and modernity is to be found in many places in the mainstream of Catholic thought and theology, in both conservative and liberal forms. It begins with the Catholic Tübingen School in the early nineteenth century, above all in the work of Johan Sebastian Drey.[26] It can be followed through such thinkers as John Henry Newman and the theologians of the "new theology" with whom we became acquainted in chapter 1. They were distinguished by a common commitment to *ressourcement* and *aggiornamento*. Going back to the sources and bringing up to date are not contradictory impulses if both are governed, as they were in all these thinkers, by a constant attention to the historicality of tradition. Nostalgia is controlled by an urgent sense of the particular needs of the present moment, while a keen sense of the historical treasure house of tradition guards against a foolish repetition of the errors of history.

There has been a great deal written about the Catholic Church and its relationship to modernity, by no one better than the distinguished American ecclesiologist, Joseph Komonchak.[27] Komonchak has consistently tried to get beyond the left- and right-wing stereotypes of the Vatican Council and its aftermath and has sought to explain it by nuancing the more recent history of the church. Where most commentators have tended to think of the church from the sixteenth century to the present as a ghetto church, Komonchak has argued that the nineteenth-century Catholic Church took a distinct turn from what preceded it. It became clearly antimodernist, as modernism took shape and the forces of liberalism and progressive thought that Pius IX so detested seemed in the ascendant. But at precisely the same time as the church was refining its antimodernist rhetoric, it was adopting patterns of organization that were distinctly modernist in nature. The centralized authoritarian church that came into existence in the nineteenth century, and that will always be associated with Popes Pius IX, Pius X, and Pius XII, says Komonchak, "represents a classic illustration of that self-conscious, rationalized, and bureaucratized mode of thought in which Max Weber saw the distinctive mark of modernity." And, he concludes, "this anti-modern Roman Catholicism was very modern indeed."[28]

If Komonchak's analysis of the church of the past two centuries is correct, then the reforms of the Vatican Council come into clear focus as correctives to this particular vision of the church. In *Lumen Gentium* the bishops present an ideal of the church as communion, which is a direct challenge to the excessively centralized and bureaucratically obsessed "church of the three Piuses." In *Gaudium et Spes* above all, but also in documents like the Declaration on Religious Liberty (*Dignitatis Humanae*), Vatican II decisively rejects the defensive, fear-laden attitude to modernity distinctive of the preconciliar church. Finally, as Komonchak himself points out in words that echo Karl Rahner's famous essay on the coming of the world church, the entire council "challenged the normative character of European and especially Roman ways of understanding and realizing Catholicism."[29]

The tension between the preconciliar church and the ecclesial vision of the council is one of two conceptions of the church in the world. However, the truism is usually understood to refer to the church that fears the Enlightenment legacy, and the one that is ready at least cautiously to embrace some of its insights. This remains valid. But at the same time, as Komonchak leads us to see quite clearly, it is a struggle between a vision of the church that models itself on the modern bureaucratic state (and sometimes upon the modern transnational corporation), and one that seeks to promote a far more human model of communion. In this regard, it seems clear that the church of preconciliar Roman Catholicism is a species of ecclesiastical fundamentalism. Like other fundamentalist movements in the nineteenth century, it is primarily motivated by a fear of modernity. And, like the TV evangelism and crystal cathedrals of contemporary Protestant fundamentalism, it is a modern phenomenon and adopts many of the organizational patterns and practices of modernity (and now postmodernity) in order to perpetuate itself.

The patterns of restoration that we had occasion to document in chapter 4 can now be seen as attempts to insist anew on the particular attitudes to modernity enshrined in the church of the three Piuses, which should perhaps be renamed, "the church of the three Piuses and a John Paul." The consistent message of John Paul's impressive list of encyclical letters is a deep suspicion of modernity, in its social, political, and economic organisms, in its underlying conception of the human, in its consumerism, and in its moral relativism. But the clear pattern of Vatican practice during the same pontificate has been a reassertion of centralization and bureacratization against the devolutionary and collegial directions clearly laid down in Vatican II. To switch images for a moment, at no time in history has the institution behaved more like a corporate giant than it does today, with head offices in Rome and branches throughout the world, staffed by local managers called bishops. This ecclesial vision is wrong. It contradicts Vatican II. But it has been promoted by Rome and effectively imposed by a pattern of episcopal appointments that has stressed loyalty to the head office over capacity to lead the local church. While such loyalty is an effective centralizing force, with the local bishop becoming a conduit for Vatican policy, it carries with it a great risk. The near collapse of episcopal leadership in major American dioceses in the first years of the twentieth century is a sign of what happens when qualifications for pastoral leadership are equated to those of corporate middle management.

This long digression on modernity has been necessary in order to make the point that the articulation of the church's mission will vary according to the conception of the church we possess. Equally truly, our vision of the church in the world will have implications for how we view the church "in itself." As we try in the next few pages to frame an understanding of the mission of the church, we shall be employing a vision of the church as communion, certainly, but in the particular form of communion that Komonchak and Rahner lead us to see as the vision of the council. The church's mission in the modern world must be seen as collaborative and challenging, but not as fearful and still less as dismissive. The capacity to conduct this mission effectively also requires the reversal of the slide into bureaucratic centralism that has marked the past two centuries. If we cannot become decentralized, then the kind of effective grass-roots conduct of the mission that conforms to local circumstances becomes impossible. We end up constantly engaged in a deductive enterprise that imposes bureaucratic edicts upon circumstances for which they are not suited. We live in one world, and so the strategic plan for the mission will reflect the universal communion of Catholicism. But we also live in a multiplicity of social locations, each with its culture and its traditions. The tactics by which the mission will be accomplished are forged at the grass roots, where we find the laity at work.

In the end, we have to choose between two ways in which we can encounter our contemporary world and address its needs. In a book published some years ago, Harvey Cox wrote of two forms of church that he saw as the principal alternatives from which the Christian church would choose, and was choosing. They were contemporary "televangelism," with its strange combination of biblical fundamentalism and postmodern technologies, and base Christian communities as they had developed in Latin America, insisting on a low-tech and localized approach to the Christian life. We have seen enough to know that the Roman Catholic Church is too often on the side of the TV evangelists. But it is clear that Vatican II favored the option for the local church. And, interestingly enough, the entrapment of the institutional church in modern bureaucracy means that it can only accommodate to modernity in its worst aspects. At the same time, the freedom of the church of the poor from bureaucratic models, and its preference for communion, has enabled it to mount the most sustained challenge to date to the antihuman and antigospel imperatives of modernity. It can be no surprise, of course, that the Latin American church of the poor has suffered almost equally from two directions, the "national security state" so common in Latin America and the Vatican, which has chosen to share so many of that state's methods.

THE MISSION OF THE CHURCH TODAY:
COMBATING THE ANTIHUMAN

Belief in God is the basis of a prophetic praxis which renews the world.
—*Edward Schillebeeckx*

In this section of the current chapter we have to articulate a vision of the mission of the church. But it must be one that respects the positive dimensions of modernity while challenging its negative elements. It must also be one that attends to the variegated character of world Catholicism and which rejects the hegemony of European models of thought and action. And it must be one that both issues from a conception of the church with which it is compatible and suggests directions in which the future shape of the church might lie. Those directions we shall try to sketch out in the final chapter of the book. For now, we shall proceed in three stages, examining in turn the relationship of mission to the negative and positive dimensions of modernity, and articulating an ecclesiology that holds fidelity to the gospel together with openness to the pluralism of the contemporary world.

The Terror of Modernity:
Prophecy and the Mission of the Church

As a Christian I cannot tolerate the immeasurable torturing of men and women in our history.

—*Edward Schillebeeckx*

Liberals are often critical of capitalism for all sorts of reasons, and their complaints are frequently easily dismissed by pointing out, for example, that these same complainers depend in so many ways on the capitalist system for the style of life they enjoy, with its attendant comforts. Those who from a religious perspective defend capitalism—Michael Novak comes to mind instantly[30]—find it all too easy to invoke the liberal tradition of rights and the constitutional freedoms we enjoy to paint a picture of a harmonious whole in which the capitalist economic system, the democratic political system, and the pluralistic and tolerant cultural system dance together in an almost trinitarian perichoresis to ensure the fruits of the American way of life and to offer them generously to those around the world who would embrace the American way. The liberal critics who are so easily swept aside usually point to capitalism's subversion of the rights of others, especially of the poor. The counterargument is easily made, that at its worst capitalism is suffering from a partial failure in the delivery system, and that it is and will continue to be the best form of wealth creation in the world. When coupled with democracy, the argument goes, it is the likeliest deliverer of relative peace and prosperity to the "developing" world. Hence, for example, the capitalist critique of Muslim fundamentalism and the attendant terror tactics of some of its adherents, focuses on the failure of Islam to deliver economic prosperity and proposes a new Marshall Plan in which increasing prosperity will supposedly overwhelm any religiously inspired critique of the West.

Earlier in this chapter we discussed the ideas of Daniel Bell. We saw that he employed the insights of several French theorists and the Latin American social critic Franz Hinkelammert to present capitalism as much more than an economic system that has triumphed over other alternatives. It is an ontological system that through its technologies fashions human beings in particular directions by orchestrating their *eros*, their distinctive patterns of desires. As we might say adopting a more familiar vocabulary, capitalism succeeds by persuading people to embrace its scale of values and build their lives accordingly, either enjoying what capitalism tells them are the fruits of success, or striving for some if not all of those rewards. What capitalism names "achievement" or "healthy competition" is revealed as a way of being (an "ontology") that prioritizes violence. It is not just the victory of an economic system; it is the triumph of a particular conception of the human and of human society.

Bell's narrative of modern global capitalism, building on the work of Hinkelammert, is full of insight. Of course, how persuasive it is to this or that individual depends on a whole lot of factors, not least the willingness to stand back from the personal benefits of living in a successful capitalist system and examine the overall systemic impact it has on human society. Thus, liberation theology has frequently argued that to know the world as it really is one has to find a way to see it through the eyes of the poor. Because the poor have nothing to lose, they can see the truth with a clarity that those seduced by the system cannot. One of the values of Bell's picture is to show that it is not quite that simple. Capitalism seduces even those who have not benefited from it, into accepting its discipline of desire. Being poor, then, is not enough. It is being poor and drawing upon the power of Christianity's competing vision of what a human society should look like that offers the true counter to capitalism. This "savage capitalism" can be countered by Christianity's own technologies of desire, in the name of the humanity that is changed for the worse through the ontology of capitalism. Christianity is a therapy of desire, says Bell.

Borrowing from Bell, while avoiding the romanticism of his solutions and the implicit totalitarianism of much of radical orthodoxy, we can surely see that one major dimension of Christian mission must be the struggle against the dehumanizing program of global capitalism. Capitalism has all but triumphed in the world. Viewed in the context of globalization as an ontology of desire rather than as a simple economic system, its power dwarfs the power of political communities to counter or control it. But the scale of values of capitalism is not the scale of values of the gospel. The world that capitalism envisages, and which it expends such wealth and power to accomplish, is an inversion of the values of the gospel. To capitalism, the world is for the strong, or at least for the enterprising. The gospel is addressed to sinners, in the name of the defense of the defenseless. For everyone, rich and poor alike, it is a mixture of call to repentance and a message of forgiveness and reconciliation. But it is not the same mixture for all. The more fully invested we are in a world system which denies so many of the values of the gospel, the louder is the call to repentance and the more dependent is the fullness of forgiveness and reconciliation upon the reality of conversion. To be "born again of water and the Holy Spirit" is to make a fundamental option for an entirely different scale of values to that of global capitalism. The Lexus and the olive tree, to return to Friedman's images, must be balanced by the all-embracing vision of the whole expressed in the gospel.

The Christian alternative vision to that of global capitalism's discipline of desire is a prophetic challenge to the negative face of postmodernity. The Enlightenment is often criticized for being godless and promoting atheistic humanism, but the limitations of Enlightenment are more surely found in its over-valorization of the individual. Human reason is at the core of our God-given natures, and we would be foolish to see the Enlightenment's impetus to secular reason as anything other than providential. But Kant and his successors make a terrible mistake when they see the autonomous human being as mastering the world through the exercise of his or her unaided intellect. Their real mistake is not to try to do without God, but to try to do without one another. And the negative consequences of Enlightenment are not to be seen in the achievements of human intellect, but are found in the picture of the human person as an autonomous individual. Contra liberal political philosophy, we are all in this together. But the ontology of capitalism requires the atomized human being. A vibrant lifeworld would be able to marshal resistance to the system in ways which you or I alone cannot accomplish.

Christian mission in the face of global capitalism is a blend of resistance and witness. It is not enough to name an evil. One must also offer an alternative vision of how to live. But, and here we part company with radical orthodoxy, it is not enough to proclaim a way of life of peaceful human relations as an ideal vision, a counter-image to the violence that is endemic in social relations within capitalist society. In other words, witness is not a full account of mission. To use traditional categories, witness is insufficiently evangelistic. Evangelism, in this sense, is persuasive life in the world. The evangelist is a person—usually a lay person—whose way of life reveals constructive possibility for the future of the world. This kind of evangelist may or may not be a leader in the normal sense of the term, holding political office, running a business, or heading up a professional organization. Obviously, most of us are not this kind of leader. However, a life of constructive possibility is leadership in another and at least equally important way. When a person's life is built up of decisions, big and small, that consistently affirm human possibility and resist every tendency in our world to diminish human freedom and responsibility, that person is a saint. Lay evangelists as we view them here, then, may or may not be "leaders" but they are surely saints.

In our discussion of the theology of Yves Congar, the reader will hopefully recall, we spent some considerable time distinguishing between different kinds of lay activity, and the church of the twentieth century consistently recognized three. There is, first, lay involvement in the internal ministries of the church. This has grown enormously since the Second Vatican Council, but questions remain—at least in some minds—about whether this is truly "lay ministry" or whether it is a matter of lay assistance for practical reasons in what is in principle the work of ordained ministers. We saw Congar and Rahner argue over this question. Second, there are organized apostolic associations led by laypeople but in some sense officially recognized by the institutional church (so-called "Catholic Action"). The language of papal approbation for such "Catholic Action" consistently used the term "cooperation in the ministry of the hierarchical priesthood" to describe it, and thus suggested that this work is not the proper work of laypeople in the church. Finally, there is the daily life of laypeople in the world, informed by the gospel, sometimes conducted privately, sometimes in association with others. But this is not to be understood simply as the life of pious lay folk beloved of conservative church leaders. This is not the "simple faithful," carrying the grace of the sacraments into lives which are shining examples of holy obedience to their pastors and dutiful good citizenship. No, this is the mission of the church, conducted by adult laypeople in virtue of their baptism and confirmation, independently of ecclesiastical oversight, exercising their status as priests, prophets, and servant leaders.

The mission of the church in the world is primarily conducted through countless millions of individual decisions made by laypeople, independently of ecclesiastical authority. The decisions we make, which individually speaking reflect who we are and also make us who we are becoming, are collectively of extraordinary importance for the world. But we do not make them under orders of the magisterium. Rather, we are free and independent citizens of the world, though guided by the Christian narrative. Theologically speaking, our decisions represent the church shouldering its co-creative responsibilities. Divine grace is visible in the life of any human being where she or he acts in a pro-human fashion. But the church is an intentional community, and when the community of faith lives up to its responsibilities the grace of God is particularly evident in its consistent solidarity with the suffering world. This is much if not all of what it means to talk of the church as sacrament, as a light to the nations or a leaven in the mass.

A life lived out on a consistent pattern of pro-human decisions, which is a life of mission, is not easy, and it needs the church. The chances of our making decisions in a consistently pro-human fashion are enhanced in several ways by the fellowship of the community of faith. Within the church as it should be, prayer is encouraged, Scripture is read, the sacraments are celebrated, the memory of Jesus is kept alive, the narrative of the community is nourished, while its members offer one another support and encouragement. But any sense that we retire into the church for refueling, or emerge from it to practice our missionary magic, should be avoided. The church, as we saw in chapter five, is a part of the secular world. We live simultaneously as churchly and secular. We are not oriented to God in the first instance, and to the human community in the second. Rather, we find God both in prayer and worship, and in the encounter with our fellow human beings in daily life. At the same time it remains true that some of our energies must go into cultivating the community of faith, not because it is an end in itself, but because we want our local church to illustrate that the fullness of the human that we work for in the world is indeed possible.

While the church is important both in the way it strengthens its members for the mission of human solidarity and the way it models a community of fellowship, the secular world is also vital to Christian mission. We shall have more to say about this in the next sub-section of this chapter. Here we can simply note that while there is a vision of human freedom and fulfillment that the gospel proposes and the church proclaims, the difficult business of figuring out precisely what kinds of initiatives in the world will further this vision cannot be left to the church. There are simply some things that the world knows, that the church does not, and here the church depends for enlightenment upon the secular world. The implications for mission are quite clear. Mission requires not only deep faith and a living relationship with God, but also an informed understanding of the world and intelligent calculation of the various strategies and options that suggest themselves for action. The cultivation of such secular expertise is primarily a lay activity, though the ordained are not excused from knowledge of worldly reality.

To summarize this section, the prophetic dimension of the church's mission is to stand up in defense of a truly human world, which is of course a world that sees human beings as a part of a larger cosmic whole. This requires discerning where in our particular moment in history the forces of the anti-human are located, in order to mount a resistance to them. In today's world, the ontology of global capitalism's "technologies of desire" represents the greatest threat to human freedom and fulfillment, and consequently it is capitalism's vision of the human (rather than simply its economic preferences) that must be countered, in the name of freedom for the entire human community. This prophetic work, while it is aided by the ordained ministers of the church, is primarily conducted by laypeople, as they build lives of human solidarity, demonstrating a consistent choice for the more human over the less human. By living in this way, they show what it means to cherish God's free gift of life together in the world.

The Beauty of Modernity: Enlightenment Values and the Mission of the Church

> The crisis of the Enlightenment was historically not only possible, but even "inevitable."
>
> —*Edward Schillebeeckx*

The story of the church's mission is not simply one of confrontation with modernity but also one of cooperation. Indeed, the story is partially one of learning from modernity. Fundamentalisms in general, and more sophisticated forms of contemporary theology like radical orthodoxy, reject anything other than a negative evaluation of modernity. The church's weakness today, on this view, is a direct consequence of accommodating to modernity. The way forward is to return to a premodern harmony of one Christian community of peace, in which the secular is not a separate realm from the sacred, but both are gathered in an organic union of life within the church. Modernity adds nothing to the sum total of human happiness. It only subtracts, replacing peace with violence.

Charles Taylor offers a resoundingly different picture of Catholicism's encounter with modernity.[31] Taylor reminds us that the Greek word *katholou* means universality through wholeness. The "great historical temptation" of Catholicism has been to go straight for unity, without recognizing the element of diversity. Incarnation, through which redemption happens, is "the weaving of God's life into human lives, but these lives are different, plural, irreducible to each other."[32] Today we have to carry this Catholic taste for diversity into a modern world in which we are partially quite at home, while it is one that under its non-Christian aspects seems deliberately to exclude the Christian kerygma. Modern culture, says Taylor, mingles together both authentic developments and negations of the gospel. Like the sixteenth-century Jesuit missionary to China, Matteo Ricci, we have to face the difficult task of "making new discriminations," determining what in the culture we encounter is a "valid human difference" and what conflicts with Christian faith.

The novelty of Taylor's view lies in his conviction that modern culture, while it broke with Christendom in many respects, advances some aspects of Christianity in ways that they had not developed previously, and even in ways that would not have occurred without this secular moment. Catholics must face "the humbling realization that the breakout was a necessary condition of the development." From somewhere within Christendom, Christian faith was "dethroned" and often sidelined. But these developments "made possible what we now recognize as a great advance in the practical penetration of the gospel in human life." For example, modern "rights culture" has produced "the attempt to call political power to book against a yardstick of fundamental human requirements, universally applied." So a vote of thanks is due to Voltaire and his like for helping us "to live the gospel in a purer way, free of that continual and often bloody forcing of conscience which was the sin and blight of all those 'Christian' centuries."[33] Violence, in other words, is certainly internal to the practice of Christendom, and, if peace is to be won, on Taylor's assessment, it needs the help of that modernity that radical orthodoxy identifies with violence, over against the peaceable kingdom of Christendom.

Taylor is primarily interested in how to live as Christians within modernity, which is essentially the same question we have asked about the character of Christian mission in today's world, and he concludes that this is no simple task. We cannot reject modernity outright, since it has advanced our understanding of Christian ideals of justice and human rights. Nor can we just accept, say, the human rights tradition and dismiss either the ideas that gave rise to it or the necessary moment of breakout from Christianity. But at the same time, we cannot give wholehearted and comprehensive approval to a modernity that includes within it an "exclusive humanism" that denies transcendence. The sense that there is "something more than life" must pervade our thought and praxis and will bring us into conflict with some at least of those with whom we share a commitment to human rights. At the same time it shows a way beyond the despair that can issue from the realization that the project of philanthropy constantly fails. Christian hope in God's reign, paradoxically enough, makes us less likely to abandon the mission for a more human world.

Taylor's picture of a Catholic modernity adds important dimensions to the prophetic element in mission that we considered in the previous section. In the first place, he paints a picture of an alliance with modernity in which Christians, with suitable humility, accept the insights into their own most cherished values that have been won for them by what are often atheistic currents of thought. Of course, the day is long past when the majority of Christians would simply ignore the achievements of secular or atheistic inquiry. Where would we be without Marx, Nietzsche, Freud, and Darwin? How impoverished would be our understanding of human nature if every creative work by agnostics were still on some Index of forbidden books? But even liberal Christians have a tendency to view intellectual or artistic creativity in a kind of "inclusivist" perspective. The work of nonbelievers is fine insofar as it chimes in with Christian revelation. But Taylor is suggesting another kind of far more comprehensive openness. If he is right that we have learned about our Christian tradition from nonbelievers, then there is no reason to believe this process is over. The grace of God can work through the secular world to bring Christians to a deeper sense of what God requires of them.

A second important idea Taylor offers us is that the "something more than life" that transcendence implies takes Christian mission beyond a mere hope in the capacity of the human. Mission remains the struggle for human fulfillment and freedom, but the very strength of commitment in a context in which the struggle is one of frequent failure is testimony to a belief that life, particularly the individual human life, is not the last word. God, who empowers the struggle, who cheers it on and who consoles the weary, is the last word. Here, mission and witness are closely tied together. For the most part, the church's work for the humanization of the world will be indistinguishable from the genuinely philanthropic activity of nonbelievers. But where there are differences, they will reflect the commitment to transcendence. From the purely secular perspective, Taylor's "exclusive humanism," the human is what we have and the individual human life is the basic value, though it is often the case that a life may be freely surrendered for the sake of the human race. In Catholic mission, the root of human value lies in our origin as God's creatures, and our lives are gifts of God. Jesus Christ is the model for Christian self-surrender. But Jesus' death is not simply for the sake of human life, though it is for the salvation of human beings. As Taylor pithily points out, while God of course wills human flourishing, "thy will be done" is not the same thing as "let human beings flourish."[34]

The paradox of Christian mission is that while it is inspired in the final analysis not solely by love of the world but by a love of God who gives us the world, and while God, and not human flourishing, is the ultimate value, the consequence of love of God is a renewed commitment to human flourishing. We explored this idea in chapter 5, but a brief recall is in order. What we know of God is what God communicates to us. We know God as creator and giver of the gift of life. But we know God better through Jesus Christ, in whom God's loving relationship to the world is scaled down to a human level. All this knowledge of God is ours only within the human world, and our response to it must take place here and now. Christian mission is worldly activity, as the church strives to do for the world what God wants, which is what Christ did for the world. Discipleship is world-building, a commitment to what Taylor called "human flourishing." Christian attitudes to life and death are transformed by belief in the resurrection, but they do not lead to a focus on renunciation. This would be an undialectical reduction of Christian witness. On the contrary, they lead to an intensified commitment to human flourishing that Taylor calls *agapē* and which he associates with the Buddhist vision of loving-kindness and compassion.

In all this talk about mission we have said very little about what we might consider to be "religious" messages. There isn't much here about evangelization in the normal usage of the word, largely because mission—if it is to be "received"—must be tailored to the world in which it is to be carried out. In the commitment to human flourishing, the church establishes its credentials as a friend of humanity, not by proclaiming high-sounding truths but by feeding the hungry and working for the structural transformation of the world. The struggle for justice, as the Rome Synod of Bishops said in 1980, is "a constitutive dimension of the preaching of the gospel."[35] In other words, the good news that God loves the world and "sent his only son" rings hollow if it is proclaimed by a community that is either not fully involved in the messy business of protecting human life against the forces of the antihuman or not conducting its own internal workings according to the scale of values it proclaims to the world at large. Justice must be worked for in the world, and it must be done within the church itself. Then and only then, perhaps, can any "religious" message be heard.

The mission of the church is conducted within the one world we share with unbelievers and people of all other religious traditions, and it is primarily present in the ordinary lives of laypeople. (Taylor calls it "the affirmation of ordinary life.") In virtue of their baptism they are authorized. Through the power of the Spirit they are moved to right action. Through scripture and the teachings of wise leaders, they are informed, guided, and occasionally corrected. But it is through their actions, their lives in the world, that the church gains what credibility it deserves. Credibility is a reward for what we stand for, not simply for what we say we stand for. Here above all lies the responsibility of ordained ministers in their teaching capacity. They gain their credibility at one remove, in the credibility of the missionary church. Insofar as they teach and support laypeople in lives of commitment to human flourishing and tend to a community that is itself a model of human flourishing, they will be playing their proper role in mission.

Dialogue with Modernity: Pluralism and the Mission of the Church

> As I brought Israel out of Egypt, so I brought the Philistines from Caphtor, and Aram from Kir.
>
> —*Amos 9:7*

In the last section our dialogue with Charles Taylor led us to see the work of the church relative to nonbelievers as a process of cooperation with and learning from the secular world, on the one hand, and of witnessing to the "something more than life" that constitutes a commitment to transcendence, on the other. But what of the church's relationship to the many other world religions that similarly testify to transcendence? Just as it is a truism to say that the church in the West has existed for the past two hundred years within a modernity that seems not to need and often not to value religious faith, so it is an all-too-obvious fact that the church is one member of a large family of religious communities. How does the mission of the church, in its confrontation with global capitalism, its commitment to human flourishing and its proclamation of transcendence, have to take account of a religiously pluralistic world?

The fact of the matter is that Catholic laypeople today, like their counterparts in other Christian churches, do not believe that their way possesses all truth and that other world religions are simply false. Nor do they think that there is nothing to learn from Buddhism, Hinduism, Islam, and so on. *Lumen Gentium* spoke generously of the possibility of salvation for those of other faiths, thus terminating (in principle if not in practice) the confusion in Catholic (and much Protestant) theology between a claim to the uniqueness of Catholic Christianity and a claim to its absoluteness. However, open-heartedness to the truth and value of other religions is not the same thing as the bare claim that "all religions are equal," or all equally relative to some underlying but unarticulated essence of the divine. Obviously, if such were the claims of the Christian church, then it would be difficult to explain how the church would summon the energy to engage in evangelism at all. "Try Christianity, we're as good as all the others," would—to put it crassly—be an unconvincing advertising slogan.

No contemporary ecclesiologist has explored this set of problems more sensitively than Edward Schillebeeckx.[36] Unlike those who engage in the debates about religious relativism (are all religions equally true? equally false?) and those who espouse absolutistic claims about Christianity, Schillebeeckx focuses on the "hermeneutical circle" within which any truth question is raised. In other words, no one can take a God's-eye view of truth. Christians, like everyone else, raise the question of truth and confess the truth of Christianity within their own interpreted, intensely particular, and historically contingent world. Such particularity is part of the human condition. Given that constraint, "it continues to be true for Christian believers that they find salvation 'only in the name of Jesus of Nazareth.'"[37] But claims to truth, which are implicit in the act of faith, are not the same thing as claims to superiority. It is pointless to claim superiority, Schillebeeckx seems to imply, because the claim would only make sense if we were able to inhabit two or more distinct interpreted worlds simultaneously. The definitive answer to the truth question can only be eschatological, and, since we do not stand at that privileged point of the end of history, we had better leave it alone and concentrate on more fruitful questions like the relationship of the Christian community to those of other faiths.

Schillebeeckx suggests that the foundation for an open attitude to other religions lies in Jesus' proclamation and enactment of the reign of God. Christians confess Jesus of Nazareth as "the personally human manifestation of God," but this uniqueness is also contingent. To call Jesus contingent is to focus on his humanity, which is circumscribed in time, space, culture, and so on. If we overlook the humanity of Jesus, he stops being human and becomes "a necessary divine emanation as a result of which all other religions are volatilized into nothingness." To make such a claim also conflicts "with the very being of God as absolute freedom." Moreover, Jesus points to God beyond himself. And so "God points via Jesus Christ in the Spirit to himself as creator and redeemer, as a God of men and women, of *all* men and women."[38] God is absolute, but no single religion is absolute, and so we ought to rejoice in the variety of religions. At the same time, as Christians we proclaim Jesus as the universal redeemer, but it is in the praxis, not the proclamation, that redemption lies. So it is only meaningful to talk about the uniqueness or distinctiveness of Christianity if discipleship goes beyond confessing Jesus as Lord to following Jesus' concrete praxis. This way of life, concludes Schillebeeckx in language that confirms our orientation in the two previous sections of this chapter, has two essential characteristics: it is marked by rejection of power and commitment to the poor and oppressed in a solidarity of love that opposes oppressive powers, and it is the way of the cross.

This view of the uniqueness of Jesus and the openness of God has consequences for Christian mission. It means, in the first instance, that mission cannot be conducted out of assumptions that what we have to offer is superior to the culture in which we conduct the mission. Second, there must be an awareness that it is God who saves, not the church, and that while the church has an important role to play and is the possessor of the revelation of God's saving purpose, God saved before the church was, and saves where the church is not present. Third, the particularity of Jesus suggests an attention to the particularity of our own context. As we saw in the previous section, how we understand the gospel is partially a product of our particular present day. But in our times, as we said above, most people in the world suffer under oppressive structures of a political or economic character. So the universality of the gospel today is distinguished less by "caritative diakonia" than by "political diakonia, which seeks to remove the causes of this structural injustice and in so doing recognizes the universality of human rights and human worth."[39]

LAYPEOPLE
AND THE MISSION OF THE CHURCH

Our discussion here, inasmuch as we have stayed within the present cleric/lay division in church structures, has led to the conclusion that the more broadly the mission of the church is construed, the more heavily the responsibility for mission falls upon laypeople. The proper role of ordained ministers is leadership of the worshiping community and the preaching of the word. For many centuries, these activities, narrowly understood, were identified as the mission of the church. But the moment that we disconnect the church as community of redemption from the human race as community of salvation, the moment we see that mission is more about saving praxis than it is about saving proclamation, clergy shift into an indispensable but ancillary role. Since they also live in a church within the modern world, clergy will and sometimes must take political responsibilities upon themselves. But such political *diakonia* is proper to the role of the layperson. Need we say once again that this does not mean some crude division between church and world? Church and world are inseparable precisely because the work of the church is mission. Whether it is internal mission to Catholics themselves, mission to unbelievers, or mission in the context of other religions, it is human beings speaking and acting in the company of other human beings who inhabit the same world, in the name of God's plan that the whole world be saved. The church is a divinely instituted human means to an end that dwarfs the importance of the church.

If the mission of the church is primarily conducted by laypeople, acting in the Spirit and on their own initiative as baptized Christians, we need to ask what will happen to this claim if and when sufficient structural reform in the church changes the patterns of ordained ministry. If ordination to ministry becomes something other than ordination to the separate culture of clerical life, what happens to the "lay vocation"? Even now, laypeople are not simply taking instructions from their ecclesiastical leaders and heading "out" into the world to carry them out. And the success of mission is a collective responsibility, not just that of laypeople. In the final chapter we turn our attention to these questions of structure and imagine a church that is organized very differently from the present one. In this reconfigured community, some ministries will be more directed toward the life of the community of faith, while others will be more directed toward the wider world. But because the different kinds of ministries will not be accompanied by distinct lifestyles, it will be easier to see that all have a responsibility for communion and all have a responsibility for mission.

8

An Accountable Church

IN THESE EARLY YEARS OF THE TWENTY-FIRST CENTURY, the
Catholic Church in North America stands at a critical point in its history. The particular occasion for the crisis in the church is well known.
The extent of clerical abuse of minors has come as a great shock to
Catholic people in the United States. For many, it has undermined
their trust in the church, and for not a few it has presented a serious
challenge to their continuing allegiance. But far more significant than
the acts of abuse—tragic and indefensible as they undoubtedly are—
is the revelation that church leadership has failed to address the crisis
adequately. Many bishops have been guilty of failures of judgment and
lapses of imagination, and some of plain deceit. Their insulation from
the lives of ordinary people is apparent. And their inability to see that
accountability for their actions is not primarily due to Rome but in
fact to the people they are consecrated to serve is perhaps the most
distressing phenomenon of all.

A crisis occasioned by sexual abuse has become a much deeper crisis of leadership. The Catholic Church in the United States will never
be the same again. Even if the problems of sexual abuse pass, and even
if a different kind of bishop comes to the fore, lay consciousness is forever changed. Never again will people find it easy to hear a bishop say,
"Just trust me." Henceforward, laypeople will look upon the clerical
culture of an enclosed society of celibate men as irreversibly dysfunctional, though they would be very wise not to imagine that an end to
mandatory celibacy or the opening of ministry to women will usher us
into a new age where the institution will have no problems. If the
church fails to take its problems seriously at this point in history, many

laypeople will simply leave the church. Worse still, those who leave will include many of the best—people full of faith who are largely responsible for the vitality of American Catholicism at the present day. What is remarkable in the Catholic Church in America today is primarily due to the level of lay involvement in ministry that sprang up in response to Vatican II. In so many informal ways, we already live in a lay-led church. The collapse of episcopal leadership at the national level and the unwillingness of the Vatican to look at the problems with any sensitivity only make this clearer.

It is a truism that North American Catholic laypeople are collectively the best-educated laity in the history of the church. However, we also bear the marks, for better or worse, of late-twentieth-century culture. We must struggle, like all citizens of the affluent world, with our tendencies to acquisitiveness and our blindness to the needs of the less affluent. We have trouble finding time for all that needs to be felt, thought, and done, beyond the energy-consuming tasks of domestic life and professional achievement. But we are also filled with convictions about the significance of private judgments, the centrality of personal freedoms, and the continuing value—despite its frequent follies —of the democratic ordering of life. If, as Americans, we need to awaken to the pains of the world that lead people to desperate measures to gain our attention, we rightly continue to insist on the superiority of a free society over authoritarian political systems, including those which masquerade as theocracy. If, as Catholics, we look for the reform of our church, we naturally enough expect that some of the changes will express both our human and our political values.

If the current crisis in the church is to be dealt with in any lasting fashion, it will have to involve a serious role for lay Catholics. The price of not doing this will be mass defection of the most active members of the faith community. But if laypeople are called into a central position in addressing the ills of the church, the clerical culture of the past will have to bow to lay convictions about the value of an open, democratic, and pluralistic society. The ways in which the church operates and the visible structures of the institution will have to change radically, if there is to be a vibrant future for American Catholicism. Of course, other futures are possible. Conservative response to the crisis, some of it lay, stresses the need to return to an earlier ecclesial world. Even if this were possible, the majority of active Catholic laypeople would not tolerate it, and the result would be a much smaller church. A more likely scenario would be for the church to bumble along in its present fashion, like a lazy householder, patching the roof here and there when too much rain comes pouring in, and hoping against hope that the whole thing won't come tumbling down any time soon. One of the things that makes this more likely is that it mirrors the worst of our American political culture, in which we ignore the lessons of history and imagine that our way of life is impervious to the effect of outside pressures, or is unaffected by the law of entropy. But this too would fail to satisfy the current temper of the more active Catholic laity, who are, on the whole, unhappy about the present and determined that it has to change. To return to the housing metaphor, there has been far too much deferred maintenance, and it cannot be postponed any longer.

In this final chapter I want to address just how change might occur in the church. I also want to speculate a bit about the kinds of change that might occur in the church without abandoning what is essential to the traditions of the community. But before tackling these two risky and perhaps tendentious topics, I need to try to answer the question why significant structural change in the church today is not only possible but perhaps even essential, if the Catholic Church is not to become simply a historical curiosity. Let us have no illusions about it. Failure to address this crisis will lead to the serious further debilitation of the American church. Vatican I may finally triumph over Vatican II.

DOES THE CHURCH HAVE A FUTURE?

In a recent book, the Canadian Catholic philosopher Charles Taylor has written eloquently about the face of religion today, and his analysis is important to our project.[1] Taylor's point of departure is a respectful dialogue with the classic work of William James, *The Varieties of Religious Experience*.[2] In that work, James chose to discuss personal rather than institutional religion. He was interested primarily in the religious experience of the individual, and he was ambivalent at best about the value of religious communities or churches. James famously defined religion as "the feelings, acts and experiences of individual men in their solitude, so far as they apprehend themselves to stand in relation to whatever they may consider the divine."[3] In its focus on the individual, the definition is very American, and in its attention to experience, profoundly contemporary. As it stands it is congenial to the convictions of most believing American Christians, while apparently inimical to the traditions of Catholicism. Taylor's dialogue with James both values his emphasis and qualifies it. James is right that our world "will almost certainly have lots of people who are following a religious life centered on personal experience," but this does not of itself mean that they will not freely associate themselves with like-minded others. "Many people will find themselves joining extremely powerful religious communities," Taylor concludes, "because that's where many people's sense of the spiritual will lead them."[4]

More important for our purposes than Taylor's conversation with James is his typology of forms of religion. Taylor identifies three stages of religion in the modern world. First, there was the stage that was typical of medieval Catholicism, in which religious authority defined the powers and limits of the political community. Second is the denominational understanding of Christianity identifiable with American Protestantism. Third is the world of the primacy of personal spirituality, in which associations with individual churches are much more fluid, if there at all. Traditional Catholicism might hanker after the premodern world of the first type, but—particularly in its American variant—it can hope at best for the perduring of type 2. But while American Catholicism has become one very large denomination among others, its more liberal end raises a different problem. "Progressive" Catholics in general, but certainly younger Catholics as a whole, reflect the modern "expressivism" that prioritizes personal conviction above institutional adherence. As so many of the more thoughtful undergraduates raised Catholic can be heard to say today, "I'm not religious, but I am spiritual." But if we give primacy to the unbounded personal search for authenticity, finding little reason to let that search be shaped by tradition, what care can we have, in the last analysis, for the persistence of the institutional form of Catholicism?

The question about the future of American Catholicism can be phrased thus: What is the tolerance of the church for the imperatives of modern expressivism? To what degree can the Catholic tradition find itself able to adjust to forms of personal and social organization that prioritize personal authenticity and devalue the individual's sub-ordination to the collective will or to the voice of authority? The "house of authority" in Catholicism is dead.[5] Catholics bow to the authority of the word of God and may well continue to turn to bish-ops for guidance in the interpretation of scripture. Catholics will also perhaps need to look to the same leaders for moral leadership, though this is far less sure today. But in the last analysis the voice of the insti-tution will be subordinated to the test of personal authenticity. It does not matter, in the end, whether we think this is a good thing or a bad thing. It has happened, and it is difficult to imagine that the pendu-lum will ever swing back the other way. The question is whether it spells the end of the Catholic Church or a new spring. Is there Cath-olicism beyond the house of authority?

At the end of Charles Taylor's book *Varieties of Religion Today*, he suggests three correctives to James's emphasis on private religious experience, which we may find useful in moving toward an answer to our question. The first, which we have already mentioned, is a cau-tion; giving such value to a personal search for religious meaning does not of itself dictate the demise of religious communities. Taylor is right to point out that it may be that a multiplicity of personal searches will carry many people into closer relationship with the Catholic Church. We should surely add that it seems obvious that this will occur only if the community itself is able to be welcoming to the logic of expressivism, including the prevalence of a critical spirit. Second, Taylor refers to the "quasi-agonistic" relationship between the con-tinuing denominationalism and the emergence of expressivism. He provides the helpful example of the struggle between the Christian right and more liberal groups, Christian or not, on the issue of school prayer. But we could also see this tension as internal to Catholicism. The hopes for the future of the church that we have discussed here in this book are clearly those of a liberal sensibility, but no one with an ounce of common sense can envisage a future in which there will not be a struggle with those of a more conservative temperament. Indeed, the tension may be very helpful, particularly in countering the easy optimism of a progressive mentality. Third, Taylor reminds James and us that an emphasis on personal religious experience can actually lead to quite demanding spiritual practices. One thinks, for example, of current interest in Eastern systems of meditation like Zen or, more generally, the commonly heard claim mentioned above that "I am spiritual but not religious." Taylor's point is easily adaptable to our context here. The future of the church will have to involve serious spiritual discipline, as serious as that which lies in the church's past, if the roots are to continue to flourish.

The question about the future of the church comes down to consideration of its adaptability to dramatic change, particularly to a transformed role for the laity, and to its capacity to distinguish between what is essential and what is not. A church built on a sense of unfolding tradition should not be frightened by such challenges. The problem is that our collective memory tends to be short, so that we may too easily identify essentials with matters that are only a century or two old. So, the papacy is essential to Catholicism, but the nineteenth- or twentieth-century vision of the papacy is not. Episcopal leadership is crucial to the church's sense of apostolicity, but the gender or marital status of the bishop is not significant. There would not be a Catholic Church without bishops, but cardinals and the entire Roman Curia and the Vatican city-state and the Vatican diplomatic service are expendable. The Word of God is unchanging while theological opinion is ephemeral. Popes must be chosen, bishops must be appointed, ministers must be called. But how these things happen is open to change and probably needs to change. Above all, there will always be laypeople, but they have grown up, and they want their adulthood to be recognized.

BEYOND VATICAN II

It is one of the ironies of twentieth-century Catholic history that Vatican II was outdated before it began. This does not mean that it was neither important nor necessary. It was both, but it was at heart a grand effort to bring the church into an age that was already waning. By the 1960s modernity was giving way to postmodernity; the so-called "communications explosion" was well under way, and the mixed economies of welfare capitalism were beginning to feel the pressures of transnational corporations that would redefine the political and economic landscape. The 1960s were the years in which Charles Taylor's "expressivism" took off. Books like Rachel Carson's

Silent Spring, Michael Harrington's *The Other America,* and Harvey Cox's *Secular City* were alerting the American public to just how much old paradigms were disappearing and new acts of imagination and will were needed.[6] Meanwhile, the bishops at Vatican II fought battles about putting the liturgy in a language that people could understand, recognizing that the church is one among many Christian communities and that Christianity is one among many religions, all worthy of respect. They recognized that people have the right to freedom of religion. They admitted that the church is not perfect. They found the collective will to talk of the church as a communion, they recognized that its monarchical history needed to be tempered by the oligarchy of episcopal collegiality and, yes, perhaps even a measure of consultative democracy. They clearly stated that laypeople have expertise that religious leaders do not always have and that their talents should be utilized. They said all these good, if quaint, things—things that ought not to have needed to be said in 1965. But many of them remain less than fully realized even today.

The legacy of Vatican II is in the first instance a story of accomplishment. The church would never be the same again. The discussions that have gone on in this book and that swirl around us among the Catholic laity and clergy in these early years of the new century are emboldened—if not actually occasioned—by the clear signals that the council fathers sent about the baptismal dignity of the laity, their full membership in the church, and the responsibilities for the church that attend on their particular vocations. These stirrings of a new theology for laypeople build upon the immensely suggestive image of the church as the People of God. And the image of the People of God itself leads directly to the central teachings of Vatican II: on the collegiality of bishops, the *sensus ecclesiae,* the role for the church in political and economic challenges, the importance of religious freedom and respect for those of other religions, the role of laypeople in ministry, and the trusting humility that should attend the passage of a "pilgrim church" through the world of God's creative will. When times are hard in the church, there are frequent stirrings of nostalgia for the days when the seminaries were full and Father knew best. This is an understandable reaction to the pain of change and confusion. It is also evidence of a clear preference for community over against the atomization of our contemporary existence, for the richness of ritual and popular religion over the demystification of today. But if we have lost some things, including some genuine values that we perhaps might work to regain, we have also benefited. When a child grows up, adulthood is both a loss and a gain. Above all, it signals entry into responsibility as a player in the game. After Vatican II, we have been given the tools to exercise that responsibility.

If Vatican II is first and foremost an accomplishment, it is also a record of missed opportunities and unfulfilled promise. This is not the place to assign blame (and indeed much of that discussion took place in chapter 5), but the list of what remains to be done to fulfill the agenda of Vatican II is pretty clear. Much more work is needed to disseminate the best of liturgical renewal to the parochial structure as a whole. The proclamation of the collegiality of the bishops is not taken seriously at the "top" of the church. The implications of conciliar teaching for ecumenism and interreligious dialogue have been inadequately explored and often frustrated by institutional fears, even where some progress has been made. The clear call for cooperation between clergy and laity at all levels of church life remains seriously underdeveloped, especially beyond the grass-roots level of parish relations. In general, it is safe to say that what can be done at the parish level has been at least attempted, if not always successfully. The best example is certainly the flowering of lay ministry, but where conciliar initiatives require the energies of the institution as a whole, the impetus to reform has limped. The face of change over the past forty years look exactly the way one would expect, if one recognizes that a blueprint for reform was handed to a bureaucracy that has been, to say the least, deeply unsympathetic to the success of the program.

Beyond the story of the mixed fortunes of Vatican II, there is a pressing need to address issues that were largely untouched by the council fathers. In the event that a new council were to be called before much longer, it would not be enough for it to insist on the full implementation of Vatican II, though that would certainly be an important part of the agenda. It would need to look beyond Vatican II to the world that exists now and to ask itself what Vatican II failed to notice about the world and the imperatives of ecclesial existence within it. The mission of the church to preach the gospel does not change; but the world in which it is preached is constantly evolving, and the way in which the mandate to evangelize is interpreted must be modified to take account of the dynamism of history. So let us suppose for a moment that Vatican III is about to open, and that we are responsible for setting its agenda. What would we want to see the council addressing?

Vatican III will have to look at the possibilities for democratization of church procedures and the implications for patterns of leadership. It will have to give serious and sustained attention to the place of women in the church. It must reexamine the nature of ministry and rethink the relationship between ministry in the church and mission to the world. It has to address the status of the claims of Catholic Christianity to be a saving religion, in light of the rival claims of other world religions. It must place the problem of poverty at the center of the church's worldly attention. It must confront the cultural hegemony of world capitalism. It must engage the phenomenon of globalization in a sophisticated manner, probing the human implications of cultural transformation. Above all, perhaps, it will have to develop a vision of the church as one player among others in a global act of solidarity to reassert the primacy of the human over the power of systems and bureaucracies. To accomplish this, it must rethink itself as a community of solidarity which keeps the systemic and bureaucratic elements of its institution in a healthy relationship to the true life of the church, which lies in the presence of the Spirit in the believing community.

Prominent among this list of topics for Vatican III is the role of the laity. Of course, Vatican II had much of value to say about the roles of the laity, much of which has been underdeveloped in the years since the council. But what was missing from the council was that thorough and radical reassessment of the nature of ministry in general, which should lead to a reframing of what it means to be a layperson and what it means to have a ministry in the church. As has been suggested time and again in the preceding pages, "ministry" is a dimension of the responsibilities of all lay Catholics in different ways. Some ministries may be more central to the life of the faith community, and thus be more necessary to its vitality. What has previously been called priesthood, the ministry of unity and eucharistic presidency, is certainly essential. But there is no justification for letting it generate a hierarchy, still less allowing it to continue to foster a disastrous divide in the Body of Christ between clergy and laity. How, then, might we proceed to rethink these structures of ministry?

THE STRUCTURES OF THE CHURCH

It is easy for all but the most conservative Catholics to see that there is something sadly wrong with the present structure of leadership in the church. Putting one's finger on the exact problem is not so simple, since there are many candidates. Some would point to the anachronism of an absolute monarch appointed for life. Others would single out the complex yet inefficient bureaucratic mechanism of the Roman Curia, through which the monarch watches and directs the world church. Still others might focus on the procedures for appointing bishops, finding them unlikely to produce the kinds of leaders the church needs. Yet others home in on the concentration of all power and formal leadership in the hands of a priestly caste defined by gender and celibacy. Today not a few would suggest that the problem is intensified by the passivity of the lay majority, who have for too long failed to voice their concerns for what is, after all, their church. Doubtless, no one of these explanations is the whole truth, and they probably all play a part in the currently dysfunctional situation. But it might be more helpful, rather than dwelling on the many contributory causes, to engage in a thought experiment about just what a structurally reformed church might look like. If we all took our responsibilities as Christians seriously, in the spirit of Vatican II and hoping for Vatican III, what could the church look like? Of course, I make no attempt to claim special insight here. I have no crystal ball, and I imagine that any serious change will take a lot of time and be mightily resisted by many. But I do not believe that we can refuse the challenge to reimagine our church in a fashion that would be faithful to its heritage and faithful to its dynamic character.

The Parish

Because it is in the parish community context that Catholics by and large celebrate the Eucharist and strengthen one another in faith, it makes sense to see parish life as the heart of the matter. The Catholic Church would be far healthier if we stopped defining ourselves by episcopal oversight or papal rule and focused our attention on the quality of our own particular faith communities. There, as we can boldly say in the light of all we have learned from Yves Congar, we are distinguished by our different ministries. The primary division in the community is not between priest and people but between those who exercise a ministry within the community and those whose lay ministry is primarily carried out in the mission to the world. All of these ministries are priestly, stemming from the common priesthood of the faithful. But there is a difference between the two kinds of ministry, *ad intra* and *ad extra*. The primary purpose of the former is to build up the community of faith in the service of its mission. The primary role of the latter is to carry out the mission. Perhaps we can distinguish between *ministers of the church* and *ministers in the world*. The former are responsible for strengthening the community of faith, and this includes a variety of responsibilities, from the celebration of the Eucharist and the preaching of the Word, to visiting the sick, teaching the young, and managing the parish finances. The latter carry out the mission of the church in the world, which, as we have now said several times, foregrounds a kind of indirect evangelization through struggle in solidarity with others for the fuller humanization of the world and against all that works to devalue the human.

Ministers of the church have in the past been divided as priests, deacons, and lay ministers. This will no longer be satisfactory. There are full-time ministers and part-time ministers. A large parish now might employ a full-time music minister, at the same time as it has part-time deacons, but it is not helpful to arrange them in a hierarchy in which the deacon is somehow "higher" than the music minister. Priests can be part-time, as many Orthodox church communities can testify. And there are some music ministers who are really "married to the parish," even when they also happen to be married to someone else and have a family to support, while there are probably a few "full-time" priests who have unfortunately trimmed their responsibilities into part-time hours.

As I look at the parish of the future, I see it led by a small team of ministers, all of whom will have been ordained by the bishop to celebrate the Eucharist, though this role may not be their primary contribution to the community. It might be that one of them is a gifted preacher, another a full-time teacher in a local school, another a hospital chaplain, and perhaps another possesses a pronounced talent for administration. Their ordination to preside at the Eucharist is simultaneously the recognition that they possess the charism of leadership. These servant leaders will all possess training in theology and scripture studies, though perhaps in different degrees. Not all will be theologians, since this too is a special talent. Sunday and weekday masses will be led by one or another of the team. One of them will usually preach, though the responsibility can be passed to others in the community for good reasons. The entire team will recognize its accountability not only to the local bishop, who exercises the episcopal role of oversight (Greek *episkopē*), but most especially to the local community that they serve.

Alongside this leadership team there will be a host of other individuals exercising particular ministries within the community. The list of these is not new to us: music ministry, youth ministry, bookkeeping, catechetical instruction, visiting the sick of the parish and those in the hospital, social-justice ministry, and so on. Some of these people may be full-time workers in the parish; others may combine part-time ministry with a lay life in the world. None of them is currently ordained to celebrate the Eucharist for the community, though some of them may be in the course of time. Since they are not ordained to preside at worship, they are not designated formally as servant leaders of the community. But many may have fine leadership qualities and may, in the course of time, come to be appointed to leadership, and hence be ordained to preside at the Eucharist. What binds them all together, and together with the leadership team, is that they all, paid or volunteer, understand their work for the church as ministry rather than employment, and the community recognizes this too.

The third group in the parish, probably the largest, is those who exercise no particular ministry within the faith community but whose ministry is carried out in their daily lives in the world. These are the true "lay ministers," but should better be known as ministers in the world. Catholics are familiar with the notion that laypeople live their lives in the world, showing a good example to non-Catholics by the witness of holy lives. This remains true, though what constitutes a holy life may be open to some elaboration. In particular, we have to get beyond imagining that private piety is enough. A holy life requires much more willingness to connect faith to the social and political realities of our world, and that in turn requires good formation in the ability to understand the connections. One of the responsibilities of the parish community, then, must be to teach adult Catholics how to read the world. The Catholic whose mission is in the world has a right to expect that the faith community will help him or her to carry out the mission successfully.

All three groups are responsible together for the good governance and practice of the faith community. Each must have its representatives on a genuine parish council. The parish council will be a deliberative body, not merely consultative, charged with long-range and strategic planning for the community. Day-to-day leadership decisions will be made by the servant leaders, but they are in the end responsible both to the parish council and to the bishop. The bishop safeguards the freedom of the ministers to preach the gospel; the parish council protects the community's values and standards. The parish council is elected by the whole community. Committees of the council will have particular responsibility for oversight of finances, education, social-justice ministry, liturgy, and so on, and those committees will work with the appropriate ministers. The parish council concept symbolizes the responsibility of the whole community for the life of the parish and the accountability of its ministers to the community.

The picture of the Catholic parish of the future presented here is dramatically different from the present situation in several ways. First, there is no cultic separation between those ordained to preside and those with other ministries. Second, I have deliberately made no mention either of celibacy or of gender, since both issues seem irrelevant to these models of ministry. Celibacy as a personal commitment formally recognized by the church is in the first instance a defining characteristic of religious life. There is only an accidental connection between ministry and membership in a religious order. And there is absolutely no connection between ministry and celibacy. Celibacy is a statement about how I believe God is calling me to live out my life. It has some practical advantages and disadvantages, though its meaning is not to be found here. As for gender, after almost thirty years of thinking about the issues of ministry and women, I still cannot claim ever to have heard a good theological argument why the two do not mix, at any level in the church.[7]

The issues of cultic separation, on the one hand, and of celibacy and gender, on the other, are clearly very closely related. If particular ministries in the church, those connected most to power and leadership, are reserved to celibate men, then intentionally or not a cultic separation between these ministers and the rest of us will become a fact. From the other side, if we wish to insist on a qualitative difference between the universal priesthood of the faithful and the "hierarchical priesthood," then to define it according to lifestyle or gender can only buttress that separation. But the opposite is also true. Take away the requirement of celibacy, take away the prohibition on women, and the understanding of ministry will change. Or change the understanding of ministry and watch celibacy and gender become irrelevant.

The cultic understanding of priesthood will change also if the patterns by which appointments are made are changed. The parish of the future will appoint pastoral leaders through agreement between the community, represented by its parish council or the personnel committee of the council, and the local bishop. The apostolicity of the church is protected in two ways, by the practice of episcopal ordination of servant leaders to lead the church and therefore to preside at the Eucharist, and by the involvement of the apostolic people in the process. The accountability of leaders is symbolized in the role the community plays in their appointment. Obviously, this has to mean, on the one hand, that the bishop cannot simply impose a leader on a particular community and, on the other, that the community cannot simply tell the bishop whom it wants as its leader. The details of how such an arrangement might work would be matter for careful thought and consideration. But there is nothing in the suggested practice that contravenes a good theology of ministry.

If appointments are made for the community, with the involvement of the community in the selection of candidates, this spells the end of the "career structure" of priestly ministry. Such a change could only be a blessing to the church. Ideally, though not always, servant leaders would come from within the ranks of the local community, selected perhaps for the qualities they have displayed in other ministries. In all probability, they would remain within that faith community for many years. The notion that success in leadership leads to a bigger or wealthier parish simply must be eradicated, and was never part of the early church's understanding of ministry. In our church it has often led to the nastier side of ambition and the petty maneuvering for position that careerism always entails. It has also inevitably meant that more senior leadership positions have tended to go to those who have set out to achieve them. Both these facts are in themselves strong arguments for change.

Changes such as these would also herald the end, finally, of the infantilization of the laity. It is simply no longer acceptable for baptized adult Catholics to be treated as if they had neither expertise nor responsibility for their community. The pattern of shepherd/sheep, while it is metaphorically appropriate to the description of the relationship between Christ and his church, is destructive to the daily life of the community of faith. Shared responsibility and accountability are the characteristics that need to replace this patriarchal and patronizing relationship. It would be good for all, for the more passive members of the so-called laity most of all.

The Diocese

The bishop is the leader of the church. There is no higher authority in the local church than the bishop, and in the universal church than the bishop of Rome. The term "diocese," then, refers in the first instance to the church here in this particular corner of the world, not to some bureaucratic or juridical structure. The diocese is not a principality, not a corporation, most definitely not a branch office of a transnational conglomerate. The diocese is the church in its fullness, an association of local communities of faith bound to one another by the gospel and by their common leader in the faith, the local bishop. Episcopal responsibility extends to both internal and external ministry. The bishop is responsible for the good order of the local communities of faith and for overseeing the commitment of Catholics to the mission of the church in the world. These are major responsibilities, and this is one ministry that cannot be part-time. But it is no more all-consuming than being president of Ford Motor Company or secretary of state, and both of those positions can be held by married men or women. Why not bishops? The only reason to continue to insist on celibacy is a continuing conviction that married holiness is not as good as celibate holiness.

Where will bishops come from in our church of the future? Like local servant leaders, they will normally be selected from among the local communities by regional or national associations of bishops, with the involvement of the local communities in their selection. The pattern that we have described for the parish structure will apply also at the diocesan level. Dioceses need to have diocesan councils that are not merely consultative, presumably with elected representatives from the local communities. Some would be ordained leaders, others ministers of the church and still others ministers in the world. It might be the responsibility of this diocesan council to formulate policy for the diocese, along with the bishop. It or some ad hoc committee elected for the occasion would be charged with representing the interests of the local church in the selection of a new bishop. The preference should be for the selection of a candidate from within the diocese, with the expectation that he or she would normally serve until resignation or retirement. It would obviously be necessary to select an individual who had shown good leadership in the parochial structure, and who was willing and able to work collegially with the whole membership of the church. The process of moving bishops to more "senior" dioceses needs to be severely curtailed. It was never the practice of the early church, and it again only reinforces an unhealthy careerism. While there might well be exceptions, it is the *pattern* of the career structure that is destructive of the role of the bishop.

The diocese is the local community writ large, as it is also the universal church in miniature. Just as we described the parish, so we should envisage the diocese. It is the local church, not the diocesan offices. Surely, there is a measure of administration in any large organization, and there will be those whose ministry will be exercised at the diocesan level, as coordinators or facilitators of one type of ministry or another. But the works of the diocesan administration are done for the local communities and are accountable to them. It should also be obvious that while this work at the level of the diocese is a true ministry, it bears no connection whatsoever to ordination to lead the local community. A diocesan administration with a preponderance of administrators who were formerly ordained to preside in parishes ought to be an anomaly. A diocese should be led by a bishop, in tandem with a genuinely deliberative diocesan council. Financial responsibility for the diocese should be under the supervision of a diocesan financial council (canon law already envisages something like this). Officers of the diocese should be selected for their talents as administrators, not because they previously held leadership responsibilities in local communities.

National or Regional Bishops' Conferences

Assemblies of bishops from particular regions or countries currently take place in the church, and there are good reasons for them to continue and, indeed, to be expanded. Typically they are annual meetings of all the bishops of the particular grouping, and they meet to discuss issues of common concern, sometimes to formulate national policy on a particular matter. As they currently stand, they cannot make policy for the national church without submitting it to the Vatican for approval. At least in the U.S. context they have shown enormous deference to the Vatican, even on issues where they are clearly likely to be better informed.[8] They have large responsibilities but little power to effect change on their own authority. This would generally please those in the Vatican committed to the continued centralization of authority in the church, and those bishops—presumably the more conservative—afraid of the "tyranny of the majority" over their personal authority within their own dioceses.

Changes in the structure of national conferences should follow the same pattern of checks and balances we have already envisaged at the parochial and diocesan levels. In the first instance, there is no good reason why national conferences should include only bishops. It would seem helpful to establish more of a synodal structure, in which representatives of all four dimensions of ministry would be elected to participate: bishops, leaders of local communities, ministers of the church, and ministers in the world. Second, this should be a deliberative body with the power to act for the American church, to speak on behalf of the church, and to make the kinds of decisions that would make it easier for the gospel to be heard in the American context. Clearly, it would need powers of discernment and direction from councils of the whole church to determine what changes it could initiate on its own authority and which would require the approval of the whole church. So, for example, a change in the law on celibacy, which is purely disciplinary, might be a "local option." But a change that would admit women to leadership positions in the church, since it would require rethinking some doctrinal positions, would have to be a decision of the whole church.

The Universal Church

When we look at how the universal church would need to be organized to reflect the shifts we have already described, we may be surprised how little needs to change, and how much the picture we paint sheds light on the structures envisaged at more local levels. Currently, the bishop of Rome is elected; he can call a general council, which is a truly deliberative and not merely consultative body; and he has an administrative structure, the Roman Curia, to aid him in his task of oversight of the universal church. All of these elements would remain present in the future church, though subtly changed. The task of the church at this universal level also remains much the same as the central task of the pope today: namely, to safeguard the unity of the church and to preserve sound teaching. The parochial, diocesan, and national levels of church leadership have no responsibility for the formulation of doctrine. That remains the responsibility of the whole church, symbolized in a general council of the church led by the pope.

The pope is first and foremost the bishop of Rome and is only leader of the universal church because he is the bishop of Rome. However, because the bishop of Rome is the leader of the universal church, the procedures that would normally be used for the selection of a bishop must be different. Currently, the bishop of Rome is the only elected leader in the Catholic Church's hierarchy. This may well stay the same in the future church, but future popes will need to be elected by a different body of individuals than the present one. Cardinals are selected by the pope himself and are usually either archbishops of major dioceses around the world or heads of curial departments. Their only official function is to elect a new pope. A medieval development that had no connection whatsoever with apostolicity or the practices of the early church, the College of Cardinals is clearly an anachronism and should be dispensed with.

Once the office of cardinal is retired, it becomes necessary to determine a more representative method for the election of a pope. Clearly, every branch of the church needs to be represented. Senior bishops should be elected from national churches, the number from each being based on the size of local churches. This, incidentally, depending on the fairness of the count, would mean that the majority of the members of an electoral college would be drawn from Latin America and Africa, and the fewest would come from Europe, which is virtually the reverse of the present situation. It would also mean that the Vatican administration would be represented very little, or perhaps not at all. We need to be open to arguments for their representation, perhaps on the grounds that Vatican administrators bring a more universal perspective to the assembly than would bishops from any particular country. But there seems to be no sound theological reason why they should be involved since, ecclesiologically speaking, the Curia has no standing. It is simply a bureaucratic body. Moreover, like the diocesan administration, the future Vatican bureaucracy should not be staffed by ordained ministers, but simply by Catholics with appropriate administrative skills. The present structure, in which lesser positions are often held by priests or religious, middle-level positions have the rank of bishops (usually titular bishops of some long defunct see), and heads of department are usually archbishops or cardinals, is a sign—if one were needed—of the hopeless confusion of Rome about the meaning of ordination.

What kind of person would such a revised electoral college choose to become the bishop of Rome? Since our future church does not exclude women and married men from the ranks of servant leaders, presumably any of them could be selected. In principle, of course, any baptized adult Catholic could be chosen (even now, the cardinals could legitimately select a layman as the next pope). But the likelihood, then as now, is that the pope would be chosen from among those who had demonstrated their capacities as servant leader through long service at the diocesan level, or perhaps through service in a religious order (more about religious shortly). The requirements, then as now, for a successful pope are pretty obvious: sound teaching, charisma, good administrative skills, common sense. Above everything else, above even the role of teaching, the pope is the one who in person symbolizes the unity, the catholicity of the entire church. Leadership may sometimes require difficult and even unpopular decisions, but more often it requires the skills of speaking for the whole group, summoning their courage and gifts to the tasks at hand, and inspiring them with the words of the gospel. For these reasons, one who is centrist rather than conservative or liberal, one who is pastoral before being either profoundly intellectual or ethereally "spiritual" is to be preferred.

When we think today of the center of the church in Rome, we tend naturally enough to think and speak of "the Vatican." This is a mistake. The symbol of unity of the church is undoubtedly the person of the pope, but the authority that goes with being at the center does not reside in the Vatican. It is not "the pope and Curia" who lead the church, but "the pope and the bishops." In other words, it is a general council of the church, not a set of administrative departments, which teaches and strategizes for the whole church. Unlike a bureaucracy, the bishops are servant leaders who work in the local churches. In our future church they will have been appointed through a deliberative process that will have involved representatives of the whole community, not just of ordained ministers, and they will work within an understanding of their accountability to the local church which they serve. Their collective responsibility, then as now, is to teach with the highest authority, in the name of Christ. But they will do so as the voice of the whole community, not separated from it. Clearly, they will need to meet more often than they have in the past, or they could delegate some of their responsibilities to a smaller synod of bishops, as envisaged by Vatican II but with genuine deliberative status.

In this picture of the structure of the future church we have had little so far to say about doctrine, either of faith or morals. Principally, this is because there is nothing much to say. It is not the teaching of the church that is problematic or dysfunctional in our present situation. We are not dealing with a crisis of faith. On the contrary, our problems stem from the incapacity of the present ecclesial structure to lead with confidence and authority in the modern world. Because the structure is unsatisfactory, teaching with authority is more difficult than it needs to be, and because it has become harder to achieve, it is now sometimes surrounded with authoritarian language that is counter-productive. The erosion of authority can come through plain poor teaching (*Humanae Vitae*, Paul VI's encyclical banning "artificial" birth control) or by way of trying to achieve the impossible (John

Paul II's attempt to proclaim "closed" the discussion of women in the ministry). Either simply undermines authority, and without authority good teaching is impossible, because it is not received.

Special Tasks

Not everything that the church needs can be achieved through the parochial and diocesan structures, either in their present form or as we have envisaged them here. There are some particular skills that may not be available to every parish community, some distinct tasks that a diocese does not have the resources to accomplish. So, then as now, there will need to be special groups and organizations that have a certain independence from the parochial and diocesan structure, though not of course from the community. Three in particular deserve notice here: the role of religious orders, the standing of theologians, and the responsibilities of Catholic educational institutions.

Religious orders. Throughout the history of the church, the orders of men and women have testified in a particular way to gospel values, which are the possession of all Christians. Traditionally, the religious orders take vows of poverty, chastity, and obedience, though the first two of these might be better phrased as "simplicity of life in community" and "celibacy." One could also envisage so-called secular institutes in which married people might play a role. But in all these cases, the orders highlight the responsibility of all Christians to devote themselves to the pursuit of a life in conformity with gospel values. Attachment to personal possessions, disordered sexuality, and egotistic willfulness are primary ways in which all of us can be derailed in our progress toward God. Members of religious orders are no less susceptible to these failings than the rest of us, but they make their lives into living symbols of the need we all have to strive for holiness of life. That, by the way, is why their failings can seem so much more scandalous than those of "ordinary" Christians. It is not that they are holier than the rest of us, but that they have committed themselves to public witness to values that we must all pursue.

Over the centuries, the roles of the religious orders have been principally focused on prayer, education, and the works of mercy. They have founded and run schools and hospitals, enclosed themselves in monasteries to pray for the church and to seek their personal spiritual perfection, crisscrossed the world preaching and giving retreats, written profound theology and been spiritual directors to popes, and worked as missionaries, psychologists, and financiers. While some of these roles may have become less important and others more prominent, in every case they represent either institutions that serve across parish and diocesan boundaries or individuals whose personal expertise makes them valuable in more than one local context. Moreover, historically speaking, the free commitment of members of religious orders to celibacy has given them a personal independence to go wherever the need is greatest. While religious orders in the future might include married members, it has to be said that in the community context of the religious life, celibacy makes sense. It is a true sacrifice to good purpose, both in the symbolic roles of religious men and women and in the practical dimensions of what tends to be their way of working for the church. Nothing that we have said above about the lack of need of celibacy in the lives of servant leaders relates to the special conditions of the religious life.

In one respect the roles of religious might change dramatically in the church of the future. It will probably become far less necessary for them to be ordained to the priesthood. In monastic life historically, ordination to the priesthood was by no means the norm. In religious orders founded more recently, ordination to the priesthood has been far more common, since the work of male religious has been in tasks that the church of these more modern times deemed appropriate only to priests—preaching, professing theology, giving spiritual direction. But male or female religious are not likely to be servant leaders of local churches. By definition, their normal roles cut across parishes and dioceses. We see so many of them in the parochial structure today only because they are making up for the shortage of diocesan clergy, but this shortage would disappear with a shift to the servant leader model as we have envisaged it here. Religious would then be freed to perform their true functions for the church.

Theologians. The bishops are those who teach with final authority in the church, but this does not mean that they are the only ones who contribute to the understanding of Christian doctrine. All members of the community contribute, though bishops do so in one way, servant leaders in another, the whole believing community in yet another. Some of those bishops, servant leaders, and lay Catholics also happen to be trained theologians, and as theologians they have a responsibility to the church that is not quite the same as their other roles. Perhaps the difference would be clearest in the case of a bishop who is also a professional theologian. As bishop, the person is charged with the task of preserving the tradition and expounding it in a way that makes sense to contemporary Christians. As a member of a general council or a synod of bishops, the bishop may have the even more solemn task of deliberating upon new teaching. But as a theologian, the bishop is engaged in the intellectual exploration of the meaning of the tradition for Christian life today. This is an important task, not at all the same task as teaching with authority, and one that demands considerably more intellectual freedom, though no less sense of responsibility.

The theologian in the church of the future may be a bishop, a servant leader, a minister of the church or a minister in the world. As a theologian, however, he or she is engaged in the task of thinking responsibly, creatively, with imagination, about the ways in which the gospel can be made more accessible to contemporary people. The task of the theologian is a ministry performed within the community and at the service of the community. But because the theologian's work relates to doctrine, it is not authoritative in itself or for the community in which the theologian participates. It is one voice in the general conversation of the church through which the Spirit guides the community into new understandings of its ancient faith. Given this understanding of theology, it is most important that the theologian be free to pursue intellectual inquiry without being policed by some episcopal or Vatican watchdog organization. There can surely be bad theology, just as there can be bad preaching or poor spiritual direction. But the checks on bad theology are the conversations of theologians among themselves, episcopal teaching, and the sense of the faithful. In other words, the Spirit that leads the church into truth will filter out what is not of God.

Catholic colleges and universities. Many though not most Catholic dioceses in this country have Catholic institutions of higher education within their boundaries. Most though not all of these are separately incorporated in such ways that they are not directly under the control of, nor directly responsible to, the local bishop. They also vary enormously in size, quality, financial stability, and the manner in which they promote their Catholic status. Pope John Paul's 1990 Apostolic Constitution, *Ex Corde Ecclesiae*, stressed the importance of these institutions in the life of the church and their responsibility to promote the Catholicism's commitment to the intellectual life. In some ways, the value of the papal letter has been overshadowed by subsequent wrangling about the attempt to impose juridical norms governing the conduct of Catholics teaching theology in these institutions. However, the central point of *Ex Corde* is beyond dispute. A school that claims the name "Catholic" is responsible to the Catholic community.

Catholic institutions of higher education are indeed responsible to the Catholic community, but we have to be clear about what they are responsible *for*. They are not primarily places of catechetical instruction, nor where ministers are supplied with professional ministerial training, though both of these activities may go on to a degree in at least some Catholic colleges and universities. Their primary purpose is intellectual inquiry and the training of their students in habits of critical thinking. This is what makes them colleges and universities. What makes them Catholic is that this teaching function is conducted with an expressed commitment to the Catholic vision of the real. They pursue scientific truth with the same unqualified commitment to truth that their secular counterparts possess. They are committed to the moral truth of life that the humanities and the arts seek to express, but they also have profound existential commitments that grow directly out of their claim to be Catholic.[9]

While secular academics may sometimes scoff at the possibility of being scientifically objective while committed to a particular vision of the real, and thus may tend toward George Bernard Shaw's oft-repeated dictum that a Catholic university is a contradiction in terms, the real problem for Catholic schools tends to come from within the church. Some Catholics, including some in positions of authority, have trouble seeing how unfettered inquiry and faithfulness to the teaching of the church can coexist. Thus, theologians have recently been required to obtain a mandate, which testifies that they teach the Catholic tradition faithfully. Of course, this is not the real issue. Most Catholic theologians faithfully represent the tradition of the church.

The problem arises when they wish to think and teach like theologians, which means that they sometimes must press beyond what the church teaches, not so much to criticize it as to seek new avenues of expression for what is the faith of the church. Theologians writing for their fellow theologians in learned journals have always been given great latitude by the church, but when their words reach the "simple faithful" it has been another story. So in the life of Catholic institutions, the question comes down to one of what is going on in the classroom. Are students in theology classes being taught catechetics, or are they being taught to think critically, in an informed manner, about how their faith relates to their lives?

The primary role of the Catholic university as *Catholic* is to teach the church.[10] This inevitably means a creative and sometimes stressful role for the Catholic university. Teaching is never simple rote repetition, but involves teaching people to think. When the Catholic university teaches Catholics to think within the tradition, it is training them for an informed but creative appropriation of that tradition and, it is hoped, giving them the tools to participate more fully in the life of the church. In these pluralistic days when Catholic schools do not only teach Catholics, it can only be one of their functions to "educate good Catholics." But insofar as that remains one of their responsibilities, they will fulfill it only when the Catholic products of the schools have internalized the vision of the real that the school inculcates, are informed about their own tradition, and are ready to engage in their local communities in the fashioning of the tradition to meet the needs of the times.

Most Catholics graduating from Catholic colleges and universities will never exercise ministry to the church, though all should be trained to see that their Catholic identity requires that they minister in the world. Readers will recall that we have suggested that mission in the postmodern world is in large part about dealing with the challenges of global capitalism, since this is the biggest force at the root of antihuman impulses today. We should therefore expect Catholic institutions of higher education to train their students, Catholic or not, to understand these powers and structures in the world, and to know why and how and when to resist them. All education is at the service of the human community, and all of it needs to be placed in a moral context. This is why, though all academic institutions must be committed to scientific objectivity, all of them need to be explicit about the vision of the real by which they live. Catholic institutions should never be shy about their vision of the real.

THE END OF THE LAITY?

In the last few pages we have been engaged in what people sometimes call "thinking outside the box." Given the history of the last thousand years of the church, such an exercise may seem futile to some, naïve to others, and plain heretical to not a few more. But we have set aside nothing essential in order to think of the future of the church in this way. Papacy, episcopacy, and ordained leadership remain. Prayer, worship, and doctrine are intact. The parochial and diocesan structures continue. Grace, holiness, saints, pilgrimage, incense and eucharistic adoration, veneration of the Virgin, the rosary, the liturgical year, all are untouched in this vision of the future. If the picture above presents consternation, it will be for one or both of the following reasons. Either we do not take seriously the adult equality of all the baptized, or we are wedded to the outmoded cultural forms in which the indispensable office of ordained ministry is currently cloaked.

There is one further set of questions that we must address in defense of this picture of the future church. If we are all called to be ministers, whether ministers to the church or ministers in the world, does that mean that there are no laity any longer? And if there are no laity, are there no clergy? Would this not be the nightmare conclusion of the "laicization of the clergy and the clericalization of the laity" that we saw John Paul II warning against in *Christifideles Laici*? If there are no longer distinctions between ordained and nonordained, have we not settled for the Protestant polity that Yves Congar so carefully distinguished from the Catholic? For Congar in *Lay People in the Catholic Church* the essential note of Catholic ordained priesthood was that it was derived not from the common priesthood of all the baptized, but from a special commission by Christ. When we involve the community in the selection of their priests and bishops, are we not transgressing against this distinction between the two priesthoods?

The first response to this genuine and important question must be to clear away the deadwood of irrelevance. When we talk of ordained ministry and other ministries, and we wish to recognize a difference between them, the difference has absolutely nothing to do with lifestyle. Celibacy is not a mark of priesthood. After all, the church recognizes the orders of Orthodox priests, many of whom are married, and there are quite a number of former Episcopalian married priests now serving within the ranks of the Catholic priesthood. Gender, I would also maintain, is not a mark of priesthood, but there is no question the church is mostly divided on this issue between conservatives who deny the possibility of ordaining women and liberals who welcome it. More importantly, the details of the entire structure of the institution, which have developed over history, including the enclosed priestly culture, the princely trappings of episcopal office, and the regal splendor of the Vatican with its medieval court, even the city-state status of the Vatican—all of these have nothing whatsoever to do with priesthood. To remove any or all of these features from the church today would in itself say nothing about the nature of priesthood. It would be possible to be absolutely committed to the qualitative distinction between ordained and common priesthood and still want to see an end to mandatory celibacy and dramatic reform of the Vatican.

The second point we need to make is that a venerable centrist theologian like Yves Congar came to see in his later years that starting from the clerical/lay divide was not helpful in discussing the role of laypeople in the church. As we have had frequent occasion to mention, Congar eventually reframed his views in terms of different ministries. Moreover, in a vision that is reflected on time and again in the second half of this book, he was happy to designate as ministry not only priestly ministry and those lay ministries that take place within the ecclesial community but also both the ministries of Catholic Action and the ministries that individual Catholics exercise in the world in virtue of their baptism, without ecclesiastical supervision. This does not mean that Congar would necessarily subscribe to the picture of the future church outlined in this chapter. But it certainly suggests that there is a greater closeness between "lay" and "clerical" ministry than might formerly have been thought. Moreover, it finally gives the lie, it would seem, to any suggestion that "lay ministry" within the church is simply a matter of the laity standing in for the clergy where circumstances temporarily require it.

With these two provisos, we can say that the picture of ministry suggested in this chapter does indeed preserve a distinction between the ministerial calling of servant leaders and that of other ministers to the church and in the world. First, we all of us who are baptized adults exercise a ministry in the world by working toward the "vision of the real" that the Catholic tradition proclaims. No one in the church calls us to that ministry. Christ calls us to it in our adult membership in his church. Relative to this ministry, the church's responsibility is to provide us with a rich sacramental life and good teaching about the relation of the Catholic vision of the real to the realities of our contemporary world. Second, some of us develop particular talents, which are utilized within the local community. We become ministers to the church, but we do not simply decide to become ministers. We offer ourselves to the community, or the community comes to us and asks us to serve in whatever capacity. The community thus confirms our calling to minister, but this is not strictly ordination. We are called to be music ministers or financial overseers, but we are not ordained to these roles.

When the time comes for the community to have new servant leaders, or when the community is so moved by the qualities of one of its members that it wishes to have that person called to servant leadership, the bishop becomes part of the mix. The church is not just the local church but also the universal church, and the role of the bishop here is as the symbolic focus of unity of the church and leader of the diocese. It is the bishop who confirms the calling of the new servant leader in the laying on of hands, but he should never take this step except in response to the expressed will of the community that this particular individual be appointed to minister as a servant leader in their midst. This two-sided process preserves the responsibility of the local community and of the bishop for protecting the genuineness of the calling. The community says, "This one!" and the bishop answers, "Yes, in the name of the whole church!" The community's role is an expression of their adulthood in the Christian life. The bishop's role is the confirmation of the apostolic tradition. Whether or not the servant leader serves for life, turns out to be a howling success or an abject failure, goes on to become a bishop or even pope, the community has had its say and the ordination by the bishop has come in the name of the universal church. The difference between the ministry of the servant leader and the ministries of the rest of us has surely been appropriately preserved, while other values of equal importance have been expressed through the participation of the local community.

To come full circle, the picture of ministries outlined here approximates that which seems to have marked the early church. A clergy/lay distinction was foreign to the consciousness of early Christians. As we saw in chapter 1, all were God's people (the laity) and all were "heirs according to the promise" (the *klēroi*, the called, the "clergy"). Some were undoubtedly called to leadership positions that the majority would not occupy, but this in no way introduced a hierarchical distinction among Christians, still less two separate orders of life. Only later, when secular models of leadership and the holiness of the monastic vocation came to cloud the picture, did something like the lay/clerical divide become a reality in the church. Not everything that the early church did is neatly transferable to the present day. But when its understanding of ministry, put into modern dress, seems so well tailored to address the ills of our present ecclesial condition, perhaps the time has come to look again at the wisdom of the first Christians, imbued as they were with the Spirit, too young in the faith to be hidebound by custom.

Notes

1. This point is made extremely well by Richard R. Gaillardetz in "Shifting Meanings in the Lay-Clergy Distinction," *Irish Theological Quarterly* 64 (1999): 115–39. The pneumatological perspective is explored especially in pp. 134–39.

Introduction:
The Idea of the Laity

1. Avery Dulles, *Models of the Church* (Garden City, N.Y.: Doubleday, 1978), 178.

2. For this brief historical sketch I rely primarily on three texts: Alexandre Faivre, *The Emergence of the Laity in the Early Church* (New York/Mahwah, N.J.: Paulist, 1990); Yves Congar, *Lay People in the Church* (Westminster, Md.: Newman, 1965), especially pp. 3–27; and Congar's article "Laic et laicat," in *Dictionnaire de spiritualité ascétique et mystique*, ed. Marcel Viller et al. (Paris: Beauchesne, 1976), vol. 9, cols. 79–108. Both Faivre and Congar refer respectfully to the work of I. de la Potterie, "L'origine et le sens primitif du mot 'laic,'" *Nouvelle revue théologique* 80 (1958): 840–53. De la Potterie's research produces many secular citations in which the laity are distinguished from those with some special role in a particular context, so that the laity can be taken to be those without any particular office or role. But de la Potterie is in agreement with Faivre and Congar about the absence of such usage in the early church. The same article also appears in his book *La vie selon l'Esprit* (Paris: Cerf, 1965).

3. Faivre, *Emergence of the Laity*, 7.

4. Congar, *Lay People in the Church*, 3.

5. Ibid., 4.

6. For a discussion of Clement's so-called "First Letter," see Faivre, *Emergence of the Laity*, 15–24. For the text of the letter, see *Early Christian Fathers*, trans. and ed. Cyril C. Richardson (New York: Macmillan, 1970), 43–73.

7. Congar, *Lay People in the Church,* 5.
8. Faivre, *Emergence of the Laity,* 40.
9. Ibid., 35–40.
10. Congar, *Lay People in the Church,* 9.
11. Ibid., 12.
12. Ibid., 17–18.

Chapter 1
The Road to Vatican II

1. The literature on the Catholic Church and liberalism is extensive. The best-known and perhaps still the best introduction to the subject is E. E. Y. Hales, *The Catholic Church in the Modern World: A Survey from the French Revolution to the Present* (Garden City, N.Y.: Hanover House, 1958). A most interesting collection of essays on the subject is *Catholicism and Liberalism: Contributions to American Public Philosophy,* ed. R. Bruce Douglass and David Hollenbach (Cambridge: Cambridge University Press, 1994). See also Joseph A. Komonchak, "Modernity and the Construction of Roman Catholicism," *Cristianesimo nella Storia* 18 (1997): 353–85.

2. The flavor of the council is very well presented in James J. Hennessy, *The First Vatican Council: The American Experience* (New York: Herder, 1963).

3. My discussion of the French church in the first half of the twentieth century owes a great debt to the work of Etienne Fouilloux, in particular to his fine book *Une église en quête de liberté : La pensée catholique française entre modernisme et Vatican II, 1914–1962* (Paris: Desclée de Brouwer, 1998).

4. *Pascendi,* Eng. trans., *The Papal Encyclicals,* vol. 3, ed. Claudia Carlen (New York: McGrath, 1981), 71–98.

5. For general studies of modernism, see Alec R. Vidler, *The Modernist Movement in the Roman Church* (Cambridge: Cambridge University Press, 1934), the more accessible *A Variety of Catholic Modernists* (Cambridge: Cambridge University Press, 1970), and the relevant portions of Vidler's *The Church in the Age of Revolution: 1789 to the Present Day* (Baltimore: Penguin, 1961). The best short discussion is the chapter by Bernard M. G. Reardon in volume 2 of *Nineteenth Century Religious thought in the West,* ed. Ninian Smart (Cambridge: Cambridge University Press, 1985), 141–77. Two more recent works of merit are Lester R. Kurtz, *The Politics of Heresy: The Modernist Crisis in Roman Catholicism* (Berkeley: University of California Press, 1986), and Marvin R. O'Connell, *Critics on Trial: An Introduction to the Catholic Modernist Crisis* (Washington, D.C.: Catholic University of America Press, 1994). Most recently there is an outstanding collection of essays that leans more toward a political or social reading of the modernist crisis

than one which explains it entirely in intraecclesial terms. See *Catholicism Contending With Modernity: Roman Catholic Modernism and Anti-Modernism in Historical Context*, ed. Darrell Jodock (Cambridge: Cambridge University Press, 2000).

6. In Pius X's letter *Pascendi* (see n. 4) and in the decree *Lamentabile*. While there was no such school as modernism, there was certainly a movement within the church to open up both scriptural studies and theology to the implications of the historical method. But the principals in this intellectual shift in Catholicism were certainly not all of one mind. The best introduction to the movement in general is Marvin O'Connell's book *Critics on Trial* (see n. 5).

7. Alfred Loisy, *The Gospel and the Church* (Philadelphia: Fortress, 1976).

8. Adolf von Harnack, *Das Wesen des Christentums*, translated as *What is Christianity?* (New York: Harper, 1957).

9. For a brief account of Benigni's influence, see O'Connell, *Critics on Trial*, 361–64.

10. Jacques Maritain (1882–1973) was a French Thomist philosopher. Reginald Garrigou-Lagrange, O.P. (1877–1964), a neoscholastic theologian and Chenu's teacher in Rome, became an arch-enemy of the new theology. Pierre Rousselot (1878–1915), a brilliant young historian of philosophy, argued for a historically sensitive approach to the study of Thomas and died tragically in the First World War. Joseph Maréchal (1878–1944), Jesuit metaphysician and Kantian scholar, is principally appreciated today as a formative influence on the transcendental Thomism of Karl Rahner.

11. *Humani Generis*, Eng. trans., *The Papal Encyclicals*, vol. 4, ed. Claudia Carlen (New York: McGrath, 1981), 175–84.

12. Jean Daniélou, "Les orientations présentes de la pensée religieuse," *Études* 249 (1946): 5–21.

13. The best insights into this aspect of liberation theology are afforded in a series of interviews conducted and edited by Mev Puleo and published as *The Struggle Is One: Voices and Visions of Liberation Theology* (Albany, N.Y.: SUNY Press, 1994). The classical sources are probably the two works by Gustavo Gutiérrez, *Liberation Theology* and *We Drink from Our Own Wells* (Maryknoll, N.Y.: Orbis, 1972, 1990).

14. Henri Godin and Yvan Daniel, *France, pays de mission?* (Paris: Les Editions ouvrières, 1943). The text of this book, slightly abbreviated, is contained in a work by Maisie Ward, *France Pagan? The Mission of Abbé Godin* (New York: Sheed & Ward, 1949). Ward's book begins with a short biography of the extraordinary Abbé Godin and concludes by discussing the ways in which the work he initiated grew after his untimely death in 1944. Godin was the more influential of the two authors, and the book is usually treated, perhaps unfairly, as his work alone.

15. Ward, *France Pagan?* 9.

16. Ibid. The thesis from which Ward quotes is entitled *D'éclassement, religion et culture humaine: Essai de psychologie sociale.*

17. Godin, quoted in Ward, *France Pagan?* 89.

18. Ibid., 92.

19. Ibid., 49.

20. For one example among many, see the pope's letter of July 30, 1928, to Mme. F. Steenberghe-Engerich, president of the International Union of Catholic Women's Associations in *The Lay Apostolate,* selected and arranged by the Benedictine Monks of Solesmes (Boston: St. Paul, 1960), 274–77.

21. Ibid., 275.

22. *Restoring All Things: A Guide to Catholic Action,* ed. John Fitzsimons and Paul McGuire (New York: Sheed & Ward, 1938), viii.

23. This interest was brought to its heights in the work of Emile Mersch, especially *The Theology of the Mystical Body* (St. Louis: Herder, 1951).

24. Ward, *France Pagan?* 21.

25. Ibid., 24.

26. On this see Jean-Guy Vaillancourt, *Papal Power: A Study of Vatican Control Over Lay Catholic Elites* (Berkeley: University of California Press, 1950).

27. Ironically enough, one of the few organizations today calling for a renewal of Catholic Action is the Catholic Research Institute, run by a congregation of traditionalist nuns, who favor the Latin mass, consider Vatican II a tragedy, and supply papal encyclicals, but only up to Pius XII!

28. See Elizabeth Teresa Groppe, "The Contribution of Yves Congar's Theology of the Holy Spirit," *Theological Studies* 62 (2001): 451–78.

29. Ambroise Gardeil (1859–1931). His major work is *Le donné révélé et la théologie* (Paris: Cerf, 1932), with an introduction by Chenu.

30. Maurice Blondel (1861–1949), a French philosopher, had an incalculable but important influence on both the modernist generation and that of the new theologians.

31. Marie-Dominique Chenu, *Une école de théologie: Le Saulchoir.* The text is most easily obtainable as reprinted in a book by the same name, which also includes interpretive essays by Giuseppe Alberigo, Etienne Fouilloux, Jean-Pierre Jossua and Jean Ladrière and a brief postscript by Chenu himself (Paris: Cerf, 1985).

32. Ibid., 8.

33. *History of Vatican II,* vol. 2, ed. Giuseppe Alberigo and Joseph A. Komonchak (Maryknoll, N.Y.: Orbis, 1997), 3–4, 52–54.

34. See Alberigo's essay in *Le Saulchoir,* "Christianisme en tant qu'histoire et théologie confessante," 11–35.

35. *Le Saulchoir,* 133.

36. Ibid., 148–49.

37. The text of these propositions is reproduced on p. 35 of *Le Saulchoir.*

38. Yves Congar, *Chrétiens désunis* (Paris: Cerf, 1935); Eng. trans., *Divided Christendom* (London: Geoffrey Bles, 1939).

39. Yves Congar, "The Call and the Quest, 1929–1963," in *Dialogue Between Christians: Catholic Contributions to Ecumenism* (Westminster, Md.: Newman, 1966), 1–51.

40. Ibid., 3.

41. Ibid., 21.

42. Ibid., 29.

43. This stormy period of Congar's life is admirably documented in a collection of his autobiographical writings, *Journal d'un théologien, 1946–1956,* ed. Etienne Fouilloux (Paris: Cerf, 2001).

44. Pius XII's encyclical attacking the work of the new theologians eventually appeared in 1950 and is discussed later in the chapter.

45. Yves Congar, *Jalons pour une théologie du laicat* (Paris: Cerf, 1953); Eng. trans., *Lay People in the Church* (Westminster, Md: Newman, 1957; rev. ed., 1965), quotation from p. 40 (all quotations are from the revised edition).

46. Jean Daniélou, "Les orientations présentes de la pensée religieuse," *Études* 249 (1946): 5–21.

47. Ibid., 7.

48. Ibid., 14.

49. Teilhard de Chardin's work is best represented by his two most widely read works, *The Divine Milieu* (New York: Harper, 1960) and *The Phenomenon of Man* (New York: Harper, 1959). The most sophisticated exposition of the theological import of his work is to be found in Christopher F. Mooney, *Teilhard de Chardin and the Mystery of Christ* (New York: Harper & Row, 1966).

50. Ibid., 17.

51. Ibid., 20.

52. Reginald Garrigou-Lagrange, "La nouvelle théologie: Où va-t-elle?" *Angelicum* 23 (1946): 126–45.

53. On Garrigou-Lagrange's unfairness, see Philip J. Donnelly's critique of his treatment of Bouillard in "On the Development of Dogma and the Supernatural," *Theological Studies* 8 (September 1947): 471–91.

54. Ibid., 481.

55. Quoted in Fouilloux, *Une église en quête de liberté,* 283.

56. There are two principal places where de Lubac addresses this issue directly and at length, *Surnaturel: Études historiques* (Paris: Aubier, 1946), inexplicably never translated into English, and *Le mystère du surnaturel* (Paris: Aubier, 1965); Eng. trans., *The Mystery of the Supernatural* (New York: Herder & Herder, 1967).

57. Henri Bouillard, *Conversion et grâce chez St. Thomas d'Aquin* (Paris: Aubier, 1944).

58. This idea of tradition as incorporating both remembering and forgetting is well developed by John E. Thiel, *Senses of Tradition* (Oxford: Oxford University Press, 2000).

59. Thiel is particularly good on this "retrospective" reading of tradition (*Senses of Tradition*).

60. For the history of the worker priest movement, see *Worker Priests: A Collective Documentation*, trans. John Petrie (New York: Macmillan, 1956).

61. Fouilloux, *Une église en quête de liberté*, 202.

62. It is particularly close to the notion of the theologian as "professional insider" developed by Ada María Isasi-Díaz in her *mujerista* theology. See *En La Lucha: A Hispanic Women's Liberation Theology* (Minneapolis: Fortress, 1993), and *Mujerista Theology* (Louisville, Ky.: Westminster John Knox, 1996).

63. See n. 45 above.

64. François Varillon, "Sacerdoce et laicat," *Masses ouvrières* (March 1947): 50–62; Yves de Montcheuil, in a collection of his essays, *Mélanges théologiques* (Paris: Cerf, 1946). There is a good selection of his essays in English in *For Men of Action* (South Bend, Ind.: Fides, n.d.). De Montcheuil was executed by the Nazis in 1944.

65. Henri de Lubac, *Three Jesuits Speak* (San Francisco: Ignatius, n.d.).

66. Ibid., 113.

67. The English translation appeared the following year (Chicago: Fides, 1956).

68. Philips, *Role of the Laity*, 21.

69. Ibid., 26, 27.

70. Ibid., 171.

71. Ibid., 174.

72. In a conversation with Jean Guitton, September 8, 1950, quoted in Peter Hebblethwaite, *Paul VI: The First Modern Pope* (Mahwah, N.J.: Paulist, 1993), 236.

Chapter 2
The Achievement of Yves Congar

1. Yves Congar, *Jalons pour une théologie du laicat* (Paris: Cerf, 1953; rev. ed. 1964). Eng. trans., *Lay People in the Church: A Study for a Theology of the Laity* (Westminster, Md.: Newman, 1955; rev. ed. 1965). All references are to the revised edition.

2. Yves Congar, "My Pathfindings in the Theology of Laity and Ministries," *The Jurist* 2 (1972): 169–88; idem, introduction to *Christifideles laici* (Paris: Cerf, 1989).

3. See especially "Ministères et laicat dans les recherches actuelles de la théologie catholique romaine," *Verbum Caro* 18 (1964): 127–48; "Min-

istères et structuration de l'Eglise," *La Maison Dieu* 102 (1970): 7–20; "Quelques problemes touchant les ministères," *Nouvelle revue théologique* 93 (1971): 785–800.

4. Congar, *Lay People*, xxi.

5. Congar, "My Pathfindings," 174.

6. *Fifty Years of Catholic Theology: Conversations with Yves Congar,* edited and introduced by Bernard Lauret (Philadelphia: Fortress, 1988), 65.

7. Yves Congar, "L'apostolat des laics," *Nouvelle revue théologique* 78 (1956): 5–52.

8. This masterly discussion of priesthood occupies pp. 194–233 of *Lay People in the Church.*

9. Quoted and discussed in Avery Dulles, *Models of the Church* (Garden City, N.Y.: Doubleday, 1987), 20.

10. Charles Péguy, *Oeuvres complètes*, 9:180–81, quoted in *Lay People in the Church*, 434.

11. Congar leans heavily here on the work of R. A. Gauthier, *Magnanimité: L'idéal de la grandeur dans la philosophie païenne et dans la théologie chrétienne* (Paris: J. Vrin, 1951). Gauthier's work is very suggestive for a lay apostolic spirituality, combining as it does the formative role of magnanimity in individual life with the call to social justice on the plane of communal life.

12. Congar, "My Pathfindings," 177.

13. Ibid., 177–78.

14. Ibid., 182–83.

15. Karl Rahner, "Notes on the Lay Apostolate," in *Theological Investigations, II, Man in the Church* (Baltimore: Helicon Press, 1963), 319–52.

16. In addition to "My Pathfindings," see the articles listed at n. 3 above.

17. Congar, "Ministères et laicat," 145.

18. Ibid.

19. Congar, "My Pathfindings," 178.

20. Ibid., 181–82.

21. This issue is discussed much more fully in chapter 4.

22. These remarks are contained in an unpublished paper by Pellitero, "Congar's Developing Understanding of the Laity and Their Mission," presented at the Catholic Theological Society of America annual meeting, June 2000, in San Jose, California.

Chapter 3
Collegiality, Coresponsibiliity, and the Council

1. Leon-Joseph Suenens, *Coresponsibility in the Church* (New York: Herder & Herder, 1968).

2. Yves Congar, *Jalons pour une théologie du laicat* (Paris: Cerf, 1953; rev. ed. 1964); Eng. trans., *Lay People in the Church: A Study for a Theology of the*

Laity (Westminster, Md.: Newman, 1955; rev. ed. 1965). All quotations are from the revised edition.

3. The text of the Vatican documents is taken throughout from *Vatican Council II: The Conciliar and Post Conciliar Documents, Study Edition*, ed. Austin Flannery, O.P. (Northport, N.Y.: Costello, 1987). References are to the numbered sections of the documents.

4. The most important text is the multivolume *History of Vatican II*, ed. Giuseppe Alberigo and Joseph A. Komonchak (Maryknoll, N.Y.: Orbis, 1995–2000). Thus far, three volumes of a projected five have appeared.

5. Suenens, *Memories and Hopes* (Dublin: Veritas, 1992), 56.

6. *History of Vatican II*, ed. Alberigo and Komonchak, 2:72.

7. See Suenens, *Memories and Hopes*, 60; and *History of Vatican II*, ed. Alberigo and Komonchak, 2:5.

8. *History of Vatican II*, ed. Alberigo and Komonchak, 2:411.

9. George A. Lindbeck, *The Future of Roman Catholic Theology: Vatican II—Catalyst for Change* (Philadelphia: Fortress, 1970). Lindbeck is perhaps here only echoing the words of John XXIII in his opening address to the council.

10. Paul J. Roy, S.J., "The Developing Sense of Community (*Gaudium et Spes*)," in *Vatican II, the Unfinished Agenda: A Look to the Future*," ed. Lucien Richard, Daniel Harrington, and John. W. O'Malley (Mahwah, N.J.: Paulist, 1987), 190–202. This entire collection of articles is a valuable resource for appreciating how Vatican II was evaluated some fifteen years ago. The time may be ripe for a new study.

11. Rahner's famous article on this topic is included in the same volume: "Towards a Fundamental Theological Interpretation of Vatican II," in *Vatican II, the Unfinished Agenda*, ed. Richard et al., 9–21.

12. Suenens, *Coresponsibility*, 187.

13. Suenens also admits here that the inclusion of laywomen was "not without some difficulty" (*Coresponsibility*, 187). One of the best evidences of this is the decision of the council fathers during the debate in the third session on *Lumen Gentium* not to allow Barbara Ward to address them on the topic of world poverty, on which she was certainly the leading expert present at the council and one of the best-known voices in the world. They chose James Norris, a Catholic layman instead, on the dubious grounds that it would be "premature" to have a woman address the assembly. As Xavier Rynne dryly comments, "Obviously, the thought was still too much for the masculine-oriented, Italian-dominated bureaucracy of the Council" (*The Third Session* [New York: Farrar, Straus & Giroux, 1965], 178). Perhaps it was just as well, since at least one relatively liberal council father had criticized what he perceived to be a weakness of purpose in the document, calling it "too feminine."

14. Suenens, *Coresponsibility*, 188.

15. Ibid., 189, 191.

16. Ibid., 190, 192.

17. Quoted in Suenens, *Memories and Hopes*, 152–53.

18. Ibid., 330.

19. See especially Edward Schillebeeckx, *The Layman in the Church and Other Essays* (New York: St. Paul, 1963); *The Real Achievement of Vatican II* (New York: Herder & Herder, 1967); *The Mission of the Church* (New York: Seabury, 1973); and, above all, *Church: The Human Story of God* (New York: Crossroad, 1990).

20. Schillebeeckx, *Mission of the Church*, 122.

21. Gustavo Gutiérrez, *A Theology of Liberation: History, Politics, and Salvation* (Maryknoll, N.Y.: Orbis, 1973), 56–58.

Chapter 4
Theology and the Laity since Vatican II

1. *The Vocation and Mission of the Lay Faithful in the Church and in the World*, Post-Synodal Apostolic Exhortation, December 30, 1988, Publication No. 274-8 (Washington, D.C.: U.S. Catholic Conference, 1989).

2. The possibilities here are endless, but we shall restrict ourselves to writings by Hans Urs von Balthasar, Ramon Pellitero, Bonaventure Kloppenburg, Hans Küng, Edward Schillebeeckx, Leonardo Boff, and Rosemary Radford Ruether.

3. Peter Hebblethwaite, *The Runaway Church: Postconciliar Growth or Decline?* (New York: Seabury, 1975).

4. *The Challenge of Peace: God's Promise and Our Response: A Pastoral Letter on War and Peace* (Washington, D.C.: U.S. Catholic Conference, 1983); and *Pastoral Letter on Catholic Social Teaching and the U.S. Economy* (Washington, D.C.: U.S. Catholic Conference, 1985).

5. On national bishops' conferences, see Thomas J. Reese, S.J., *A Flock of Shepherds: The National Conference of Catholic Bishops* (Kansas City: Sheed & Ward, 1992); and Joseph Komonchak, "On the Authority of Bishops' Conferences," *America*, September 12, 1998.

6. "On Human Work" (Washington, D.C.: U.S. Catholic Conference, 1981).

7. Leon-Joseph Suenens, *Coresponsibility in the Church* (New York: Herder & Herder, 1968), 190.

8. Hebblethwaite, *Runaway Church*, 50.

9. For a thorough discussion of the impact of John Paul's authoritarianism on the fortunes of the church, see John Cornwell, *Breaking Faith: The Pope, the People and the Fate of Catholicism* (New York: Viking Compass, 2001).

10. Xavier Rynne, *The Second Session* (New York: Farrar, Straus, 1964) 223.

11. An outstanding discussion of Catholicism and public life can be found in Claire E. Wolfteich, *American Catholics in the Twentieth Century: Spirituality, Lay Experience and Public Life* (New York: Crossroad, 2001).

12. "Visiting Pope Listened, Rejected 'Lay Ministry,'" by Peter Hebblethwaite, *National Catholic Reporter*, October 2, 1987, 5.

13. Ibid.

14. See Peter Hebblethwaite, "Unloved Synod Dies Unmourned with Few Assets," *National Catholic Reporter*, November 6, 1987, 17–18.

15. *Commonweal*, December 4, 1987, 682.

16. Publication No. 5-268, Washington, DC: U.S. Catholic Conference, 1998.

17. See http://www.usao.edu/~facshaferi/STECHER2.HTM.

18. This is a central issue for Karl Rahner, who insisted that a layperson acting in such a capacity is no longer a layperson. His purpose seemed to be to expand the understanding of "ordained" ministry, while at the same time safeguarding the integrity of "true" lay ministry in the world, exercised in virtue of baptism and without direct ecclesiastical oversight . See "Notes on the Lay Apostolate," in *Theological Investigations, II, Man in the Church* (Baltimore: Helicon, 1963), 319–52.

19. "Reflections of the American Bishops Commemorating the Fifteenth Anniversary of the Issuance of the Decree on the Apostolate of the Laity," Publication No. 727-8 (Washington, D.C.: U.S. Catholic Conference, 1980).

20. *Called and Gifted*, 4.

21. Ibid., 6.

22. Ibid., 8.

23. Ibid., 9.

24. Publication No. 5-002 (Washington, DC: U.S. Catholic Conference, 1995).

25. Quoted in "Instruction," 1.i-ii.

26. Ramiro Pellitero, *La teología del laicado en la obra de Yves Congar* (Pamplona: Servicio de Publicaciones de la Universidad de Navarra, 1996). See also an unpublished paper given at the meeting of the Catholic Theological Society of America in June 2000, "Congar's Developing Understanding of the Laity and Their Mission."

27. Hans Urs von Balthasar, *A Short Primer for Unsettled Laymen* (San Francisco: Ignatius, 1985).

28. Ibid., 11.

29. *The Von Balthasar Reader*, ed. Medard Kehl and Werner Löser (New York: Crossroad, 1982), 292.

30. Ibid., 293.

31. Ibid., 292.

32. Bonaventure Kloppenburg, *The Ecclesiology of Vatican II* (Chicago: Franciscan Herald, 1975).

33. Ibid., 319.

34. Ibid., 314.

35. On the relationship of priest and layperson, see Edward Schille-beeckx, *Ministry: Leadership in the Community of Jesus Christ* (New York: Crossroad, 1981); on the ecclesiological vision of Vatican II, see *Church: The Human Story of God* (New York: Crossroad, 1990).

36. Schillebeeckx, *Ministry*, 135.

37. Leonardo Boff, *Church, Charism and Power: Liberation Theology and the Institutional Church* (New York: Crossroad, 1985). The book was origi-nally published in Portuguese in 1981.

38. Ibid., 30.

39. Boff expands this particular discussion in a later book, *Ecclesiogenesis: The Base Communities Re-Invent the Church* (Maryknoll, N.Y.: Orbis, 1985).

40. Among Ruether's many writings, the crucial text here is *Women-Church: Theology and Practice of Feminist Liturgical Communities* (San Fran-cisco: Harper & Row, 1985).

41. Ruether, *Women-Church*, 3.

42. Ibid., 5.

43. Ibid., 87.

44. Ibid., 89.

45. Hans Küng, *Structures of the Church* (Garden City, N.Y.: Doubleday, 1971) and *The Church* (Garden City, N.Y.: Doubleday, 1976).

46. Hans Küng, *Reforming the Church Today: Keeping Hope Alive* (New York: Crossroad, 1990).

47. Ibid., 82.

48. Ibid., 83.

49. Ibid., 91.

50. Much harsher criticisms than those of Küng can be found in Stephan Pfurtner's article "Pathology of the Catholic Church," in *Ongoing Reform of the Church*, ed. Alois Muller and Norbert Greinacher (New York: Herder & Herder, 1972), 24–32. The same volume includes an interesting piece by Yves Congar entitled "Renewal of the Spirit and Reform of the Institution" (pp. 39–49), in which he gently chides criticisms that do not approach the reality of the church "with a sufficiently inward and spiritual orientation" (p. 46). He argues for "a union of the Spirit and an effort to renew the struc-tures," and cites "basic groups" as a positive example of such an alliance (p. 49).

Chapter 5
Secularity

1. Yves Congar, *Lay People in the Church: A Study for a Theology of the Laity* (Westminster, Md.: Newman, 1955; rev. ed. 1965), 19. All quotations are from the revised edition.

2. See pp. 31–34 above.

3. Georges Bernanos, *The Diary of a Country Priest* (New York: Carroll & Graf, 1983), 298.

4. "I've got more faith in Hitler than in anyone else. He's the only one who's kept his promises, all his promises, to the Jewish people" (Elie Wiesel, *Night* [New York: Bantam, 1982], 77).

5. Congar, *Lay People*, 19

6. Dietrich Bonhoeffer, *Letters and Papers from Prison, The Enlarged Edition*, ed. Eberhard Bethge (London: Folio Society, 2000).

7. A good example of this kind of appropriation can be found in John A. T. Robinson's best-seller from the 1960s, *Honest to God* (Philadelphia: Westminster, 1963).

8. William F. Lynch, *Christ and Prometheus: A New Image of the Secular* (Notre Dame, Ind.: University of Notre Dame Press, 1970).

9. William O. Fennell, "The Theology of True Secularity," in *New Theology no. 2*, ed. Martin E. Marty and Dean G. Peerman (New York: Macmillan, 1965), 28–38. Lynch quotes from pp. 29–30.

10. This brief treatment of Habermas is greatly expanded in my work *Theology and Critical Theory: The Discourse of the Church* (Nashville: Abingdon, 1990).

11. Harvey Cox, *The Secular City: Secularization and Urbanization in Theological Perspective* (New York: Macmillan, 1965).

12. *Religion in a Secular City: Essays in Honor of Harvey Cox*, ed. Arvind Sharma (Harrisburg, Pa.: Trinity Press International, 2001).

13. All quotations from documents of Vatican II are taken from *Vatican Council II: The Conciliar and Post Conciliar Documents*, ed. Austin Flannery, O.P. (Northport, N.Y.: Costello, 1987).

Chapter 6
The Liberation of the Laity, the Liberation of the Church

1. Rembert Weakland, "What 'Restorationists' Are Doing to the Liturgy, and Why They Should Be Resisted," *Commonweal*, January 11, 2002.

2. "A Crisis of Clergy, Not of Faith," *New York Times*, March 6, 2002, A21.

3. John Henry Newman, *On Consulting the Faithful in Matters of Doctrine*, edited with an introduction by John Coulson (New York: Sheed & Ward, 1961).

4. Ibid., 110.

5. "Womanist" is the self-designation of black feminists, and "*mujerista*" is the term preferred by many Latina women.

6. A recent and notable exception to this judgment is Bernard J. Lee, *The*

Future Church of 140 B.C.E.: A Hidden Revolution (New York: Crossroad, 1995).

7. Penny Lernoux, *Cry of the People: The Struggle for Human Rights in Latin America—The Catholic Church in Conflict with U.S. Policy* (New York: Penguin, 1982), 17.

8. Consult http://www.votf.org

9. In a private conversation over a cup of coffee in London in 1976.

10. Accounts of individuals like Charles Curran and Leonardo Boff of the processes to which they were subjected show how basic human rights and legal due process are seemingly ignored by the Sacred Congregation for the Doctrine of the Faith. On this whole question of authority, see Patrick Granfield, *The Limits of the Papacy: Authority and Autonomy in the Church* (New York: Crossroad, 1987). For Yves Congar's own account of his ill-treatment at the hands of the then Holy Office, see the fascinating *Journal d'un théologien, 1946–56*, ed. Etienne Fouilloux (Paris: Cerf, 2001).

11. Ada María Isasi-Díaz, *In the Struggle: A Hispanic Women's Liberation Theology* (Minneapolis: Fortress, 1993).

12. On Gramsci and the theologian, see my article "For Whom Do We Write? The Responsibility of the Theologian," in *The Promise of Critical Theology: Essays in Honour of Charles Davis*, ed. Marc P. Lalonde (Waterloo, Ont.: Wilfrid Laurier University Press, 1995), 33–48.

13. Paul Lakeland, "The Lay Theologian in the Church," *The Month* 25 (January 1992): 19–25.

14. Yves Congar, *Lay People in the Church: A Study for a Theology of the Laity* (Westminster, Md.: Newman, 1955; rev. ed. 1965). All references are to the revised edition.

15. See Avery Dulles, *Models of the Church* (Garden City, N.Y.: Doubleday, 1974), passim.

16. Pius XII, address to the International Congress of the Catholic Press, Rome, 1950, quoted in Congar, *Lay People*, 265.

17. *Vatican Council II: The Conciliar and Post Conciliar Documents*, ed. Austin Flannery, O.P. (Northport, N.Y.: Costello, 1987), 790–91.

Chapter 7
Mission in the (Post) Modern World

1. For documents of Vatican II, see *Vatican II: The Conciliar and Post-conciliar Documents*, ed. Austin Flannery, O.P. (Northport, N.Y.: Costello, 1987). For *Gaudium et Spes,* see 903–1101.

2. Dennis Doyle, *Communion Ecclesiology: Visions and Versions* (Maryknoll, N.Y.: Orbis, 2000).

3. Ibid., 12.

4. Doyle correctly insists on the need to allow a range of versions of communion ecclesiology, in the name of the catholicity of the church's vision. He is irenic about all the views he recounts, except for those at the left-wing extreme. Hans Küng and Leonardo Boff are thus obviously suspect, though Doyle admits that they offer necessary correctives.

5. Tertullian, *Apologeticus*, chap. 39, in *Tertullian: Apologetical Works* (Washington, D.C.: Catholic University Press, 1950), 98–102.

6. A nuanced case about the negative effects of global capitalism in the context of the globalization phenomenon is made, e.g., in Michael Hardt and Antonio Negri, *Empire* (Cambridge, Mass.: Harvard University Press, 2001); and James H. Mittelman, *The Globalization Syndrome* (Princeton, N.J.: Princeton University Press, 2000). A more popular treatment of the phenomenon of globalization is Thomas L. Friedman, *The Lexus and the Olive Tree* (New York: Anchor, 2000). From the perspective of Christian theology, see *Religions/Globalizations: Theories and Cases*, ed. Dwight N. Hopkins, David Batstone, Eduardo Mendieta, and Lois Ann Lorentzen (Durham, N.C.: Duke University Press, 2001); and Daniel M. Bell, *Liberation Theology after the End of History: The Refusal to Cease Suffering* (New York: Routledge, 2001).

7. Friedman, *Lexus and the Olive Tree*, 8.

8. Ibid., 9, 31, 42, 418.

9. Ibid., 364.

10. More sophisticated treatments of globalization than Friedman's recognize the essentially political nature of the questions that global capitalism provoke. Most significant in this respect is Hardt and Negri's *Empire* (see n. 6 above).

11. Bell, *Liberation Theology after the End of History;* see also the other works listed in n. 6 above.

12. The principal voices of radical orthodoxy are the British scholars John Milbank, Catherine Pickstock, and Graham Ward, though the numbers increase daily, and they have found allies in such eminent American theologians as Stanley Hauerwas. A representative sample of key works include the following: John Milbank, *Theology and Social Theory: Beyond Secular Reason* (Oxford: Blackwell, 1990); Catherine Pickstock, *After Writing: On the Liturgical Consummation of Philosophy* (Oxford: Blackwell: 1997); Graham Ward, *Cities of God* (New York: Routledge, 2000); and *Radical Orthodoxy: A New Theology*, ed. John Milbank, Catherine Pickstock, and Graham Ward (New York: Routledge, 1998).

13. Milbank, *Theology and Social Theory*, 434.

14. For a critique of Milbank, see Lakeland, *Postmodernity*, 68–76.

15. See Gilles Deleuze and Felix Guattari, *A Thousand Plateaus: Capitalism and Schizophrenia* (Minneapolis: University of Minnesota Press, 1987); and Michel Foucault, *Technologies of the Self: A Seminar with Michel Foucault,*

ed. Luther H. Martin, Huck Gutman, and Patrick H. Gutman (Amherst, Mass.: University of Massachusetts Press, 1988).

16. Franz Hinkelammert, *Cultura de la Esperanza y Sociedad sin Exclusión* (San José: DEI, 1995).

17. See *A Catholic Modernity? Charles Taylor's Marianist Award Lecture. With responses by William M. Shea, Rosemary Luling Haughton, George Marsden and Jean Bethke Elshtain*, ed. James L. Heft (New York: Oxford University Press, 1999).

18. Edward Schillebeeckx, *Church: The Human Story of God* (New York: Crossroad, 1990), 51.

19. Max Horkheimer and Theodor Adorno, *Dialectic of Enlightenment* (New York: Herder, 1972).

20. For an elaboration of this typology, see Paul Lakeland, *Postmodernity: Christian Identity in a Fragmented Age* (Minneapolis: Fortress, 1997).

21. Harvey Cox, *Religion in the Secular City: Toward a Postmodern Theology* (New York: Simon & Schuster, 1984).

22. Karen Armstrong, *The Battle for God* (New York: Knopf, 2000).

23. The Bible of this theological school is George Lindbeck, *The Nature of Doctrine: Religion and Theology in a Postliberal Age* (Philadelphia: Westminster, 1984).

24. For *Humanae Vitae,* see the publication of Ignatius Press, 1978. The other encyclicals and the apostolic letter have been published by the U.S. Catholic Conference, Washington, D.C. All these papal documents are most easily available at the Vatican website, http://www.vatican.va.

25. See, e.g., Gabriel Vahanian, *The Death of God: The Culture of Our Post-Christian Era* (New York: Braziller, 1961); and Thomas Altizer, *The Gospel of Christian Atheism* (Philadelphia: Westminster, 1966).

26. For the Tübingen School, see James Tunstead Burtchaell, "Drey, Möhler and the Tübingen School," in *Nineteenth Century Religious Thought in the West*, volume 2, ed. Ninian Smart, John Clayton, Patrick Sherry, and Steven T. Katz (Cambridge: Cambridge University Press, 1985), 111–39. Burtchaell appends a detailed bibliography.

27. The bibliography is immense. A representative threesome of serious works might be *Vatikanum II und Modernisierung: Historische, theologische and soziologische Perspektiven*, ed. Franz-Xaver Kaufmannn and Arnold Zingerle (Paderborn: Schöningh, 1996); *Catholicism and Liberalism: Contributions to American Public Philosophy*, ed. R. Bruce Douglass and David Hollenbach (Cambridge: Cambridge University Press, 1994); and *Catholicism Contending with Modernity: Roman Catholic Modernism and Anti-Modernism in Historical Context*, ed. Darrell Jodock (Cambridge: Cambridge University Press, 2000).

See in particular two essays by Joseph Komonchak: "Modernity and the Construction of Roman Catholicism," *Cristianesimo nella Storia* 18 (1997):

353–85, and "Vatican II and the Encounter between Catholicism and Liberalism," in *Catholicism and Liberalism*, ed. Douglass and Hollenbach, 76–99.

28. Komonchak, "Modernity and the Construction of Roman Catholicism," 383.

29. Karl Rahner, "Towards a Fundamental Theological Interpretation of Vatican II," in *Vatican II: The Unfinished Agenda: A Look to the Future*, ed. Lucien Richard, Daniel Harrington, and John W. O'Malley (New York: Paulist, 1987), 9–21; Komonchak, "Modernity and the Construction of Roman Catholicism," 385.

30. For a representative text from his prolific output, see Michael Novak's *The Catholic Ethic and the Spirit of Capitalism* (New York: Free Press, 1993).

31. *A Catholic Modernity?* (see n. 17 above).

32. Ibid., 13.

33. Ibid., 16, 18.

34. Ibid., 20.

35. "Justice in the World" §6, in *Proclaiming Justice & Peace*, ed. Michael Walsh and Brian Davies (Mystic, Conn.: Twenty-Third Publications, 1984), 190.

36. See, above all, Schillebeeckx, *Church: The Human Story of God*, 5–15, 159–86.

37. Ibid., 164.

38. Ibid., 165, 166.

39. Ibid., 169.

Chapter 8
An Accountable Church

1. Charles Taylor, *Varieties of Religion Today: William James Revisited* (Cambridge, Mass.: Harvard University Press, 2002).

2. In William James, *Writings 1902–1910* (New York: Library of America, 1987), 1–477. This edition reproduces the first edition text (New York and London: Longmans, 1902), together with James's own authorial emendations.

3. James, *Writings*, 36.

4. Taylor, *Varieties of Religion Today*, 112.

5. Edward Farley's resonant phrase in *Ecclesial Reflection: An Anatomy of Theological Method* (Philadelphia: Fortress, 1982), 3–168. Farley is describing the way in which traditional Protestantism has been governed by the authority of scripture, and Catholicism by the voice of the "magisterium."

6. Rachel Carson, *Silent Spring* (Boston: Houghton Mifflin, 1962);

Michael Harrington, *The Other America: Poverty in the United States* (New York: Macmillan, 1969); Harvey Cox, *The Secular City: Secularization and Urbanization in Theological Perspective* (New York: Macmillan, 1966).

7. While I would write it very differently where I to be working on it today, I retract nothing contained in my brief first book, *Can Women Be Priests?* (Cork: Mercier, 1977).

8. The best recent example of this would be the debates in the late 1990s over establishing norms for the application of the Apostolic Constitution *Ex Corde Ecclesiae* to the American context. See *Apostolic Constitution "Ex corde ecclesiae" of the Supreme Pontiff John Paul II On Catholic Universities* (Washington, D.C.: U.S. Catholic Conference, 1990), and the extensive documentation and commentary to be found at the website of the Association of Catholic Colleges and Universities (http://www.accunet.org/ece/exc.asp).

9. Here see the immensely valuable work of George Dennis O'Brien, *The Idea of a Catholic University* (Chicago and London: University of Chicago Press, 2002).

10. See Merrimon Cunningim, *Uneasy Partners: The College and the Church* (Nashville: Abingdon, 1994).

Index

Abraham, 155
accountability, 200, 214, 219, 230
Acts of the Apostles, 103
Action Française, 23
Adam and Eve, 179
Adorno, Theodor, 235
Agaganian, Grégoire-Pierre Cardinal, 119
Alfrink, Bernard Jan Cardinal, 84
American church, 116-17, 124,
    131-35, 186, 203
    crisis in, 257-85
Amos, 175
Angelicum, 38
anointing of the sick, sacrament of,
    128
anthropocentrism, 163, 182
apartheid, 195
apostolicity, 62-64, 72, 127, 144,
    274
Aquinas, St. Thomas, 40, 49, 58,
    60, 93, 156
Arianism, 191
atheism, 100, 151, 166, 181
atheistic humanism, 60
Athanasius, Saint, 191
Augustine, Saint, 40, 232, 234
authority, "fatherly," 211

Balasuriya, Tissa, 99
Baltimore Catechism, 160
baptism, 81, 89, 105-6, 109, 126,
    132, 139, 252

Barth, Karl, 159
base Christian communities, 26,
    59, 76, 80, 141-42, 216-18,
    233-34
Bea, Augustine Cardinal, 86
Bell, Daniel M., Jr., 232-35, 243-
    44
Bellarmine, St. Robert, 58, 79, 81,
    149
Benigni, Umberto, 22
Bernanos, Georges, 151
Bethge, Eberhard, 158
bishops
    appointment of, 72, 106, 201,
        271-73, 276
    authority of, 212, 279
    college of, 102, 103
    collegiality of, 104, 115, 118-
        20, 144, 223, 264
    Committee on the Laity, U.S.,
        132
    failure of leadership, 188-92,
        198, 227, 240, 257
    married, 214
    national conferences of, 114,
        273-74
    retirement of, 115
    Roman synods of, 114, 120-25,
        251
    selection of, 209
    timidity of American, 131-32
    U.S. national conference of,
        114, 132

Blondel, Maurice, 30, 39, 289 n.30
Boff, Leonardo, 44, 140-41, 222, 292 n.39, 298 n.10
Bonhoeffer, Dietrich, 158-62, 163, 168, 173, 174
Boston, Massachusetts, 198
Bouillard, Henri, 40, 48
Bush, President George Herbert Walker, 190

Cahill, Lisa Sowle, 189
Cajetan, Cardinal, 58, 79
Call to Action, 194
Called and Gifted, 132-33
Called and Gifted for the Third Millennium, 133-34
Camus, Albert, 169
canon law, 210-11, 224
capitalism, 230-35, 243, 265, 281
Cardenal, Ernesto, 204
Cardijn, Joseph-Léon Cardinal, 26
cardinals, 115, 274
careerism in the church, 209, 271, 272
Carson, Rachel, 262
catechetics, 69
Catholic Action, 26, 27-29, 35, 67-70, 86, 88, 97, 109, 289 n.27
Catholic colleges and universities, 279-82
Catholic-Lutheran Commission, 49
Celestine I, Pope Saint, 209
celibacy, 57, 72, 74, 94, 105, 130, 144, 157, 203, 267, 269
charismatic renewal, 225
Charlemagne, Emperor, 210
Chenu, Marie-Dominique, 22, 23, 29-32, 42, 48, 151
Chiffon, Archbishop Donate, 125
Christifideles Laici, 50, 111, 124, 125-28, 134, 282
Christ, 161, 172, 202, 251
    commissioning of the apostles, 62-64, 128, 137

divinity of, 191-92
Mystical Body of, 28
spiritual authority of, 54
temporal authority of, 54
Christianity, religionless, 159
church
    authority in, 56-57, 64
    as communion, 62-64, 102, 126, 140, 192, 220-27
    democracy in, 57, 102-7
    executive power in, 211-12
    gender and, 190
    hierarchical constitution of, 56, 88, 212
    homosexuality in, 188
    institutional model of, 8
    kingly function, 208-15
    lay/clergy distinction, 7-13, 103, 176
    leadership, 176-77, 240
    leadership crisis in, 187-92
    local, 123, 126, 199, 205
    as people of God, 11, 28, 63, 70, 81, 87, 88, 102, 105-7, 109, 118, 157, 172, 221, 263
    as pilgrim, 88, 263
    prophetic element, 64-65
    public opinion in, 212
    secularity of, 126, 149-85
    as spouse, 171-72
    structure/life distinction, 56-57, 58, 62-64, 212-13
    structures, 266-82
    universal, 274-77
    women in, 123, 130, 133, 142-44, 190, 202
    world and, 98-100, 136, 140, 171, 234-35
Cicognani, Gaetano Cardinal, 84
Clement of Rome, 11, 12
clergy
    careerism, 209
    celibacy of, 57, 72, 74, 94, 105, 130, 200, 227, 269

education of, 59
lifestyle of, 200
shortage of, 142
See "laity"
clericalism, 143, 189-90, 195
clericalization
of the church, 53, 144
of the laity, 74, 121, 127
Commonweal, 124-25
communicative action, 166-67
Communion and Liberation, 123,
138, 237
communion ecclesiology, 62-64,
102, 126, 140, 192, 220-27,
231
confirmation, sacrament of, 91
Congar, Yves, 1, 3, 11, 12, 13, 22,
23, 27, 29, 30, 32-35, 42,
44, 45, 47, 49-77, 78, 79-80,
92-94, 101, 109, 127, 135,
149, 151, 156, 175, 180,
184, 208-15, 224, 245-46,
266, 282, 283, 286 n.2, 290
n.43, 291 n.1, 291 n.2, 291
n.3, 296 n.50, 298 n.10, 298
n.14
Divided Christendom, 33-35
Lay People in the Church, 35, 49-
77, 79-80, 93, 149, 208-15,
282
*True and False Reform in the
Church*, 49
conscientization, 198, 200, 202,
203, 205-7, 217
consent, principle of, 56-57, 209,
212-13, 216, 218-19, 225
contraception, 188, 201
coresponsibility in the church, 101-
7, 117-20
Cornwell, John, 294 n.9
cosmocentrism, 163
councils of the church, 209-10
Council of Jerusalem, 103, 209

Cox, Harvey, 99, 168-71, 241, 263
creation, 150
theology of, 164, 170
cross, the, 150
Cuomo, Mario, 121
Curia, Roman, 83, 112, 129, 131,
215, 262, 274, 275
internationalization of, 114
Curran, Charles, 44, 298 n.10
Cyprian, Saint, 209, 210
Cyrus, King of Persia, 154

Daniel, Yvan, 25
Daniélou, Jean, 23, 29, 35-39, 41,
42, 47, 53, 151
Darwin, Charles, 250
deacons, 128, 267
de Chardin, Pierre Teilhard, 37,
290 n.49
de la Potterie, Ignace, 286 n.2
Deleuze, Gilles, 233
de Lubac, Henri, 23, 29, 39-42, 4,
48, 151, 290 n.56
democracy, 167, 183, 243
in the church, 57, 118, 144,
207-15, 265
de Montcheuil, Yves, 44-45
diocesan councils, 272
diocese, 271-73
discourse ethics, 167
dissent, 200, 202
doctrine, 218
Doepfner, Julius Cardinal, 84, 119
Donnelly, Philip, 38, 290 n.53
Doyle, Dennis, 222, 298 n.4
Drey, Johann Sebastian, 238
Dulles, Avery Cardinal, 8, 215,
222, 286 n.1
Duquesne, Jacques, 30

ecumenism, Congar and, 33-35
electoral college, 275
Enlightenment, the, 60, 163, 233,
234, 236, 239, 244

episcopate, 56
ethics, 61
Etudes, 35
eucharist, 72, 92, 97, 132, 143,
  195, 221, 266-68
evangelization, 24-29, 100, 127,
  139, 174, 245
Ex Corde Ecclesiae, 280, 302 n.8
existentialism, 37, 169

faith
  act of, 155
  seeking understanding, 153
Faivre, Alexandre, 11, 12, 286 n.2
Farley, Edward, 301 n.5
fellowship, 62-64, 229
feminism, 142-44, 167, 193
Fennell, William O., 164-65
Ferraro, Geraldine, 121
Feuerbach, Ludwig, 181
Foucault, Michel, 233
Fouilloux, Etienne, 22, 43, 287
  n.3, 290 n.43
Fourvière, 29, 48
Frankenstein, 235
freedom, 178-80, 186-219, 229-30
Freud, Sigmund, 181, 250
Friedman, Thomas L., 231, 232,
  244
fundamentalism, 236, 240

Gaillardetz, Richard R., 286 n.1
Gardeil, Ambrose, 30
Garrigou-Lagrange, Reginald, 23,
  30, 32, 38-39, 41, 288 n.10
Gaudium et Spes, 81, 85, 87, 98-
  100, 116, 135, 138, 221,
  234, 239
Genesis, Book of, 168
Gilson, Etienne, 32
globalization, 231, 264, 299 n.6,
  10
God, transcendence of, 160

Godin, Henri, 25-28, 159, 288
  n.14
gospel, proclamation of, 229
Gramsci, Antonio, 203
Gratian, 13
Gregory of Nyssa, 36
Grootaers, Jan, 87
Gutiérrez, Gustavo, 110

Habermas, Jürgen, 166-68, 176,
  189, 235
Harnack, Adolf von, 21
Harrington, Michael, 263
Hebblethwaite, Peter, 113, 118,
  122
hierarchical apostolate, 27, 67, 97
Hinkelammert, Franz, 233, 243
historical-critical method, 31
historicity, 9, 140
Hitler, Adolf, 155
holiness, universal call to, 88
homosexuality in the church, 188,
  201, 203
Horkheimer, Max, 235
Hughes, Patrick, 122
Humanae Vitae, 104, 114
Humani Generis, 34, 39, 47-48
On Human Work, 116, 177
humanism, "exclusive," 249

imagination, 161-66, 167-68
  sacramental, 164
Immaculate Conception, 191
incarnation, 150, 164
inculturation, 26
Index of Forbidden Books, 31
infallibility
  in the church, 118
  of the pope, 17, 18, 213
infantilization of the laity, 200, 211
internal mission, 27
International Theological Commission, 49, 117

Irenaeus of Lyons, 12, 36
Isasi-Díaz, Ada María, 43, 203-5, 217
Islam, 180, 243

James, William, 259-62
Jesus of Nazareth, 155, 157, 158, 169, 170, 183-84
John Paul II, Pope, 3, 49, 105, 111-13, 115-18, 125-28, 134, 177, 236, 237, 280
  Christifideles Laici, 50, 111, 124, 125-28, 134, 282
  Laborem Exercens, 116, 177
John XXIII, Pope, 19, 32, 48, 49, 77-78, 82, 83, 113, 115, 208, 232, 238
Judaism, 117, 173
Jurist, The, 50
justice, 229, 249

Kant, Immanuel, 245
Kennedy, John Fitzgerald, 121
kenosis, 61
kingdom of God, 155, 161
Kloppenburg, Bonaventure, 138-39
Komonchak, Joseph, 220, 238-40
König, Franz Cardinal, 84
Küng, Hans, 44, 144-45

Laborem Exercens, 116, 177
laity
  authority of, 211-12
  clericalization of, 74, 121, 127
  decision-making and, 144
  hierarchical ministry and, 53
  infantilization of, 200, 211
  liberation of, 186-219
  mission of, 100, 125-34, 247, 255-56
  oppression of, 187-219
  passivity of, 58-59, 63, 68, 216
  Pontifical Council for, 122, 134

priesthood of, 53, 55-56, 89-95
role in councils, 209-10
Roman Synod on, 121-25
secularity of, 52-54, 98, 100, 125-26, 135, 139, 149-85
solidarity with clergy, 95, 264
teaching role of, 64-67
theology of the, 1, 7-13, 17-19, 44-47, 52-77, 81, 88-95, 107-9, 111, 117-18, 121-25, 131-34, 135-45
Vatican "Instruction" on, 128-31
voice of, 197-99, 201, 213, 216, 218
Lao-Tzu, 156
lay apostolate, 61, 67-70, 98-100, 108, 157, 258
lay/clergy distinction, 195-97
lay consent, principle of, 56-57, 209
lay ecclesiology, 100
lay ministry, 89, 91, 122, 123, 125-34, 245, 264
Lauret, Bernard, 50
Law, Bernard Cardinal, 198
League of Women Voters, 173
Lee, Bernard J., 297 n.6
Leo XIII, Pope, 28, 29
Lercaro, Giacomo Cardinal, 119
Lernoux, Penny, 197
Le Saulchoir, 29-32
Leo XIII, Pope, 232
liberation, 165
  of the laity, 186-219
  theology, 24, 54, 59, 76-77, 113, 141-42, 193, 199, 202, 216, 222, 233-34, 243
Lindbeck, George, 88-89, 293 n.9
liturgy, 132
Loisy, Alfred, 20, 21-22
Lumen Gentium, 60, 80, 87, 88-95, 102, 115, 119-20, 139, 171, 222, 239, 253

Lutheran Church, German, 162
Lynch, William F., 162-66, 167,
    169, 173, 174, 180, 181

magisterium, 64, 224
Maréchal, Joseph, 22, 32, 288 n.10
Maritain, Jacques, 22, 23, 288 n.10
marriage, sacrament of, 128
Marshall Plan, 243
Martini, Carlo Maria Cardinal, 113
Marx, Karl, 181, 250
Marxism, 37
Mersch, Émile, 289 n.23
Metz, Johann Baptist, 9
Milbank, John, 233
ministers of Holy Communion
    of the church, 267-71
    extraordinary, 128
    in the world, 267-71
ministry, 70-75, 76, 156, 184-85
misogynism, 142
mission, 100, 220-56, 247
    of the laity, 100, 125-34, 247,
        255-56
Mission de France, 26, 29
Mission de Paris, 26
modernism, 3, 19-23, 36, 239, 288
    n.6
modernity, 163, 239, 242-55
Möhler, Johann Adam, 34
monasticism, 12-13, 69
Montini, Giovanni Battista Cardi-
    nal, 86
Mooney, Christopher F., 290 n.49
mujerista theology, 193, 204, 217
mystery, 152-53, 174
mysticism, 156

national security, church of, 202
natural desire for God, 39-42
natural law, 182, 203
natural theology, 153
nature and grace, 151

Nazism, 162
neocolonialism, 100
neoscholasticism, 3, 19-23, 37, 40
Newman, John Henry Cardinal,
    191, 238
new theology, the, 3, 20, 23-44,
    78, 82, 238
Nicaea, Council of, 191
Nietzsche, Friedrich, 181, 250
nihilism, 154
nostalgia, 236-37
Novak, Michael, 242

O'Brien, George Dennis, 302 n.9
Orange, Council of, 209
oppression, structural, 194, 228-29
Opus Dei, 123, 124, 135, 138,
    236
ordination
    of married men, 188, 190
    of women, 188, 190, 197, 203,
        269
Origen, 36
Osservatore Romano, 34
Ottaviani, Alfredo Cardinal, 85,
    119

Pacelli, Eugenio Cardinal, 34
papacy, 115-18
parish, 266-71
passivity of the laity, 58-59, 63, 68,
    216
pastoral councils, 128, 269
Paul, Saint, 10, 28, 153, 213
    Galatians, Letter to the, 10
    Romans, Letter to the, 153
    Timothy, First Letter to, 214
Paul VI, Pope, 49, 83, 101-2, 104,
    112-20, 237, 238
    Humanae Vitae, 276
    Populorum Progressio, 114
pedophilia, 189, 192, 203
people of God, 11, 28, 63, 70, 81,

87, 88, 102, 105-7, 109, 118, 157, 172, 221, 263
Péguy, Charles, 60
Pellitero, Ramon, 76, 135-36, 137, 138, 292 n.22
Peter, First Letter of, 10
Pfürtner, Stephan, 296 n.50
Philips, Gerard, 45-47
Pius IX, 191, 239
Pius X, Pope Saint, 17, 18, 20, 22, 47, 239
Pius XI, Pope, 27, 29, 34, 35, 66, 67, 88
Pius XII, Pope, 23, 35, 36, 44, 58-59, 88, 115, 216, 219, 239
pluralism, 252-56
Poland, 116
politics, 231-32
poor, the, 100
  preferential option for, 141, 199
pope
  appointment of, 106, 274
  infallibility of, 17-18
  primacy of, 58
Populorum Progressio, 114
postmodernity, 163, 233, 236-38
pragmatism, 169
praxis, 152
preaching, ministry of, 93, 128, 139
priesthood
  of all believers, 27, 80-81, 103, 122
  celibacy and, 57, 72, 74, 94, 105, 130, 144, 157, 203, 267, 269
  gender and, 57, 73, 94, 142-44, 269
  of the laity, 53, 55-56, 89-95
  "ministerial," 53-54, 55-56, 103, 144
  women and, 75, 270, 302 n.7
priestly formation, 59

priestly identity, 72-75, 94
priests
  councils of, 128
  laicization of, 115
  selection of, 72
"profanity," 169-70
prometheanism, 163, 167, 169, 175, 180
Prometheus, 163, 167, 169, 175, 178-80
prophecy, 242-48
Protestant Reformation, 210
Proudhon, Pierre-Joseph, 169
Puleo, Mev, 288 n.13

Qur'an, 156

racism, 195
radical orthodoxy, 232, 244, 249, 299 n.12
Rahner, Karl, 42, 44, 52, 68, 84, 99, 109, 151, 165, 239, 241, 245, 295 n.18
Rambler, The, 191
Ratzinger, Joseph Cardinal, 114, 129, 222
religious imagination, 161-66
religious life, 73, 269, 275
religious orders, 277-78
ressourcement, 3, 35-39, 238
resurrection, 150, 152, 160
revelation, 31, 154, 159, 173
Revue Thomiste, 38
rights, human, 142, 233-34, 242, 249
Rite of Christian Initiation of Adults, 69
Robinson, John A. T., 297 n.7
Rousselot, Pierre, 22, 30, 32, 288 n.10
Roy, Paul J., S.J., 99-100
Ruether, Rosemary Radford, 142
Rynne, Xavier, 293 n.13

sacramentality, 160

Sacred Congregation for the Doctrine of the Faith, 114, 117, 119

Schillebeeckx, Edward, 30, 44, 101, 107-9, 139-40, 184, 235, 242, 248, 253-54

sacrifice, 92

secular, unconditionality of, 150, 164-66

secularity, 149-85
  of the laity, 52-54, 98, 100, 125-26, 135, 139, 149-85
  theology of, 158-71

secularization, 168

sensus ecclesiae, 212

sensus fidelium, 64, 118, 191, 223, 225

servant leaders, 210, 269, 270

sexual abuse, 1, 189, 192, 201, 213, 219, 225, 257

sexual orientation, 192, 193

sexism, 195

Shaw, George Bernard, 280

Siena, Council of, 210

signs of the times, 223, 227-35

sin, structural, 228-29

Siri, Giuseppe Cardinal, 85

slavery, 187, 195, 213, 228

Sobrino, Jon, 202

Sodalitium Pianum, 22

solidarity, 229

soteriology, 54

Spirit, Holy, 58, 63, 69, 75, 82, 90, 92, 106, 118, 155, 194, 208, 212-13, 217, 221, 225, 244, 265
  gifts of, 96

spirituality, 59-62, 154
  of freedom, 178-80
  of the laity, 96-97, 177-85
  of limitation, 180-83
  of responsibility, 183-85

Stecher, Bishop Reinhold, 129-30

structural oppression, 194-95

structures of the church, 266-82

Suenens, Léon Joseph Cardinal, 3, 82-87, 101-7, 117-19, 126, 145, 188, 211, 225, 293 n.13

Suhard, Emmanuel Célestin Cardinal, 26, 31

Taylor, Charles, 235, 248-51, 259-62

technopolis, 170

Tertullian, 226

theocracy, 183, 258

Theological Studies, 38

theologians, 203-7, 217, 268, 278-79
  identity of, 193
  lay, 205-7
  as organic intellectuals, 203-4
  as professional insider, 203, 217

theology, 64-67, 107-9
  of creation, 164
  feminist, 193
  of the laity, 1, 7-13, 17-19, 44-47, 52-77, 81, 88-95, 107-9, 111, 117-18, 121-25, 131-34, 135-45, 204
  lay experience in, 193
  liberation, 24, 54, 59, 76-77, 113, 141-42, 193, 202, 204, 216, 222, 233-34
  mujerista, 193, 204, 217
  natural, 153
  new, 3, 20, 23-44, 78, 82, 238
  role of context in, 193
  secularization of, 137
  womanist, 193

Thiel, John E., 291 n.58, 291 n.59

Thomas à Kempis, 154

Thomism, 22, 32, 36

tradition, 7, 31, 64

transcendence, 250

Trent, Council of, 18

Unam Sanctam, 34
United Nations, 173
urbanization, 168

van Roey, Jozef Ernest Cardinal, 84
Varillon, François, 44, 291 n.64
Vatican, 17, 201, 262, 273, 276
Vatican Council, First, 2, 10, 17-
    20, 118, 149, 209
Vatican Council, Second, 1, 10, 13,
    18, 20, 31, 32, 41, 64, 70,
    71, 75, 78-110, 119, 122,
    136-37, 162, 188, 192, 219,
    221, 238, 240, 245, 258,
    262-65
    Ad Gentes Divinitus, 81, 97,
        107
    Apostolicam Actuositatem, 80,
        87, 92, 95-98
    Dignitatis Humanae, 239
    Gaudium et Spes, 81, 85, 87, 98-
        100, 116, 135, 138, 221,
        234, 239
    Lumen Gentium, 60, 80, 87, 88-
        95, 102, 115, 119-20, 139,
        171, 222, 239, 253
    preparatory commission, 83, 84
Vatican Council, Third, 265
violence, 249

vocation, 71-74, 91, 156-57, 184,
    256
Voice of the Faithful (VOTF), 198,
    201
voice of the laity, 197-99, 201,
    213, 216, 218
Voltaire, 249
von Balthasar, Hans Urs, 136-38

Ward, Barbara, 293 n.13
Ward, Maisie, 26, 28, 288 n.14
Weakland, Archbishop Rembert,
    124-25, 188
Weber, Max, 239
white supremacy, 195
Wiesel, Elie, 154, 297 n.4
witness, 226-27, 245
Wittgenstein, Ludwig, 174
Wolfteich, Claire E., 295 n.11
Women Church, 142-44
world
    engagement in, 61
    gift-character of, 153
    responsibility for, 61
    theology of, 170
worldliness, 178-80
worship, 175

Young Christian Workers, 26, 28-
    29